CW01021020

Hemingway and *The Sun* Set

Ernest Hemingway decked out as an American soldier, Michigan, 1919.
Collection of Donald St. John.

A Bruccoli Clark Book

HEMINGWAY AND *The Sun* SET

by BERTRAM D. SARASON

Microcard Editions
901 Twenty-Sixth Street, N.W.
Washington, D.C.

The editor wishes to thank Charles Scribner's Sons for permission to quote passages from Ernest Hemingway's The Sun Also Rises, *and Berenice Abbott, Carlos Baker, Kathleen Cannell, James Charters, Morrill Cody, the Gale Research Company, Leah Rice Koontz, Harold Loeb, William B. Smith and Donald St. John for their kind permission to publish photographs from their respective collections.*

Copyright © 1972 by The National Cash Register Company
Library of Congress Catalog Card Number: 72-76990
ISBN: 0-910972-06-0
Published by NCR/Microcard Editions,
901 26th St., N.W., Washington, D.C. 20037
Printed in the United States of America

To my wife Kerin
    and to Lawrence Agonne

Contents

Preface

It requires no great measure of boldness to predict healthy sales for almost any decently written *roman à clef*, for this particular genre excites a very special kind of interest which does not emanate exclusively from the "literary" public. Even people who rarely read novels are driven by curiosity to investigate a story supposedly based on real people and events. When such a novel is additionally acclaimed by the critics and widely hailed as the Bible of a whole generation, the furor increases geometrically. Over a period of years bits of information purported to be "the truth" about the novel and its prototypes multiply and are synthesized, resulting in a confusing array of legends which not infrequently contradict one another. Thus has it been with Ernest Hemingway's *The Sun Also Rises*.

Today we are fairly certain of the identity of many of the persons whom Hemingway fictionalized. As a matter of fact, some of them are still alive and they have their say about former friend Ernest in Part II of this book. Who they were, how they felt about Hemingway's treatment of them, what he did or didn't know about them, what he made up, what facts he traded on, are told in "Hemingway and *The Sun* Set," which comprises Part I. In Part III we have an opportunity to see Hemingway's characters as viewed by others who knew them. I do not wish to suggest by the foregoing remarks, however, that the game of identification is all but over. Allen Churchill, for example, in his recent book, *The Literary Decade*, names many former celebrities of the Left Bank as persons who figure in *The Sun Also Rises*. Among those named are Laurence Vail, Robert McAlmon, and Harry Crosby. There is no evidence that Hemingway fictionalized these persons. But Mr. Churchill is a responsible writer and what he sets down as fact may have stemmed from rumors that had once circulated. Hemingway himself liked to make up tall stories about *The Sun Also Rises*. About two years after its publication he told Chicago bookseller Georgia Lingafelt that *The Sun Also Rises* was written on a train en route from Madrid to Berlin, that he became drunk before reaching his destination, that he gave the manuscript to a friend, and that the friend never returned it. This bit of apocrypha was the forerunner of subsequent myths Hemingway told Hotchner and others. Indeed, the living persons whom Hemingway fictionalized became the subject of myths from many sources and the myths continue even today. Just recently, Kenneth Rexroth in his *American Poetry: In the Twentieth Century* reported that Harold Loeb knocked Hemingway out on a beach in Spain as the result of a quarrel over a "slut."

I have attempted in Part I to get all the information I could about the real persons in the novel without cramming in every possible reference to them which has already appeared in print. More interested in discovering what has not yet been printed, I wanted to reveal how *The Sun Also Rises* fictionalized their biographies and failed to take into account some of the realities of their lives. The reader who wants to know more about Ford Madox Ford's relationship to Hemingway should pore over Nicholas Joost's *Hemingway and The Little Magazines*, Bernard Poli's *Hemingway and the transatlantic review*, and Ford's *It Must Be the Nightingale*. But to include every possible relevant item from these works for the man fictionalized as Braddocks, who occupies three minutes reading time in the novel, would be far out of proportion—worse, would be mere repetitiveness. Nor have I gleaned minutely from the many memoirs of the 1920's and the accounts of life in Montparnasse to reiterate every reference in them to the Hemingway characters. James Charters' *This Must Be the Place* is still the reference book for those persons and that era. Whoever wishes to get to the minutiae should read Charters, along with Kay Boyle, Robert McAlmon, Samuel Putnam, Matthew Josephson, John Dos Passos, and historians such as George Wickes, all of whom I have drawn on sparsely. I have drawn on Carlos Baker's *Ernest Hemingway, A Life Story* considerably.

In relating in Part I what one person thought about another, I have done so quite aware that their judgments about each other are open to question. Let me add that they are not necessarily my own. If I only reported nice things, I would not be reporting accurately—perhaps I would not have much to report. I have attempted to apprise all those whose lives are the subject of comment in these pages that my purpose is to present the raw material out of which Hemingway fashioned his novel without neglecting emphasis on the raw deal that Hemingway gave most of the persons who became his fictions. To obtain what information I did, I had the help of a considerable number of persons.

Preface xi

My thanks are owing to Berenice Abbot; Margaret Anderson; Jerome Bahr; Professor Carlos Baker; Jacques Baron; Paul Blum; Professor Matthew Bruccoli; Mrs. Dana Suess Burr; Kathleen Cannell; Mr. and Mrs. Stuart Chase; Louise Chiaraluce; C. E. Frazer Clark, Jr.; Morrill Cody; James Charters; Mrs. Louis Henry Cohn; Mrs. Peter Dickens; Mrs. Anne Fellowes; Edward Fisher; Dorothy Fribble; Florence Gilliam; Dr. and Mrs. Edward Harkavy; William Hoffmann; William D. Horne; Sister Mary Joachim; Clinton King; Professor Leah Rice Koontz; the late Professor L. B. Kreitner; Mrs. Dorothy Kreymborg; Arthur Lett-Haines; Harold Loeb; His Worship, The Mayor of Richmond, Yorkshire; Professor Charles Mann; Professor Arthur Mizener; Mrs. Doreen Moss; Charles Norman; Professor Norman Holmes Pearson; Professor Bernard Poli; Juanito Quintana; Man Ray; Mrs. John Rogers, Jr.; the late William B. Smith; Lady Castle Stewart; Donald Ogden Stewart; Donald St. John; Malcolm Tooze; Peter Townend; Elizabeth Aileen Twysden; the late Sir William Twysden; and Professor Philip Young. I would also like to express my gratitude for her editorial assistance to Ms. Carole Jacobs.

The notes to Part I require a few comments. The date of communication from all persons who were sources of data is generally given, but not for Harold Loeb and Kathleen Cannell. What I learned from them was not restricted to a particular day. In conversation with Loeb and in both letters and conversation with Mrs. Cannell, we went over familiar territory time and again. It would have been possible, of course, to settle arbitrarily on some particular day when this or that matter became finally clarified; however, the record-keeping would have been enormous. Therefore, I have just given their names as sources without specifying times. Communication with Loeb took place from 1965–1970, with Mrs. Cannell from 1967–1970.

References to Baker in the notes apply to *Ernest Hemingway, A Life Story* unless otherwise indicated. No pagination appears for documentation of Morrill Cody's *"The Sun Also Rises* Revisited," because this article, a copy of which I had in advance of its publication, had not yet appeared in print while this manuscript was being prepared. Allusions in the notes to a "Hemingway" recording made by the Canadian Broadcasting System in 1970 require a comment. CBC recorded some dozen voices of persons who were close to Hemingway in his lifetime on two LP records. Sometimes it is not clear who the speaker is; therefore the simple acknowledgement to CBC is all that can be prudently made.

In addition, certain acknowledgements are to be made: For permission to quote from *The Sun Also Rises* to Charles Scribner's Sons; for permission to reprint from *The Way It Was* to Harold Loeb and Sidney Phillips, publisher of Criterion Books; for permission to quote from Kathleen Cannell's articles on Ford Madox Ford to *The Providence Journal* and *The Christian Science Monitor;* for permission to reprint Harold Loeb's "Hemingway's Bitterness," Kathleen Cannell's "Scenes with a Hero," Bertram D. Sarason's "Lady Brett Ashley and Lady Duff Twysden," James Charters' "Pat and Duff, Some Memories," and Donald St. John's "Interview with Hemingway's 'Bill Gorton'" to the editor of the *Connecticut Review* on behalf of The Board of Trustees for the Connecticut State Colleges; for permission to reprint Sam Adams' "The Sun Also Sets" to *Time Inc.* and the Estate of the late Sam Adams; for permission to reprint F. Scott Fitzgerald's letter to Ernest Hemingway to the editors of the *Fitzgerald/Hemingway Annual* and Harold Ober Associates; and for permission to reprint "Fitzgerald's *Sun Also Rises:* Notes and Comments" by Philip Young and Charles W. Mann to the editors of the *Fitzgerald/Hemingway Annual.* The essay on "Montoya" by Leah Rice Koontz, the essay on "Duke Zizi" by James Charters, the essay on Ford by Bernard Poli, the letter from Robert McAlmon to Norman Holmes Pearson, Donald St. John's interview with Donald Ogden Stewart, and the whole of Part I have not appeared in print previously.

BERTRAM D. SARASON

Northford, Connecticut
1965–1971

Hemingway and *The Sun* Set

Part I THE BACKGROUND

Hemingway and
The Sun Set

IN the summer of 1965 I discovered that the Robert Cohn of *The Sun Also Rises* lived less than a ten minute drive from my home. That was Harold Loeb, and he cordially invited me to visit him. Before the third visit Loeb and I were talking about Hemingway and, of course, about Duff Twysden, the model for Lady Brett Ashley. And we did that on and off for five years. But there were many questions he could not answer about her and about other members of *The Sun* set. He suggested names of old acquaintances of Duff and he knew where those characters, still alive, whom Hemingway had put in his novel, might be found. I was curious to meet them or to correspond with them, the originals of the novel as well as their friends. I wanted to know what they thought about the novel in which they had been depicted and what they thought about the author. I wanted to know what they were like and what likeness, if any, Hemingway had drawn. I wanted to know the facts.

And, over the course of trips to New York, Maine, Massachusetts, London, Paris and Sicily, I acquired a great deal of information that had not been printed before or which was at variance with a good deal that had appeared in print, especially in memoirs of the 1920's. Much that was corrective and new came from correspondents in Santa Fe, Key West, Tokyo, and Tunis. Occasionally, I met with resistance or with reluctance. The characters of *The Sun Also Rises* had been the subjects of loose talk and, some people thought, even looser fictionalizing at the hands of Hemingway. Friends of those characters had good

3

reason to believe that gossip was my passion, and, certainly, those facts I came to acquire—aside from dates of birth and addresses—were sometimes beyond verification and sometimes beyond belief, but often within the purlieu of scandal. I have omitted in the pages that follow matters of questionable passports, probable bigamy, and alleged sexual perversion, especially when such matters were merely tangential to the points of my inquiry; and where I have felt compelled to report what I had been told, I have done so only to be informative. Whenever I could, I tried to assemble all the data pertinent to a fact, especially if it was not too flattering a fact. Gossip, however, was never my motive.

Yet, I would be reporting tall stories, myths, and legends. It was the fate of *The Sun* set to inspire fantasies, almost at once after Hemingway's novel was published and ever since. The fight between Loeb and Cayetano, the bullfighter, was not as violent as Hemingway reported of their fictionalized versions—so said the hotelkeeper at the lodging in Pamplona where Hemingway and friends stayed for the fiesta of San Fermin.[1] A reliable source? That comment sounds like the report of an onlooker. But, in fact, Loeb and Cayetano met only for an instant, just long enough to shake hands. There never was a fight nor a quarrel nor any time for nor reason for hostility.[2] The untrue and the improbable, reported to me as fact—I don't think anyone deliberately lied to me—must be set down as part of my account. A case in point is the assertion that Jake Barnes, the narrator of the novel whom Hemingway identified with himself, was drawn, in part, from one of Hemingway's oldest friends. This friend had told someone (absolutely no doubt that he did) of his being sexually incapacitated as a result of war experiences. Of course, he may have been making the story up. Another person, however, had heard that story; she had had it from still another person. But, I was told, the so-called invalid had a wild imagination and what he said was to be taken with a grain of salt. A very close friend of that man said he had no imagination whatsoever, and a member of the so-called invalid's family said the whole idea was without foundation. There is nothing to do but report this story and dismiss it at once. There are many such stories about *The Sun* set. Some of these stories must have seemed plausible because Hemingway's characters belonged to the zany world of Montparnasse of the 1920's. He himself was accused of reporting that world inaccurately.[3] Let us say that some there worked, some played. I lump them all together in reporting the impact of *The Sun Also Rises* when the novel first appeared.

Among the girls who had come to Paris in the early 1920's to paint or write, to be wed or merely to be seduced willingly, and among their male friends, the writers, painters, photographers, musicians, critics, and drinkers, few had any difficulty in recognizing the real persons on whom Ernest Hemingway drew for his characters in *The Sun Also Rises*. That recognition was most extensive around the cafés and boulevards of Montparnasse,[4] but it was not limited to the Quarter. As soon as the novel appeared in the fall of 1926, the reviewers of the book across the Atlantic could inform the general reader that Mr. Hemingway had drawn on living persons. "Anyone," wrote Cleveland Chase in *The Saturday Review of Literature*, "who is acquainted with the habitués of the cafés of the Boulevard Montparnasse will recognize most of the characters at once. Not one of them, I think, is the product of the author's imagination. Even the fishing trip about which the story centers is an actual event that took place, if my memory is not at fault, in the spring of 1924."[5] Irishman Ernest Boyd commented that, "Those familiar with the particular world of Paris which is the axis of the narrative will further note with amusement how Mr. Hemingway has managed to introduce several easily identifiable people .... Robert Cohn ... is something more than an impression of a certain American editor in exile."[6] Boyd knew that American editor. Harold Loeb had met him in Dublin;[7] in another year Boyd and his wife Madeline visited Loeb in New York just as Loeb was about to launch *Broom*, his expatriate magazine of the arts.[8] Others might have seen Loeb and Bill Smith, Hemingway's childhood friend,—who was also to be fictionalized—in the rotogravure sections of the *New York Times* and *Tribune*.[9] Photographers in Pamplona (where the novel reaches its climax and the dénouement begins to unfurl) caught Smith being butted and Loeb "born aloft" on a "bull's head." This is not to say that Loeb and Smith by the summer of 1925 were already known nation-wide or that everyone in Montparnasse identified them at once in Hemingway's novel, or that they became notorious because Hemingway's novel was a bestseller. It was a success, but not nearly as successful as, for example, Wilder's *The Bridge of San Luis Rey*. *The Sun Also Rises* was in sufficient demand to make Hemingway known beyond the small circle of admirers who had been impressed by *in our time* (1924) and *Three Stories and Ten Poems* (1923). He became a public figure and was on his way to becoming a famous public figure. But not because he had drawn ruthlessly some of his friends, or without pity travestied them, or had depicted recognizably friends of friends. It was the epigraph quoted from Gertrude Stein, "You are all a lost generation," that established Hemingway as the artist who recorded the plight of his time.[10] And this distinction overshadowed quickly all the gossip that had been stirred up and which, had it continued, might have made the novel a mere *succès de scandale.*

Hemingway wondered whether his novel might be bought up for the movies. Fitzgerald didn't think so—unless, he said, it made its mark as a *succès de scandale.*[11] Given a good public relations man, Hemingway might have achieved that mark. All the elements to make for sensationalism were there. In the Quarter a jest started up that the novel should have been entitled, "Six Characters in Search of an Author—with a Gun Apiece."[12] The idea, based, of course, on Pirandello's play which was then new and in vogue, was intended as wit.[13] The cleverness caught on and the wit began to be taken seriously. Soon there were reports that Harold Loeb was going about with a gun and an intent to kill Hemingway on sight.[14] Never mind that the man Hemingway had fictionalized into Robert Cohn was one who abhorred cruelty. He had been represented as a cross between a boob and a bore. It was logical—was it not?—that he should defend his honor. Somewhat later this rumor took on a romantic tinge. It was bruited about that Loeb was really hurt by the loss of Duff Twysden, the model for the heroine, Lady Brett Ashley; and that when she left him for Hemingway, he became so enraged that then he acquired a gun to fulfill schemes of homicide.[15] There was a logic in this legend too. Hemingway depicted Robert Cohn as a man possessed when under the influence of love. He had glued himself to Brett Ashley and offered to fight for her honor when challenged by Jake Barnes, under whose name Hemingway himself was disguised. And Duff Twysden? In the novel she was shown treating men as her wardrobe, trying on one after another and discarding one after another as easily as one might tire of last week's new garment. It was well known that the novel was heavily weighted with reportage. The living Loeb had had a liaison with the viable Twysden and assumedly she had intimacies with the real Hemingway as well. If so much of fiction was founded on so much of fact, the new fictions outside the novel, but deductible from it, carried conviction. Hemingway might well have stolen Duff from Loeb. Quite in character, Duff would have allowed the looting; and also in character, Loeb would have lost himself in a jealous rage. The annals of imagined violence did not stop there. One could impute uncontrollable anger to still another person whom Hemingway fictionalized. That was Kitty Cannell recognizable in Frances Clyne, the mistress of Robert Cohn in the early chapters. Bad enough to be made the mistress of a boob and boor, she was also made out to have designs on Cohn's money with nothing more to offer on her part but a wealth of ill-nature. You can well understand Kitty Cannell's joining the local gun and rifle set. But after all, ladies don't as a rule seek revenge either by means so direct or so obvious. So the rumor for her was that when she and Loeb parted, she acquired a new boyfriend, six feet three in height[16] and presumably with the strength and skills of the tribe of Mendoza, Dempsey, and Cassius Clay. He might knock out Hemingway on sight. What weapons for Duff? Her new husband. She married a Texan artist, Clinton King, in 1928. No matter that King has been described by several who knew him as the gentlest of men. Allegedly, he confronted Hemingway and pasted him to the floor.[17]

You will find similar twice-told tales in A. E. Hotchner's *Papa Hemingway*, and, if Hotchner had been available to young Hemingway in the 1920's, some of these stories would have been widely columnized and might have given the Hall-Mills Case and the Peaches-Daddy Browning affair stiff competition. Of course, *The Sun Also Rises* made the movies on its own steam; but long afterwards Hemingway himself could not resist the temptation to revive the scandals of an earlier day. Yes, he told Hotchner, he had heard that Loeb was out to kill him;[18] that those days with Duff had ruined Loeb permanently, and indeed, Duff Twysden's coffin was borne by a flock of former lovers.[19] Who knows how many of these legends were originated by Hemingway in the first place? But the point is they were circulated and believed, and once again we must regret the unavailable public relations man who would have had his glamor to make. Loeb was a product of the multi-millionaire Loebs and Guggenheims. Duff Twysden claimed descent from the Stuart Kings of England[20] and, *pièce de résistance*, Bill Smith, it was said, tried out for the St. Louis Cardinals[21] to end up in later years writing some of Harry Truman's labor speeches.[22] These were the boys and girls of the so-called Lost Generation. They were not, as Malcolm Cowley described them, mere folksy types out of the Protestant midwest,[23] uprooted from the soil and uneasy therefore in the Village and the Left Bank. But Cowley's sentimentalism is itself part of the mythology about the characters of *The Sun Also Rises*, and the novel mothered fictions about itself. Even Hemingway could not stop the legend that he was depicting the Lost Generation.[24] He protested that the Earth and not Jake Barnes, not even the matador, Pedro Romero, was the hero. Few critics believe Hemingway even today.[25]

We are told by Cowley that the younger generation saw itself mirrored in the novel.[26] We are also told that it became a kind of guidebook for the young much like Chesterfield's *Letters* and Castiglione's *Courtier* for the young of an earlier day. Thornton Wilder remembered undergraduates at Yale taking on the hard-boiled mannerisms of Jake Barnes.[27] Other sources tell us that Smith College alumnae made Brett Ashley their model.[28] Cowley reported that it was not unusual to see young men assuming the stance of bullfighters, then stepping aside to clear from the charge of an imaginary bull.[29] Most of these stories should be placed in the same category as the stories about Loeb and his revolver, Kitty Cannell and her gigantic boyfriend, and Duff Twysden's smashing funeral. At any rate, the living characters whom Hemingway transmuted into the fictive ones of his novel did not feel lost—not one to whom I have spoken felt that in his youth. A protest against the idea of one's being lost can be found in a letter sent to Gertrude Stein.[30] The writer said that Hemingway gave a false picture of their genera-tion—he was not speaking, of course, of the very young but of the group around Stein and Hemingway. In 1943 James T. Farrell clarified the issue.[31] No, Hemingway's generation was not lost; it was the younger generation, the college kids and such, who found their malaise in the pages of *The Sun Also Rises*. Perhaps so. But the consequences were not necessarily the cult of the hard-boiled or the promiscuous or the alcoholic or the matador.

Like its author, *The Sun Also Rises* had charisma; and because it did, its fictions could support fiction spun out of it. Fortunately for us some of the original characters are still alive to tell their story. Per-sons close to the deceased characters can contribute to our knowledge of the way they were and exactly who they were. It would be pleasant to be able to say that we are on the high road to fact. But we must anticipate blurred memories; we must allow for the will to believe and doubt; we must reckon with old antagonisms among the characters themselves; or with hatreds and admirations of extant friends and relatives. Out of all this some truth will emerge, and along with all this will come new legends, revived squabbles, together with myths spawned out of love and revenge. Somehow, one will get a clearer pic-ture of Hemingway's people. Certainly, one will get an inkling of how they felt to be fictionalized. Let's keep in mind that literature has many nuggets of this kind—poems and plays, as well as novels. But I can re-call no circumstance in which several of the real persons incorporated in a fiction took the opportunity to speak out, or to have spokesman for them. We start with Harold Loeb, the Robert Cohn of Heming-way's creation.

In the fall of 1926 Harold Loeb received a copy of *The Sun Also Rises* which hit him like an upper-cut. He was in St. Paul in the south of France when Hemingway's novel arrived and he was living with a

Dutch girl in a rented farmhouse set in a field of artichokes. He had found the Dutch girl in Paris; he thought her to be very beautiful but because Loeb spoke no Dutch and the girl no English, they communicated in French[32] and perhaps it was in French that Loeb fulminated about the book he had just received. There was no doubt that one of its principal characters, Robert Cohn, had been provided a biography based on the life of Harold Loeb. Depicted as the offspring of one of America's richest Jewish families, he was easily identifiable with Loeb, descended from the opulent Guggenheims and Loebs. Cohn, like Loeb, had gone to Princeton where he might have taken boxing lessons from Spider Kelly, a genuine member of the pugilistic faculty. Loeb, like Cohn, had edited an avant-garde magazine, written a novel, gone off to New York, returned to Paris, quarrelled with a so-called mistress, admired the romantic novels of W. H. Hudson, had an affair with a titled English lady, and raised a row with some of her male friends at Pamplona where they had all gone to see the bullfights. There was no doubt about the similarities between the fictive Cohn and the living Loeb. But the fictive Cohn appeared to the living Loeb as a considerable boob and a drag; there the identification ceased and the indignation began. And quite understandably. The author of *The Sun Also Rises* was considered by Loeb to have been his close personal friend. They played tennis, they boxed, they chatted over oysters and wine at their favorite cafes, and lately Loeb had gone to the trouble of introducing Hemingway to publisher Horace Liveright's agent[33]— Loeb had gone out of his way, when in New York, to help the young author be published.[34] And, of course, Loeb had told Hemingway a good deal about his current personal life.[35] The intimate disclosures became, as Loeb saw it, the betrayal; the friendship, a lie which ended in travesty. It is said—among other things which were said—that Loeb developed an ulcer. The story of the ulcer gave rise to the report of seven years of psychoanalysis.[36] There is no doubt that Loeb was outraged, and the Dutch girl was the first to witness the protest that has gone on intermittently over forty years.

In recounting the narrative of the persons whom Hemingway used in his novel and their reactions to being fictionalized, the Dutch girl would be the right person to begin with. But it was not certain that she was still alive. Loeb thought not. The poet and former surrealist, Jacques Baron, said she was, that she was married to a physician and that she lived in Paris.[37] Interesting as her testimony might be, it has been omitted for certain reasons of which delicacy is one. Sufficient to say, she became Loeb's wife, travelled with him to the Near East, and became involved with an officer of the French Foreign Legion. Loeb discovered them, but was powerless because the officer carried a revolver and looked menacing.[38] So Loeb abandoned her "in the desert," as he said. Out of courtesy he brought her back to Paris, and then went on to obtain a divorce. Over the years he lost track of her, although for a while she sent letters asking for money. So if Loeb had exploded against Hemingway in French that fall day of 1926, we might get a still more explosive but a somewhat slanted account from our Dutch source, and had he done so in English, we would have received from her very little information indeed. At any rate, evidence from divorced wives is notoriously unreliable; evidence from divorced wives who have been abandoned in a desert is even more suspect. It is problematical, in fact, whether she knew the background of the Loeb-Hemingway relationship and it is fairly certain that she had not read *The Sun Also Rises*. At best, her report would be of a certain anger out of context. Eventually she was to find out a bit about her new husband's relationship to one of the characters in the novel. One day she saw a package of water colors enveloped in a paper on which there was familiar handwriting. She recognized the handwriting as Kitty Cannell's. Angrily she threw the package out of the porthole of the transatlantic liner they were taking to come to America where the "waif" was to charm the Lehmans and Guggenheims. Sandwiched among the water colors that sank in the Atlantic was a photograph of Duff Twysden as a teenager. That was a bit of the aftermath of Loeb's idyllic episode with Duff Twysden at St. Jean-de-Luz which Hemingway—we had better say Jake Barnes, the narrator—once held up to ridicule.

To make matters worse for Loeb, several reviewers in America, you will recall, let it be known that Hemingway had based his characters on real persons and Harold Loeb was not unknown to the American public. In Paris the identity of Hemingway's characters was no secret. Morrill Cody, presently an executive of Radio Liberty in Paris, recalled hearing that Loeb had, in fact, sought out Hemingway with a gun.[39] Such rumors sprang up at once while in peaceful southern France amidst the artichokes Loeb thought about Hemingway's deceit. If his thoughts turned to Paris or New York, he must have envisioned the jests and gossip that might ensue. That wound was too deep to allow fine distinctions as to whether the views of the narrator, Jake Barnes, might not, after all, be quite different from those of author Hemingway. Hemingway never gave Loeb or Kitty Cannell or the others the benefit of such an explanation. He allowed it to be known, in fact, that Jake Barnes represented him; and in the fall of

1925, after he had written the first draft of *The Sun Also Rises*—a secret from all but few of his Paris friends[40]—he threatened in a conversation with Kitty Cannell that he "would rip those two bastards apart." He assured Kitty he would never do that to her, but the other two....One proposed victim was Harold Loeb, the other Bill Smith: both close friends of Hemingway.[41]

Loeb felt betrayed; it is said that out of sympathy for him Kitty Cannell took to bed for three whole days.[42] Their relationship had come to an end almost a year and a half before the novel appeared.[43] Hemingway reported accurately that after Loeb had gone to New York to see to the publication of his new book—Loeb had sailed to America to settle the publication of *Doodab*, his novel—he wrote to Kitty that February 1925 from on board that he would probably not return.[44] She was miserable.[45] When he did return to Paris and to his apartment near the Eiffel Tower where they had adjacent quarters, they attempted to resume their relationship.[46] It was hopeless—"We were not on the same wave length," Kitty Cannell said[47]—and it came to an end just before Loeb went off to St. Jean-de-Luz with Duff Twysden. The end was unnerving for Kitty Cannell. She continued to correspond with Loeb, however, although she shortly became friendly with Bill Smith.[48] Loeb's affair with Duff Twysden was brief; he had ended his relationship with Kitty, and for a brief interim in the fall of 1925, he and Smith took up with two hostesses of a night club. They were Russian emigrees; one was Countess Vera, the other Princess Cleopatra. Loeb's was the princess. A real princess? "Anyone who had owned a few acres might be called a princess," he said.[49] One of the results of this double-dating was a novel by Loeb called, *The Professors Liked Vodka*. In it, Vera and Cleopatra are named by their real names; Smith is disguised as Professor Halsey and Loeb as Professor Mercado. The novel, published the year after *The Sun Also Rises*, is suggestive. Vera has an air of mystery about her. Loeb, even forty years after the episode of St. Jean-de-Luz, spoke of that quality in Duff Twysden.[50] Mercado wished to marry Cleopatra but is held back by some fear. That too was Loeb's experience with Duff. Finally, Mercado is unable to marry Cleopatra because she reveals herself to be violently anti-Semitic, although Duff gave no indication of having been so. But Loeb might have felt that in his fictive role as Robert Cohn he was getting a taste of traditional bigotry. Nevertheless, Loeb, despite all his grievances, has defended Hemingway against the charge of anti-Semitism.[51]

The place of *The Professors Liked Vodka* in the Loeb-Hemingway story is confusing because of its publication date. Though published

after *The Sun Also Rises*, it was written earlier and was not respon-
sive to Hemingway's novel. Loeb's book nominally recounts the futile
adventure with Cleopatra, but the sadness and the nostalgia were
for someone else. Not Duff Twysden, as we might think, but for Kitty
Cannell.[52] Nevertheless, during the period he began the book, or
shortly before, Loeb was corresponding with Duff Twysden. She was
in Scotland at her mother's. Her letters were friendly. Yes, she remembered—and she was touched by the memory of last summer—but
she thought it best for them to remain mere good friends.[53] Next summer, after returning once again to Paris from New York, he met Duff
at the Select.[54] Soon thereafter he met the Dutch girl—a "waif," he
thought her. She said she had run away from home—and he was with
her at his hotel when Duff reappeared.[55] He could not very well invite
her upstairs. Had there been no one with him, he and Duff might have
resumed their friendship. Who knows? Loeb might not have remarried, he might not have gone to St. Paul to write his next novel
Tumbling Mustard. He might have remained in Paris and it might have
been in the company of the heroine of Hemingway's novel that *The Sun
Also Rises* would have first reached him. She, not the Dutch girl,
would have been witness to his outrage, and Loeb would have had a
story to tell us about her reaction to being depicted as alcoholic and
promiscuous—and, like Loeb, betrayed.

I asked Loeb more than once what his reaction was when he first received a copy of *The Sun*. What did he do? What did he say? Certainly, he must have said something to his new wife. No, he could not
recall saying anything to her. He was sure that he did not discuss the
book with her. Then, one day, he asked me to read an unpublished
novel he had written in 1930. It was entitled *Leaf of Twisted Olive* and
its opening chapters were about Paris in the mid-twenties with the
Dutch girl as the principal female character for the first half of the
book. The scene I sought, the one in which Loeb received Hemingway's novel, was not there. But a character named Hank, remotely
suggestive of Hemingway, is singled out as a significant friend. Hank is
a writer who has turned his back on America and has come to Paris to
write and to drink. He is a dedicated writer with two shortcomings.
The first, the lack of a job or income, the hero of the novel (Loeb himself) is trying to remedy, just as in life, Loeb had done what he could to
find Hemingway a publisher.[56] The second fault is a lack of social and
political commitment; to Hank writing is an end in itself. While Loeb
told me that Hemingway was not to be identified with Hank, it is quite
clear that that fictional character represents the quintessence of

Hemingway and the hundreds of expatriates whom the hero of the novel—and Loeb himself in actual life—was shortly to reject. The hero dedicates himself to the Zionist cause; Loeb was to return to the United States to become an advocate of Technocracy. Loeb seemingly was rejecting Hemingway as a type rather than as the mere person who had violated the common decencies of friendship just four years before.

In the absence of witnesses we have Loeb's own account of his anger over *The Sun Also Rises*. That account excludes guns and psychoanalysis, ulcers and homicidal intents. He was embittered, but not ruined either by Hemingway, or as Hemingway would have it, by Duff Twysden. Hadley thought that Harold Loeb carried on his bitterness far too long;[57] but even most of Hemingway's close friends—Bill Horne for example—agreed that Loeb had just cause.[58] That too was the opinion of Hemingway's principal biographer, Carlos Baker.[59] It would seem that Loeb never forgave the offense. More than thirty years later in *The Way It Was* he published his account of his friendship with Hemingway and his brief love affair with Duff Twysden. That biography emphasized the idyllic character of the affair with Duff and Hemingway's betrayal of friendship. Again, in 1967, Loeb published "Hemingway's Bitterness," an essay in which he reviewed again the love affair and the betrayal. But this last essay was provoked by Hemingway's misrepresentation of the past as reported in Hotchner's *Papa Hemingway*. Loeb was so indignant at that time that he consulted an attorney here about the advisability of a libel suit[60] and he asked his cousin, Lady Castle Stewart, to obtain advice from an English attorney as to the advisability of a suit abroad.[61] He learned that libel suits are rarely remunerative and always expensive. He turned instead to the pen and began a book on—or should we say against?—Hemingway himself. It was the material for this book that formed the nucleus for his essay, "Hemingway's Bitterness."

But it would be an exaggeration to say that from 1926 onwards Hemingway was Loeb's obsession. After writing his third novel in the 1920's, he left Europe, as did so many of the expatriates by the time of the stock market crash or as a result of it. He began a new career as a government economist. Holding a responsible position with the War Production Board, he abandoned belles-lettres for such writing as, *Report on the National Survey on Potential Product Capacity* and *Full Production Without War*.[62] Apparently the animosities of 1926 were long put aside when, in 1959, Loeb published his memoirs of the earlier period. In *The Way It Was* Loeb tried to tell the actual story of the love affair and the breaking up with Kitty Cannell, the friendship with

Harold Loeb, 50, government economist. *Collection of Harold Loeb.*

Hemingway, the interlude with Duff Twysden, and the gathering in Pamplona, the scene of assault by Pat Guthrie (Duff's fiancé) with Hemingway joining in the attack.

Hemingway's comment, meant sympathetically, was that the book was more like, "It Might Have Been."[63] Yet, Loeb told me, Hemingway often had this book before him during the composition of *A Moveable Feast*—Loeb was told that by Valerie Danby-Smith, Hemingway's secretary.[64] Let us say that after many years Loeb's emotions of anger or hatred—or whatever the right term is—were revived. Yet Loeb's memories were not without gallantry. More than once Loeb was asked if part of Hemingway's discrediting him did not have its roots in anti-Semitism. No, Loeb said; he defended Hemingway from the charge of anti-Semitism.[65] Did he think Hemingway was a great writer? To be sure, he did not; but he certainly thought him to be an influential one: the novelist who had changed the style of the contemporary novel. He remembered Hemingway as having been one of the most charming of men. That made the treachery beyond Loeb's comprehension.[66] He tried to explain it away in "Hemingway's Bitterness" as something that had stemmed from early childhood. In conversations with me he defended Hemingway from the charge of homosexuality.[67] If anything, he thought Hemingway a Puritan. He might have been envious about Duff.[68]

Did he think that Hemingway had been plying him for information? After all, Hemingway knew about the quarrels and the breakup with Kitty Cannell and he knew, of course, about the affair with Duff Twysden. Loeb admitted that they had talked in Paris about his private life. Hemingway was actually present with Loeb and Kitty Cannell in the scene described in Chapter I (the kick Cohn gave Jake under the table was not real).[69]

Of course, Hemingway was never told by Loeb that his mother objected to his marrying Kitty. She was not "refined," his mother had objected.[70] In fact, a lot of pressure was being put on Loeb to drop Kitty. A second cousin, Barbara[71]—not to be confused with Loeb's present wife, Barbara Loeb—tried to divert him from Kitty by making herself available. This Barbara, who lived with Loeb's mother at the Berkeley in London, must have discussed with her possible mother-in-law the prospect of matrimony.[72] Hemingway knew nothing of these pressures being put on Loeb, but apparently he did have an outline of Loeb's earlier years.

Loeb thought that Hemingway must have known about his college

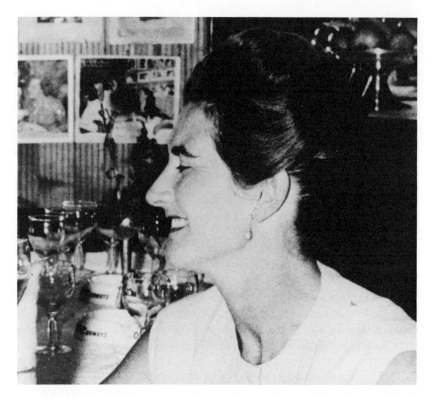

Mrs. Harold Loeb, Rome, 1965. *Collection of Harold Loeb.*

days recorded in the opening pages of *The Sun Also Rises* through classmate, Bill Horne.[73] The last surmise turned out to be debatable. Bill Horne knew little or nothing of Loeb when they were at Princeton; they became somewhat acquainted during the period that Loeb was on the War Production Board. In fact, Horne did not read *The Sun Also Rises* until an even later period. When he did, he realized that his one contribution was to have acquainted Hemingway with the name Spider Kelly in the opening lines. Horne had mentioned that name to Hemingway when they struck up a friendship in New York in Hemingway's youth. (They later served together with the Red Cross.) Hemingway seemed fascinated by the name; he told Horne that he wished that he might go to Princeton.[74] Although this friendship lasted for the rest of Hemingway's lifetime, Horne conceded that Hemingway had played Loeb a "dirty" trick.[75]

So Loeb himself was the chief source of Hemingway's knowledge

It became evident to me that after 44 years interpretations might differ and memories might clash. Loeb declared her completely unreliable; Mrs. Cannell pointed out that before writing *The Way It Was*, Loeb made two visits to Boston to check his data for the book with her. Most of the points at issue need not have aroused such strong feelings. There was much ado about cats, pants, and conversions. Mrs. Cannell had it that Hemingway was already a Roman Catholic convert before meeting Pauline Pfeiffer, his second wife. Loeb questioned that, but recently published evidence supports Mrs. Cannell's statements.[88] Mrs. Cannell mentioned Loeb's instant generosity in getting Hemingway a pair of trousers when he said his were worn through at the seat. Loeb could recall no such act. One of the main points of furor concerned the identity of the cat that they had given Hemingway. Loeb was absolutely certain that it was the cat they had rescued one night in a pit by Trajan's Column in Rome. Mrs. Cannell was equally certain that it was her mother's cat. (A scholarly note on this subject will be found in Baker's biography.)[89] But the true cause of Loeb's irritation stemmed from a comment Mrs. Cannell had made to the effect that they had established separate quarters during the period of their intimacy in Paris. Without denying there had been an affair, she mentioned it pianissimo and in a minor key. Loeb felt that she was trying to deny their essential relationship. He produced a sheaf of her letters of the year 1925 and gave me some to read. I hoped that he would not have them deposited in the Princeton Library, as he proposed to do; for, after reading a few lines it became quite evident that these were very personal letters and that the relationship was one which had been very agonising at the time for Mrs. Cannell. It also appeared evident that Hemingway had a month-by-month knowledge of the decline and fall of the affair.

She was surprised when I told her about the letters. She had never denied having had a relationship (as such things are called these days) with Loeb; but she remembered it as having been far more casual. "We were not on the same wave length," she once told me before this new quarrel broke out. Now she said, "I must have been a dumb blonde." I did not tell her that the facts Hemingway had given in the opening of Chapter II corresponded to the actual events. Her letters to Loeb showed that Loeb, as Hemingway recounted, did plan a severance on his going to New York to have his first novel published. How did Hemingway know even this detail? Had she confided in him? Certainly, not—Loeb must have done so, I suggested. But if Hemingway had access to some of the facts, Mrs. Cannell denied that his portrait of her as Frances Clyne bore much resemblance to the real person. She conceded that Hemingway had given Frances some of her typical expressions, but that the character assigned her belonged to another person: a young woman who served briefly on the staff of Loeb's magazine *Broom*. Details of the story could not be written; too many living persons were involved. It could only be related in conversation.

So I went to Boston and, over lunch at the Statler, Kitty Cannell told me a story she had heard in Paris in the early 1920's.

There was a young woman on the staff of *Broom* (who is mentioned in fact, by Frances in her quarrel with Robert in Chapter VI) with whom, allegedly Loeb had had an affair. (In the novel Frances says that it was merely a platonic relationship). That young woman may have heard, as Hemingway had heard, that Loeb still had some of the $50,000 left him by his father and that he was now getting an allowance from his mother.[90] At any rate, Loeb was equated with wealth, if not in hand then with good prospects. Someone—perhaps the girl herself—decided that Loeb should be trapped into marriage. Others were acquainted with this scheme, Mrs. Cannell said: two members of the *Broom* staff and a lady novelist called "June" whose literary talents were admired by T. S. Eliot. The novelist was evidently the chief advisor. The plan called for the girl's declaring herself pregnant and demanding that Loeb marry her. Part of the intrigue involved her calling for help while Loeb was locked in her room in the Hotel Jacob. Then there would be witnesses that she had been overcome by Loeb, or, at least, that she had been in an intimate situation with him.

This was the golddigger, Mrs. Cannell said, who was the real model for the predatory Frances Clyne. In fact, her name was Frances.

I asked her how Hemingway knew or could have known about her.

It was simple, she said. There was an excellent grapevine in Montparnasse. Everybody knew about Loeb's private life.

I thought it a good idea to check this story out with the proposed victim. I mentioned the identity of the girl to Loeb who remembered her merely as an employee who had failed to do four letters and whom he fired. Yes, she made a scene when he fired her. He denied ever having had an affair with her, and he denied her ever having made a demand of marriage and he denied her having pretended to be pregnant.

If there had been a plot, he said, he certainly would have known about it.

No, I insisted, if there had been a plot, he would have been the last to have known about it.

Well, the whole thing was nonsense, he said. This was more of Kitty

Cannell's irresponsibility, her wild imagination. Don't trust a word she says. She'll make up anything.

But Kitty Cannell did not impress me as having a wild imagination or as being irresponsible. Moreover, she made it clear that she was merely reporting.

Loeb seems to have forgotten that Hemingway knew something about his relationship with that secretary.

The novelist "June" with whom the story might be checked was still alive. A letter addressed to her in care of her publisher was un-answered. Inquiries as to her precise whereabouts—I had heard that she lived in New York City—failed to yield a telephone number or ad-dress.[91] One day I telephoned a New York rare book dealer whom I proposed to visit. I called at the wrong time, she regretted. T. S. Eliot's widow, Valerie, had arrived at her home to spend a few days there; and that day they were having lunch with "June." I proposed joining them, but, I was told, Valerie Eliot had been guaranteed pri-vacy. It was also made clear that "June" would likewise remain inac-cessible. But if Kitty Cannell's story could not be checked out through "June," there was still another source. I located one of the *Broom* staff who was in Paris at the time of the alleged plot. Yes, she remem-bered a plot against Loeb, but it was not quite the same plot that Mrs. Cannell had related to me.

There had been a Frances who gave up her job near the Washington Square Bookshop to accompany Loeb and his editorial assistants, the Kreymborgs, on their trip to Europe where *Broom* was to be launched. Frances was to serve as Loeb's secretary. Had they had an affair, I asked? No question about that, I was told. It had begun while crossing the Atlantic on the S.S. *Rotterdam*; there were eyewitnesses to the intimacies below decks. (The so-called intimacies were a hoax, Loeb told me.) Moreover, Loeb and Frances had moved into the Hotel Jacob on arrival in Paris; apparently they occupied separate rooms. On one occasion they dined out together and Loeb ordered Frances to get something on the menu less expensive than rump steak. "Pas de rump steak," he had insisted. Then he fired her. He gave her as yet unpaid wages of about $5.00 and there was Frances stranded in Paris virtually penniless.[92] "June" (who also lived at the Hotel Jacob) had become very fond of Frances and on hearing of her situation be-came incensed at Loeb. "June" persuaded Frances to call Loeb to her room. At the time of his anticipated appearance, "June" stationed her-self with a club at the head of the staircase. Soon footsteps were heard. "June" raised her club. But the man who appeared was Marsden Hartley, the writer; and he almost became the victim. This was the story told by one of the former *Broom* staff, and we must keep in mind that it was told by one with whom Loeb did not have the most cordial of relations.

There is no question but that Hemingway was familiar with at least a part of this story. He has Frances refer to Robert Cohn's having moved his secretary from Carmel, California to Provincetown where he abandoned her. He didn't even provide her with train fare back to California.[93]

I related the new version of the plot to Loeb at the same time informing him that the source was not Kitty Cannell. He listened to this account with more respect. Now he remembered an occasion when Frances urged him to come to her room and after his arrival there, she locked the door and raised a row. In retrospect, Loeb thought that she was merely protesting her dismissal, but he conceded that there might have been elements of intrigue. At a later date he told me that once Frances had asked him to her room and, suspecting a plot, he kept his foot in the door so she could not close it on him. Then, he added, somewhat gratuitously, that while crossing the Atlantic he had pretended to make love to her in front of the Kreymborgs in a cabin that they all shared jointly. It was all a hoax, he explained.

Dorothy Kreymborg knew about the plot to club Loeb; she did not know about a plot to entrap Loeb into marriage. Yet, she did think Kitty Cannell quite reliable, although she found it difficult to believe that Frances—whom she thought of as too nondescript to kindle a writer's imagination—would have been capable to playing the part of an outraged, to-be-abandoned, pregnant girl.[94]

At any rate, some sort of plot against Loeb existed, and in *The Sun* the biography of Frances Clyne coincides in part with the real Frances and in part with Kitty Cannell. The real Frances accompanied Loeb to Europe as did the fictive character;[95] the fictive character had a liaison with Robert Cohn that corresponded to the stormy relationship between Loeb and Kitty Cannell. She did not meet Loeb until he arrived in Paris. They were introduced by the Kreymborgs.[96]

It may have been that the plot against Loeb circulated by way of the Montparnasse grapevine through which source the story was embroidered on and highlighted for points of narrative interest. Certainly, Loeb was reputed to be a catch. On news of the launching of *Broom* a writer for *The Dial* hinted at Loeb's having $100,000.00 behind the project.[97] Hemingway in *The Sun* had a more realistic account of Loeb's low-five figure resources; he must have had these statistics from

Loeb himself.[98]   But it is also possible that Hemingway heard about "June" and Frances and Loeb from Alfred Kreymborg. His autobiography, *Troubadour*, published in 1925 and, no doubt, completed at least just the year before, excludes any mention of the plot to assault and club, but his wife assured me that he knew about the matter. She also told me that Hemingway and Alfred Kreymborg met at the time when the former was about to sign with Scribner's. He seemed to have had a flicker of doubt, for he asked Kreymborg whether or not to sign with Harcourt, Brace.[99] This conversation, which took place just before the revision of *The Sun*, may have been the occasion for talk about Loeb. Nothing is more usual than for two literary men to discuss what they have been doing, and here is Kreymborg who has worked under Loeb whom Hemingway knows intimately as a tennis companion, eating buddy, and father confessor. And it may be that Kreymborg also told him what he suppressed in *Troubadour* namely, that he and Dorothy could not work with Loeb because Loeb could not be made to work.[100] The published account by Kreymborg of their differences suggests mere polite inability to agree on editorial policy.[101] To this day Loeb is insistent on his conscientiousness as publisher and editor. Hemingway's account is closer to Kreymborg's. Robert Cohn is represented as a fatuous lover and a full-fledged sentimental Romanticist. He is never depicted working.

So much for the account given me by Mrs. Cannell. Whether or not Hemingway drew on Loeb's secretary to create the scheming Frances Clyne, it is beyond question that Kitty Cannell had no designs on Loeb. She remembered gratefully a fur coat he had bought for her;[102] Loeb himself recalled the gift.[103] He did give her a gift at the time of their breaking up so that she could visit friends in London, but the circumstances were quite different from those reported in Chapter VI. Loeb's was an act of kindness.[104] There was no attempt on Kitty Cannell's part to upbraid him or to double the amount of the gift through a war on his nerves. She did not rant about being stranded without a man to her name. The trip to London was understood between them as a means to making a clean break.[105] There Mrs. Cannell met good friends from the United States and through them received the hospitality of the Earl of Lathom. Her subsequent acquaintances included Noel Coward and, before long, two young men who were bona fide suitors. The remark made by Frances Clyne in Chapter VI that she doubted if she were still young and attractive enough to marry was Hemingway's invention. Invention of that sort did not surprise Mrs. Cannell when she read *The Sun Also Rises*. She never trusted Hem-

ingway, she said. She tried often to warn Harold Loeb against him.
She frequently told Loeb that Hemingway was anti-Semitic, but he
would not listen to her.[106] He trusted Hemingway. Poor Harold was
naive, she said, and when the novel came out she suffered for the attack
made on one so guileless.[107]

Loeb himself defended Kitty Cannell against Hemingway's de-
piction. She was no golddigger, he said.[108] According to Mrs. Cannell,
Loeb did attempt a reconciliation after Pamplona—a forecast made in
Chapter XVIII; she said that she would not go back to the past once a
break was made.[109]

I asked Loeb if Kitty Cannell was the tempestuous character Hemingway had drawn in the person of Frances Clyne. She had a bad
Irish temper, Loeb said. She admitted to me that she had "a terrible
temper" in those days, but she overcame it once she stopped drinking;
and she has not had a flare-up since she stopped drinking 30 years ago.
However, during the time that she was friendly with Loeb, she was
irascible. He remembered their having been at a hotel whose walls
were mere "thin partitions." She evidently was berating him in a voice
loud enough to be heard in the adjoining room. In that room was a
friend of theirs, Josephine Bennett. Loeb asked Kitty Cannell to calm
down, but in vain. This incident seems to have been the source for the
conclusion of Chapter II. Robert Cohn reports to Jake a sleepless
night. Much argument has gone on which Jake tells us he can picture.
In actuality, Loeb may have reported the incident himself. It is also
possible that Josephine told Hemingway about it. She knew the Hemingways. She was supposed to have joined them just before Christmas
of 1924 in their expedition to ski in the Austrian Alps.[110]

It would be absurd to deny that Harold Loeb and Kitty Cannell
quarreled. It would be more absurd to believe that she had more ve-
hemence in her blood than corpuscles. However, Hemingway regarded
her as formidable. She didn't need any six-foot boyfriend to beat him
up, she said, dismissing the rumor that she had acquired one for that
purpose after *The Sun Also Rises* was published.[111] If Hemingway had
met her at that time in a café and had ventured a snide remark, there
were several bartenders who would have come to her defense. They
would have laid Hemingway low. As a matter of fact, she said, Hemingway avoided her. Friends of his told her that Hemingway was
worried. What if he met Kitty face to face? And she told him off? "I
couldn't smack her," Hemingway was reported to have said.[112] I don't
want to leave the impression that Kitty Cannell was (or is) a species of
Amazon. I always found her courteous. I found her to be what is

called a sensible woman. But speaking of tempers, I was curious to know about the so called ex-boxing star of Princeton. What about Loeb's temper, I asked Kitty Cannell? Was he the touchy, sensitive soul that appeared in Hemingway's pages? No, she replied, he was nothing like that, not in those early days.[113]

Kitty Cannell, in whom there was a mixture of English, Red Indian, and Irish,[114] prides herself on a life of hard work. She had met Loeb through the Kreymborgs just after their arrival in Paris to launch *Broom*. She knew them quite well because she had performed along with Edna Millay in Alfred Kreymborg's play, "Manakin and Mini-kin," at the Provincetown Playhouse.[115] Her acquaintance with the Kreymborgs had begun even earlier when her then husband, Skipwith Cannell, a minor poet, took an interest in Kreymborg's magazine, *Others*.[116] The Cannells were on their way to divorce when she met Loeb in Paris.[117] As far as Loeb knew, she was born in Philadelphia; she was in fact born in Utica, New York.[118] Hemingway makes his Frances Clyne European educated.[119] Possibly he got that impression from Kreymborg's *Troubadour* which appeared about the time *The Sun* was being written; Kreymborg observed that she spoke as only a native Frenchwoman[120] could. Kreymborg knew her well, Mrs. Cannell told me. He was quite aware that she had lived with a French family and later had attended the Sorbonne,[121] a fact about which Loeb knew nothing, and when told about, disbelieved.[122] Her early college years, however, were at the University of Toronto (Loeb knew nothing about that either) and somewhere in her youth she was trained for ballet.[123] Through her husband she had become friends with Ford Madox Ford. She knew Pound, and later the entire Dadaist and surrealist set, particularly young Jacques Baron and Louis Aragon.[124] Which is to say, she moved in literary circles and was herself a writer, although ballet was her first love.

In the 1920's two of her short stories were commended by O'Brien. They were written during the period she knew Loeb but published in *transition* after their break-up.[125] He therefore did not know about her success, but he did remember her writing during the time they were together.[126] And during the time she was Loeb's intimate friend she was a great help with translations for *Broom*.[127] That she was of artistic temperament and literary is not even remotely suggested in Hemingway's characterization of her as Frances Clyne. He saw her merely as an intriguante and what he knew of her—apart from any tidbits he might have gotten from Kreymborg or from gossip—he got from Loeb or from the circumstances of having been in their company. Now Loeb himself was no authority on Kitty Cannell. He knew, of course, of her broken marriage, of her training to be a ballet dancer, of her having performed in Kreymborg's play, and of her friendship with Ford Madox Ford. But he did not know if and where she was educated, he did not know much about her writing. To this day he doubts that she ever attended the Sorbonne or that, even after the time he knew her, she ever had anything published. But Hemingway knew that she was educated abroad—he says that of Frances Clyne in Chapter I; he must have researched her beyond the limits of Loeb. Frances Clyne is presented to us as a shrew with the talents of a schemer or as a schemer using the pressures of a shrew. By her own admission (Chapter VI) she has not been able to find a publisher, but carefully omitted are any references to her artistic talents and to her friendship with writers. Hemingway did not forsee publication by Morrow in 1945 of *Jam Yesterday*, the autobiography of Kitty Cannell's childhood. Yet Hemingway knew Kitty Cannell well enough—she pointed out to me— to be aware of her literary friendships and aspirations during the 1920's. He made light of them.

A similar observation may be made about Harold Loeb. Depicted as Robert Cohn, a Princeton graduate, Hemingway tells us merely that he liked the *authority* of editing and that his chief accomplishment at Princeton was to have become its middleweight boxing champion, coach Spider Kelly's outstanding pupil.[128] In fact, Loeb went out for and made the wrestling team, although he did a little boxing;[129] the legend that Loeb took up boxing to beat up his anti-Semitic persecutors began with this fiction in the introductory pages of *The Sun Also Rises*.[130] However, Kitty Cannell asserts that Loeb himself told her that he took up boxing for that reason—Loeb has no recollection of ever having told her that.[131] Nowhere in *The Sun Also Rises* is it suggested that Loeb was an intellectual, one of whose relatives had published the famous Loeb Classical Library. And likewise omitted is any reference to Loeb's zeal in making *Broom*, during its brief lifetime, one of the outstanding international magazines of the arts. In *Broom* were reproduced works by painters now famous, so as to give them in the early 1920's, a larger public than they would have otherwise had. The writings of names now familiar to us—Marianne Moore, Hart Crane. E. E. Cummings, Gertrude Stein—found an outlet in Loeb's publication. *Broom* also published Pirandello, Apollinaire, the Comte de Lautréamont, and James Stephens.[132] No doubt, had Loeb met Hemingway two or three years earlier, before *Broom's* demise, he would have published Hemingway too; for, prior to publication of *The Sun Also Rises*, Loeb thought Hemingway's gifts worthy of all the help he

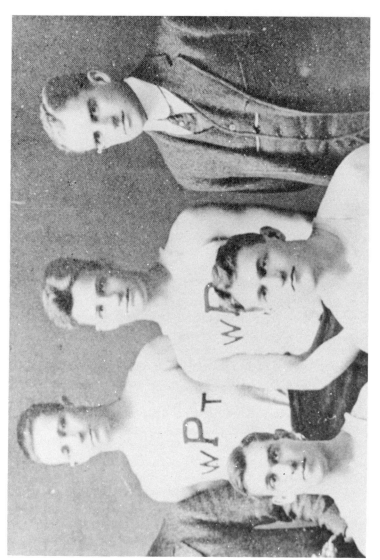

Harold Loeb (top center) on the Princeton wrestling team. *Collection of Harold Loeb.*

could give him.[133] Hemingway in turn, gives us Cohn gloomily faltering over his second book (Chapter V). But there is not the slightest
suggestion in Hemingway's novel that Loeb was involved deeply and
sincerely with modern art and literature. Robert Cohn, we are told,
was regarded as an "angel" and then found that he liked the authority
of editing (Chapter I). (Kreymborg said that he had to leave *Broom*
because Loeb insisted on being final arbiter, as was his right).[134]

   The brazen Frances Clyne who boasts that she is to get two hundred
pounds from Robert Cohn—not the mere hundred he promised her for
her trip to England (Chapter VI)—lacks the finesse of Brett but Brett
likewise has no scruples about marrying for the money Mike Campbell will some day inherit (Chapter V). Both women attract Cohn, and
it is possible Hemingway had some satiric motive over and above the
obvious satire on Cohn's inability to see these women in the fulness of
their faults. They had faults enough, certainly, without Hemingway's
having to give them a strong sense of cupidity. The emphasis on money
may have had something to do with Loeb's manifesto for *Broom*.
Called, "The Mysticism of Money," it contained ideas, Malcolm
Cowley said at the time of publication, "fresh to American literature
and which ought to revitalize it."[135] Loeb's manifesto was, in fact, a
defense of American life against its critics, the most vociferous of whom
were the expatriates. He "maintained that art was the expression of a
culture and that many artifacts spewed out by American business ac-
tivity, tools as well as music, advertisements as well as movies, were
true and often beautiful expressions of the prevailing faith of America...." Loeb designated that "prevailing faith" as "The Mysticism
of Money." Money, he said, "had become the measure of most values"
and as "values are largely subjective," they may be thought of as
mystical. Hence, money might be thought of as mystical.[136]

   Loeb's essay became editorial policy and gave rise to the publication
in *Broom* of photographs of machines and movie stills. Matthew
Josephson wrote on the "Poetic value of advertising."[137] In other
words, Loeb's ideas made their impact and Hemingway may have
known of them even before he met Loeb. I asked Loeb if he ever discussed "The Mysticism of Money" with Hemingway. Of course, he
said. And what was Hemingway's reaction? Well, Hemingway disliked theories and abstract ideas. Loeb thought he did not take this
credo seriously because of his contempt for theorizing.[138] But there
are many passages in *The Sun* which seem to be ironic commentaries,
even burlesques, on "the mysticism of money."

   If that was Hemingway's intention, he was having his fun at Loeb's
expense in creating a grasping Frances Clyne as Cohn's mistress and a

predatory Lady Brett as Cohn's romantic ideal. Since Kitty Cannell was not grasping and since Duff Twysden was not predatory, we can understand what impelled Hemingway to attribute to their fictive counterparts these particular traits. He makes much of money and a little about mysticism in the novel. Cohn won't marry her, Frances says, because he really wants a mistress. She knows. She's had a vision at the Café Select. All very mystic, she adds (Chapter VI). In *The Sun Also Rises* money works wonders, but not of the sort that inspired the former editor of *Broom*. Brett, calling on Jake in the early hours of the morning, is labeled a *poule* by the concierge (Chapter IV). By the mysticism of money—two hundred francs that she gave the concierge as a tip—she is transformed in the concierge's judgment into a lady from a very fine family (Chapter VII). Conversely, when Jake accompanies a real *poule*, Georgette, to Mme. Lavigne's restaurant— Georgette didn't think it chic—she is passed off to Jake's friends, Frances Clyne among them, as Georgette Leblanc, the opera singer; her being with Jake was a guarantee of social and economic status (Chapter III). Francs, pounds, dollars, and pesetas rustle and clink throughout the first half of the novel; and in the concluding chapters, money abounds and becomes the subject of a treatise. Early in the story we encounter Harvey Stone, an adept in the arcana of cash, who chisels a handout from Jake even though the donor knows full well that Harvey is not destitute. Just three days before he had won two hundred francs (the amount of Brett's tip) at dice from Jake (Chapter VI). Cohn himself is to bet Bill Gorton one hundred pesetas against the expected arrival of Brett and Mike at Pamplona (Chapter X). The last chapter contains passages about gambling, cheating, and usury. What works of art, we may ask, was such money producing? Earlier in the book, at one point, Cohn observes that a man might, if he had to, earn a living at bridge (Chapter II). Obviously, neither tools, music, movies, advertisements, or any sort of artifacts could come from that.

Throughout the novel money is a touchstone of character—but this is another subject. We will want to see if there are further evidences of Hemingway's burlesquing Loeb's theory. Art, Loeb had maintained, "was the expression of a culture," and the products of business, even its advertisements, might have aesthetic value. Money made such artifacts available to all, just as advertisements were in the public domain. Therefore, Loeb concluded, "if one believed in Democracy, measuring value by money was good since by this means, everyone had a vote, big or little, on the relative desirability of things." And, of course, since money made things of value accessible, money was in itself a value. As Bill Gorton is to put it—in a dialogue which otherwise seems mere drivel—you lay out your money and you buy a stuffed dog: an exchange of one value for another (Chapter VIII).

Other passages which seem to contribute little or nothing to the story suddenly become significant. For example, one morning as Jake is walking to work, he walks behind a man who was stamping out CINZANO on the sidewalk (Chapter V). There's an artistic advertisement for you! When Jake and Bill go to Madame Lecomte's restaurant, they are unable to get seats at once. The restaurant is crowded with Americans. Someone had advertised Madame Lecomte's restaurant as a place unfrequented by tourists. So, ironically, it is overcrowded with them (Chapter VIII). There's the beauty of advertisements for you! (The restaurant will lose its charm, but, Bill Gorton predicts, the owner will be rich.) Finally, in the same mail delivery in which Jake receives his bank statement, he finds an announcement of the marriage of Katherine, daughter of Mr. and Mrs. Aloysius Kirby. He knows neither bride nor groom. Jake humorously suggests that the Kirbys might be spreading the news (as in an advertisement or a public relations release) throughout Paris (Chapter IV). As Aloysius is a Catholic name—a good one at that, Jake reflects—we are invited to the conclusion that even the sacraments are being subjected to the mysticism of money.

As for the artifacts which might well be objects of beauty while being objects for sale, we have already noticed one of Hemingway's selections for ridicule. That was the stuffed dog Bill was urging Jake to buy: a lovely artifact, of course. Other dispensable objects are to be found in the very section where Jake encounters the man with the roller stamping out CINZANO on the sidewalk. He passes another man selling toy frogs and still another vending toy boxers. The inn at Burguette (where Jake and Bill feel overcharged) has its own fascinating artifacts: pictures of dead rabbits, dead pheasants, and dead ducks (Chapter XI). The selection of animal subjects seems deliberate (the pun on boxers may be allowed). There is little but the absurd available for money. The alternative is not "real toads in imaginary gardens" but real toads in real gardens. It is Bill who selects a McGinty *fly* with which to fish; no artifact for Jake: he uses a worm (Chapter XII). The symbolism suggests the natural versus the man-made. Something of that was implied when Hemingway remarked that the Earth was the hero of the novel. Something of that was implied when Jake notes that the straight line of Pedro Romero's movements is natural. The other bullfighters move like a corkscrew (Chapter XV).

But it may be objected that if Hemingway put to use Loeb's ideas for irony and satire, sometimes to the point of absurdity, Robert Cohn, the fictional version of Loeb, hardly seems the proponent of such ideas. On the contrary, he wishes to escape from society and whatever it is that, in society, money permits one to acquire. He proposes to Jake that they go to South America—at Cohn's expense. He is in quest of the never-never land of W. H. Hudson's, *The Purple Land* (Chapter II). Similarly, as a ridiculous Romantic, he idealizes Brett. Precisely because he does, he is incapable of accepting her in her reality; and, to the extent that he is incapable, he demands the artificial over the real, the imaginative over the natural. It is at this point that the imaginative Romantic, or the demanding idealist, is at one with those who prefer the artifact to the real: they are each in their way intolerant of Nature. Now, of course, we tend to think of Bill—and even Jake—in polar opposition to Cohn. They can see his follies; they are appalled by them. But Bill too is a muddled idealist. When he arrives from Vienna, conscious suddenly that it seemed much better than it actually was, he recounts a tale of heroism and generosity. He had helped a Black boxer escape from an angry mob. The boxer had not been paid off; Bill unsuccessfully tried to collect for him. The promoters argued that the Black had violated his contract. He was supposed to have thrown the fight but instead knocked out his opponent. The Black protested to Bill that he tried to throw the fight but somehow his opponent managed to get himself knocked out. For Bill, who loaned the Black money to return home, there was a tale of injustice (Chapter VIII). That the unpaid boxer had agreed to fix the fight—that in agreeing to frame it he was party to fleecing those who had bet on it—did not occur to the overwrought, idealistic Bill. Despondent, he took to a four-day drunk and he was still loaded as he expounded the idea that the world is made up of things and cash, that life is simply an exchange of one of these values for another.

And that outlook ultimately is to be Jake's. His relationship to Brett has dwindled in his eyes to a mere transfer of values, a getting and giving, a simple exchange (Chapter XIV). Unwittingly he has adopted Bill's philosophy, and from Chapter XI onwards we find Jake, hitherto generous, hitherto taking bills, tips, and loans lightly, suddenly sharp, suspicious, and argumentative about prices. Before the closing incident of the book—his reunion with Brett in Madrid—he reflects, after overtipping a waiter, that in France everything revolves about money. Friendship there is a commodity to be bought (Chapter XIX). The mysticism of money, which Loeb had declared to be good as a means to securing objects of manufactured art, has become for Jake, grown cynical, the means to things spiritual.

To be precise, it is Bill Gorton who is the spokesman for Loeb's aesthetic ideas—not, as we would expect, Robert Cohn. That is to say, Hemingway took traits from one living personage and transferred them to another whom he subsequently fictionalized. Such was Kitty Cannell's point in saying that Frances Clyne was a composite. She also believed that of Jake Barnes. Bill Gorton, also, is an admixture. As we will have occasion to see, two other friends of Hemingway went into his creation.

But we have not done with the matter of mysticism. Were my purpose here to explicate Hemingway's novel, I would catalogue examples of the author's awareness of three levels of beings: the supernatural (or mystic), the man-made, and the natural. In Chapter V, for example, the natural order is presented as we are told of the horsechestnut trees in bloom and the flowers being carried by vendors. A few lines later we are given illustrations of the artifact: the Cinzano man, and the sellers of toy frogs and boxers. Jake has observed all this as he walks from the Madelaine to the Boulevard des Capucines, the latter named after a convent, the former, site of the famous church, after Mary Magdalene. Scattered throughout the book are references to Saints and religious institutions. The bullfights are part of the fiesta of San Fermin. Jake's deterioration in the last chapter takes place in the resort of San Sebastian. The fishing episode with Bill is in the vicinity of the Roncesvalles monastery. It is in that episode that Bill harangues now about sex, now about evolution, now about natural religion—quoting Bryant's, "Forest Hymn" while he exhorts Jake to accept on faith the mysteries of Darwinism. Even as Frances Clyne sarcastically expounds her vision about Robert Cohn's wish for a mistress, she cannot resist adding that a memorial might be put up some day at the Select, like the tablets at Lourdes.

Religious allusion is appropriate, of course, in view of Jake's being a Catholic, if only nominally so (Chapter XIII), or if, as Jake has said of himself, a pretty rotten one (Chapter X). Hemingway himself, at the time of the writing of the novel, does not appear to have been much preoccupied with the Catholic Church. He admitted being a Catholic, his conversion having taken place just after the events at Fossalta when he was badly wounded.[139] One hardly gets the impression that in 1925 he was obsessed with a rage for piety. Oddly enough, though not a Catholic, one of the persons well-known to Hemingway and whom he made one of the principal characters of the novel, was allegedly a dedicated mystic. That character was Lady Brett Ashley and the person on whom she was based was Duff Twysden.

At least, that was what I was told—Duff Twysden was a mystic. To those who have equated her with Brett such a statement must be difficult to believe, and there are many, especially those who saw her drinking in the Quarter during the Lost Generation era, who insist on that equation. They believe too that the model for Brett was as promiscuous as the fiction.[140] Now, mystics are not as a rule alcoholic or promiscuous, at least, not the mystics who have earned their place in history. So for those who identify Brett and Duff it is something less than plausible that Duff Twysden was one of those visionaries. But that identification is a questionable one. At any rate, there can be no doubt that she told Harold Loeb she was a mystic. She said to him on an occasion that she was not sure "You are one of us."[141] It was her way of letting him know that spiritually they might be out of tune. Since it was no compliment, I am sure that Loeb did not make up the anecdote.

The expression used by Duff is familiar to readers of *The Sun Also Rises*. It occurs in Chapter VII after Count Mippipopolous shows the scars and welts of arrow wounds to Jake and Brett. She repeats—she has evidently told this to Jake before—that the Count was "one of us." As used by Hemingway, the expression means that the Count, like Jake and Brett, has in some way been scarred by the war. Brett, we are told (Chapter V) prior to marrying Lord Ashley, lost her lover during the war. In actuality, Duff Twysden is not known to have lost any lover during the war either from the cause given, dysentery, or from any other cause.[142] This seems to have been one of Hemingway's inventions, and it was needed to establish a theme and that special rapport between Jake and Brett.

But the fictional Ashley was based on fact. Duff had married Sir Roger Twysden and, at the time of Hemingway's writing the novel, was like Brett, awaiting a divorce (Chapter V). Hemingway implies that Brett was the plaintiff in the action—later in the book we are given the terrifying grounds (Chapter XVII)—whereas, according to Miss Aileen Twysden, the late Sir Roger's sister, it was he who sued Duff for divorce.[143] This is by way of saying that Brett should not be completely identified with Duff regardless of whose biography of her one comes to accept. There are two main biographies. One stems from the Twysden family and is, on the whole, contemptuous; the other is from Clinton King, whom Duff married not long after the publication of *The Sun Also Rises*. His version, entirely favorable, is, of course, at variance with both the Twysden account and Hemingway's fictive characterization.

In speaking of the information provided by the Twysden family, I will have occasion to mention two names that require identification, Mrs. Anne Fellowes and Mrs. Peter Dickens. The latter was the first of the Twysden family with whom I communicated, and she became

known to me through the kindness of Mr. Peter Townend, the editor
of *Burke's Peerage*. I had written to him to clear up a mystery about
Duff. According to *Burke's Peerage* she was the daughter of B. W.
Smurthwaite and she was christened Mary among other given names.
That would have made her Mary Smurthwaite, a name to me without
romantic or aristocratic association. But Harold Loeb had told me that
her maiden name was Duff Stirling, that, indeed, her sister was presented to him as Jean Stirling.[144] Arthur Lett-Haines who knew Duff
and her mother and sister also knew them under the name of Stirling.[145] Moreover, the hospital records of St. Vincent's in Sante Fe,
New Mexico, where Duff died, also showed that as her maiden name
along with a variant, "Sterling,"—her given name was listed as Duff.[146]
No one seems to have known her as the former Mary Smurthwaite,
which, without doubt, was her original name.[147]

Mr. Townend referred me to Duff's daughter-in-law, Mrs. Peter
Dickens. Readers of *The Sun Also Rises* would not be aware that there
might be such a person because Hemingway did not let them know that
his heroine had a son. He was Mrs. Dickens' first husband; after his
death in a German prison camp,[148] she remarried. Hemingway knew
that Duff had borne Sir Roger Twysden an heir to the title. On page 2
of the first deleted chapter he revealed that. Loeb also knew of the boy.
In letters to Loeb in the fall of 1925 Duff mentioned her hope of seeing
her son in the very near future.[149] Mrs. Dickens, it turned out, was a
means to, not a source of, information. She had never met her mother-
in-law, but Mrs. Anne Fellowes, Sir Roger Twysden's sister had; why
not write to her. I did. Mrs. Fellowes distinctly remembered Duff's
parents, the Smurthwaites. The father kept a wine shop in Darlington.
When Duff's son, Tony, was very young, Mrs. Smurthwaite sometimes
took care of him. Yes, she had heard that Duff could not return to
England—Loeb had told me that and I wondered if the Twysdens had
the answer; Loeb himself did not. The Twysden answer was that Duff
had ruined herself socially by having an affair with a Black man. I
could get more information, Mrs. Fellowes suggested, by calling on
another sister, Aileen Twysden. She lived in New York City and she
would be willing to see me.[150]

Elizabeth Twysden had come to think of herself by her middle name,
Aileen. She had lived in New York for many years, having previously
been involved in the production end of a famous ballet company. Now
a consultant to a well-known, New York department store, she lived in
the vicinity of Carnegie Hall. When we dined at the nearby Stage Deli-
catessen Restaurant, she ordered blintzes. She was a small woman,
vigorous though in her seventies, I would guess. I found her somewhat

reserved and with unostentatious good manners. She had read *A Fare-well to Arms* but not *The Sun Also Rises*. She had no idea that Duff was the heroine of that novel. - Hemingway, she said, was a phase one goes through. Had she heard that just before the novel was published in England under the title of *Fiesta* Duff's family tried to buy up the plates? (Loeb had told me that). No. I had not heard at that time of the alternative account, namely that the Twysden family had done its utmost to prevent the sale of *Fiesta*. So Kitty Cannell was informed by Berenice Abbott. Miss Abbott had met Duff in New York in the 1930's and was told by Duff how outraged she had been about *The Sun Also Rises*. She was incensed that Hemingway had revealed confidences about Sir Roger Twysden.[151] The Twysden family, she told Miss Abbott, tried to buy up every copy it could. Apparently, Duff herself, one can well surmise, was never forgiven; but certainly she never suspected that Hemingway was engaged in literary espionage. If the Twysdens had done what they could to spirit the novel out of existence, Miss Twysden did not volunteer that information. And since she did not, despite my having given her a quite audible cue, I did not pursue the question. We went on to talk of Duff's family. She knew the Smurthwaites although she had never been aware of Mr. Smurthwaite's having dealt in wine in Darlington. It does not appear that she ever met him. Jean Smurthwaite, Duff's flaxen-haired sister, was a fellow employee in the Signal Corps of the Admiralty during World War I. Mrs. Smurthwaite, widowed, had red hair with streaks of grey. She lived in the vicinity of Westminster Abbey. Miss Twysden once heard her say, "We have had an Age of Aristocracy, an Age of Money, the next Age will be an Age of Brains."

I wondered if Duff had been brought up to fit into the coming Age. Miss Twysden thought her clever, the café society type, with money and social position as her aims. Pretty clearly she was telling me that her brother Roger had fitted in with such designs. Duff was not stupid, she said, "Duff could have held a job like a buyer. She would have been better off if she worked. But she never did." But, it was evident, she did not know Duff well enough to recall more than an incident of their having been together. She invited Duff to a polo club in Hurling-hame, and they spent a pleasant day together. Miss Twysden recalled without comment Duff's wearing white stockings, black patent leather shoes, a blue dress, a hat with a green ostrich feather—somewhere in this melange of color was a dab of yellow. Afterwards, Duff told her sister Jean that she liked Miss Twysden.

What about the scandal of Duff and the Black man?

Miss Twysden had never heard of that.

And then she launched into a discourse about the Scotch nobility. I didn't get the point of the discourse at that time. At a later date I could understand clearly that it had something to do with Duff. But I didn't make the connection with Duff because the subject of the Scotch nobility seemed to be one of those topics that found its way into fairly free-flowing conversation. We had talked about the present state of the British aristocracy, about country houses, about student protests, about Anacharsis Clootz, about the ballet, and about Morley Callaghan whose identity now eludes me. At any rate, Miss Twysden reminded me that centuries ago the people of Scotland were organized into clans—I nodded, having remembered this not so much from books as from having seen *The Ghost Goes West.* Any member of a clan might, and many did, adopt the surname of the head of the clan. Thus, without actually being a blood relative of a distinguished member of the Scottish nobility, many persons bore his name. Really, Miss Twysden said, just about everyone in Scotland could claim kinship with nobility on that basis.

I thought this matter a digression—I later realized it was not—and turned to some specific questions. What was Sir Roger like? What went wrong in his and Duff's marriage? Roger, she said, was handsome, charming, a good dancer, an excellent cricket player; he attracted a lot of women and he must have attracted Duff. They were married secretly after Duff was divorced by her previous husband, Luttrell Byrom—not Byron, as *Burke's Peerage,* has it; Miss Twysden had called attention to the error for several years. Perhaps, after Duff's marriage to Roger, she never had a chance to come into her own. Roger's mother opposed the marriage. She even offered to underwrite the cost of a divorce.

Although our talk was friendly up to this point and although Miss Twysden was not seemingly vindictive against Duff I did not think I could as yet ask questions in depth. What I had in mind was to ask her about the paragraph in *The Sun Also Rises* where Brett is quoted as contemptuous about her life with the British aristocracy. Ashley, her former husband, a naval officer (as Sir Roger Twysden was), is reported as refusing to sleep in a bed, making Brett sleep on the floor, threatening to kill her, and making his threats appear real by going to sleep always with a revolver (Chapter XVII). I didn't think that I could pose questions on these matters on such short acquaintance.

"Did your brother drink?" I asked.

"Not before he was married."

The reply was crisp rather than sharp, but Miss Twysden, I felt, was ready to suggest that Duff had enticed him, and that, if Sir Roger had

developed any flaws of character, they were the consequence of his having married Duff. Miss Twysden agreed that Duff might stir a man's
imagination, but she agreed with the opinion of a psychoanalyst who
knew Duff socially that she was the type who drifted from man to man;
a floater.

Duff's son, Tony, she said, was musical. His first interest was in jazz.
By the time he was 17, when he was taken to the opera in Paris, his
tastes had become more mature. The first opera he saw was *Boris
Gudonov*, which he liked immensely. After the divorce of Duff and
Roger, he had a guardian—precisely who was not made clear. But it
wasn't Duff. The child did not live with her.

That was all Miss Twysden had to say on our first meeting. She
would soon be off to England to visit her eldest brother, Sir William
Twysden. He knew more about Duff than she did. Perhaps she would
return with more information. I mentioned my own plans to visit
England in the fall. In that event, she said, I must certainly visit Sir
William. He lived in Torquay. He would be a better source of information than she had been.

My second meeting with Miss Twysden provided an opportunity to
ask about an anecdote Loeb said Duff had told him.[152] She said that
she had run off with the best man as she and the groom approached
the altar. Miss Twysden dismissed that as fiction. Byrom, her first
husband, had brought her into country society. She met Roger at a
party before her divorce from him—Roger was in no way involved in
the divorce. Well, I asked, was Duff given to making up stories? Of
course she did, but no one would believe them. But apparently it was
Duff's mother who was the target for criticism at this point. The
mother used to insist that she and her children came from a "good"
family. As on my previous visit, Miss Twysden expatiated on the clan
structure of Scotland, pointing out that all Campbells, for example,
could claim kinship with the house of Argyll. The name Stirling, she
explained, is not to be confused with the Stuart family; Stirling is
merely the name of a castle where the Stuarts resided. I made a mental
note not to confuse the castle with the family—I was still not aware of
Miss Twysden's purpose. There were some references to subjects we
had gone over at our first meeting. Miss Twysden corrected the point
of location of Duff's father's wine-shop. It was not in Darlington but
in Richmond, Yorkshire.[153] He was known to be an honest man and
probably made enough to retire to Westminster. As to the Black man,
yes, Anne Fellowes said Duff had an affair with a Black man in Paris.
Details of Duff's wedding to Roger? They were married in the home
of a Scottish minister in Edinburgh. The minister was probably Presby-

terian. Had he been a Church of England prelate, some question might
have been raised about his entering a divorced woman into matrimony.
Was there, I asked, any correspondence between Duff and the fictive
Brett who married for money? Money and title, Miss Twysden said;
and Duff married the first time for money too, but was wrong in thinking Roger wealthy: he was only comfortable. And when she married
him there was tremendous confusion about the names on the marriage
certificate.

And her reputation when she married Roger? Was she anything like
Hemingway's portrayal of her? Did she drink? Was her mother known
to be a social climber? Duff's mother had no opportunity, Miss
Twysden said, nor did she have much money. But she pushed the girls.
Duff did drink at the time she met Roger, just how much she could not
say. She was known to be chasing after a number of naval officers. Her
reputation was that of a "tart." Miss Twysden tempted me to ask how
Roger could have married a woman with that reputation, particularly
one that had been gained among his fellow officers. I simply asked,
"How would you describe Roger at that time?" "He loved cricket and
football. He was charming, spoiled, and naive."

Did Miss Twysden know about Duff's talents in music and painting?
Her brother, Sir William, said she had musical talent, but, she added,
Duff didn't want to work. She knew nothing about Duff's painting.
She remembered young Tony's saying that neither his father nor his
mother would let him study music. She had deserted Tony in Scotland
and Roger's mother had gone there to take care of him.

And what was Miss Twysden's estimate of Duff's character? She
thought Duff a bore but striking in appearance. She could understand
how Duff might have captivated a man's imagination; she could not
understand how Duff could have inspired anyone. She was intelligent,
but not interested in the Twysden family.

The hope was expressed that when I went to England I might see Sir
William. I certainly did want to see him, I said. Miss Twysden hoped
he was not too ill to receive me. She would write to him. I told her I
would let her know when I was leaving.

We corresponded briefly before my flying across that fall. One thing
I wanted to know. She had given me information in my last talk with
her that she had not given the first time we met. Did she have more to
tell as a result of seeing her brother, Sir William? In other words, had
she in reality been quoting him? She replied that that was true.

I wrote to Sir William Twysden in Torquay just before leaving. I
told him the purpose of my proposed visit and asked him to suggest a
time convenient to him—his health permitting—when I might call on

him. There was no reply to my letter. Shortly after arriving in London,
I called him long distance. A hostile voice at the other end made it instantly clear that I would not be driving to Torquay. Some intimation
of events had been given to me by Aileen Twysden in New York. Sir
William suspected me of being a New York journalist.

"What's your business asking about Duff?"

I explained calmly that I was studying the lives of the real persons
whom Hemingway had used as the basis for his characters in *The Sun
Also Rises*.

"Hemingway was just a damn journalist."

"When did you first meet Duff?"

"She was still Mrs. Luttrell Byrom. And I hated the sight of her.
She was just a damn tart."

"Do you remember what she did in the War?"

"She was a nurse," he spoke somewhat under control for a second,
"in a hospital. An R.C."

"Was she an interesting person?"

"Sure, if you like tarts."

"How did Sir Roger meet her?"

"He gave parties. He met her at one of his parties."

"What's the significance in your calling her a tart?"

"What you really want, well, I won't mention names."

"Then you know something about the scandal about the Black
man."

"Black man? I heard all kinds of stories. She didn't give a damn. I
avoided her like the plague. She avoided me like the plague. You want
to know about her? Well, in your country if you want to know about
someone like her, you go to the FBI. You go to Scotland Yard. They
could tell you more."

He was not joking about Scotland Yard. I tried to pinpoint Duff's
alleged crime. Her friend Guthrie had been on drugs. I tried that line.
Had she smuggled drugs?

"The FBI," he continued, "would know about things like dope
smuggling. She wasn't playing it straight. Let Scotland Yard tell you."

The records of Scotland Yard, a very polite public relations man explained, were confidential. He hoped I would pass this news on to
American professors from whom more and more requests for data were
coming in these days. Scotland Yard, he said, was not the equivalent
of the FBI; it was the headquarters of the London police department.
I blamed the Sherlock Holmes stories for putting American professors
under a misapprehension; I hoped he might make an exception in my
favor. No, that could not be done. Besides, the subject of my inquiry

was deceased. Once a person died, Scotland Yard destroyed the files on that individual.

I had gone to Scotland Yard to fulfill a scholarly obligation created by Sir William.

The full impact of the Twysdens' version of Duff did not become clear until Mr. Clinton King, Duff's surviving husband, kindly provided me with his knowledge of his late wife, at least, that part which was pertinent to my interests. I had, by this time, accepted the possibility of her having been a mystic. Now I was to learn that she served during World War I in the Secret Service. I was also to be told that she was a descendant of the Stuarts—the family of Mary Queen of Scots, James I, James II, and the famous Pretender of Thackeray's *Henry Esmond*. The lectures on Scotland and on its clans and on the meaninglessness of claims to nobility there had considerable significance now. Up to this point I had only heard modest claims of Duff's link with nobility. She had told her New York friend, Mrs. John Rogers Jr., that she was connected with the minor nobility of Scotland. No more than that.[154]

One can understand and even sympathize with that family pride that led the Twysdens to represent Duff as a liar and as an adventuress. Aileen Twysden, after reading the novel—or after recalling the movie; I do not remember for certain which it was—admitted that she did not recognize Duff in Hemingway's Lady Brett Ashley. However, after reading ex-bartender Jimmy Charters' account of Duff side by side at Parisian bars with Pat Guthrie, with whom she was in love, Miss Twysden recalled her in that role perfectly. Because the scenes sketched by Charters are palpably close to some in *The Sun Also Rises*, I have the impression that Miss Twysden was now conceding verisimilitude to the novel. I am quite certain the Twysden family (Aileen Twysden admitted Anne Fellowes and Sir William as her sources) was accepting the book as factual—excluding, certainly, the few derogatory references to Sir Roger—inasmuch as Duff comes off as somewhat of a drunk and a nymphomaniac. "A damn journalist," those were Sir William Twysden's words for Hemingway; and though ejaculated in anger, they meant that by and large Hemingway was reporting facts, especially, we can assume, about Duff Twysden. But of fifteen persons who knew Duff none had ever heard of her being a nurse during the war and although Sir William did not identify the specific scandal about the Black, he knew about it; yet none of Duff's acquaintances and friends had ever heard of her having had an affair with a Black man. Two of these allegations might have been derived by anyone who took the novel as an accurate piece of journalism. In Chapter V Jake tells Cohn that Brett had been a V.A.D. in war time. The exact expression used by Sir William, "in a hospital," comprises part of Jake's statement. The scandal about the Black could have its source in *The Sun Also Rises* likewise. A brief encounter by Brett with a Black drummer at Zelli's occasions the statement from Brett that he and she are wonderful friends (Chapter VII). That might be enough to convince Duff's enemies that she had in actuality such a close friendship and that certain intimacies were inevitable. Certainly, if Sir William wished to think of Duff as a "tart," he might well have taken for gospel the first two-thirds of Hemingway's novel.

In making Brett a former nurse Hemingway probably had in mind Agnes von Kurowsky with whom he was in love some years earlier. He had met her while hospitalized after the incident at Fossalta, and she was not forgotten during the days when Hemingway dined with Loeb in Paris in the mid-twenties. Once Loeb told Hemingway that if he were ever to write a novel—or become a successful writer—he would have to know more about women than he did. Hemingway then told Loeb about Agnes,[155] the nurse he had loved while in Italy and who was to become the heroine of *A Farewell to Arms*. Certainly, Hemingway had Agnes rather than Duff in mind in that section dealing with Brett's background. She was a nurse, Jake tells us, at the time of the last war in the same hospital he had been in. Quite obviously, this version of Brett's (or Duff's) background is fictionalized.

In suggesting that Sir William Twysden may have taken some parts of *The Sun Also Rises* as scripture, one is not charging him with any more credulity than, say, Matthew Josephson, who, after seeing Duff and Loeb and Guthrie over drinks one day, believed that these models for Hemingway's characters were precisely in life as they were in the novel.[156] Such was the magic of *The Sun Also Rises*.

But an entirely different picture of Duff was given to me by her last husband, Mr. Clinton King. In justice to him I must say that at no time did I embroil him in a rebuttal to the Twysden family. My efforts to obtain information from him preceded my acquaintanceship with the Twysdens. The data he gave me should not be construed therefore, as either defensive or retaliatory. Moreover, King, it is well known, has rarely discussed Duff with anyone likely to publish about her for fear of increasing the legends she left behind as the model for Lady Brett Ashley. He was aware, through the essay I had published on Duff,[157] that even her extant kind friends were influenced by the Hemingway legend and that, under the novelist's spell, they were unwittingly adding to the fund of error. I suppose that a moment of outrage caused by Hemingway's remarks about Duff in *Papa Hemingway*

led King to speak out, if only briefly. The account in that book of
Duff's funeral was so blatantly untrue that King must have been incensed. Hemingway told Hotchner that Duff's casket was borne by
her former lovers and that after the church service, as they carried the
coffin, one of them slipped. The casket fell and split wide open.[158]
This story, incidentally, is a variant of an earlier one which has it that
the funeral took place on a Mexican hillside, that Duff's friends (and
presumably former lovers) carried the casket upwards while they themselves were dead drunk, and that the casket rolled down the slope.[159]
No such happening occurred, King said, because there had been no
service, no coffin, no procession: Duff had been cremated.[160] In the
same note in which he protested against Hemingway's account of
Duff's funeral, King also answered the question about Duff's relationship to the writer. No, they had never had an affair. Hemingway was
not her type.[161]

King was induced to comment further through the persuasion of Mr.
Morrill Cody whom I had met in Paris. Here, then, is the information
King gave me.[162]

Duff was born in London, May 22, 1892. She went to school in London but mostly in Paris. She was bi-lingual. When she was very young,
her parents were divorced. He knew nothing about Mr. Smurthwaite,
nothing of his having been a wine dealer in Richmond. He, Clinton
King, gave the hospital the correct information about her parents; the
hospital recorded the information inaccurately. Whether Duff's
mother, who called herself Mrs. Stirling, had her name and that of the
children changed legally, he could not say. Stirling was her maiden
name; Duff's sister and Duff's brother, who died in battle, used it.

Duff was a sort of child prodigy in music. At the age of 12 she gave a
recital at the Trocadero in Paris. She played mostly Chopin. Two
great aunts, the Stirling sisters, had had a nocturne, possibly two, dedicated to them by Chopin. They were great beauties in their day, came
out at the Tuilleries and created quite a stir. Mrs. Charlotte Stirling,
Duff's mother, had been a beauty too. She was tall and distinguished.
Likewise musical, she had many friends among the literary and artistic
personages of her time. Duff resembled her mother. Duff was tall, five
feet, nine inches, and, of course, with very high heels she was almost six
feet. She was angular and a perfect example of the most aristocratic
breeding. She was named after her godmother, a well-known personage of her day. In Duff's mother's home in Scotland were many paintings of the Stuarts, some by Nattier.

Through her mother she was a descendant of the Stuarts. There had

not been a fancy coming-out party (as her friend Mrs. John Rogers had
thought); at the time Duff's family was quite broke. But she had come
out at Buckingham Palace. There was no abandonment of any groom
at either of Duff's weddings; she was not forced into marriage with any
nobleman (as I had been told).[163] But the account given by Hemingway
of Lord Ashley's treatment of Brett had its basis in fact. Duff evidently
had told Clinton King her story of harrassment by Sir Roger Twysden.
Moreover, contrary to all rumors, King and Duff were married, August
1928.[164] An emissary had been sent across the Atlantic, not, as I had
been led to believe, a lawyer or two, but a friend of Mr. King's
father.[165]

Robert McAlmon had once been their good friend. References in
Being Geniuses Together to their occupying a studio of his and leaving
it in shambles were not correct. At one time McAlmon, Duff, and King
were great friends. Later, King said, McAlmon cooled against them.
And Hemingway? King did not have much regard for him. There is no
truth to the statement (made to me by a close friend of King)[166] that he
knocked Hemingway out. It was a fact, however, that King and Duff
met romantically. They saw each other in mirrors behind a bar and fell
in love with each other's reflections.

Was it true that Duff would never have had an affair with Hemingway? If there were no other reason than consideration for Hadley
Hemingway, that reason, King said, would have been sufficient for de-
terring her. Duff liked Hadley too much to go to bed with Ernest.
Hemingway knew that. I asked King his opinion of Hemingway's portrayal of Duff as Lady Brett Ashley. He replied that Hemingway failed
to bring out her generous nature, and he therefore omitted one of her
essential qualities. He failed also to emphasize her cleverness and her
constant flow of wit. She was not what Hemingway suggested,
nymphomaniacal and alcoholic. He gave her no depth and little talent.
She read a great deal and devoted much time to painting. It wasn't
fair to judge her by her life in Montparnasse. She drank then as
everyone around her did. They all lived in the atmosphere of a great
and continuous party. And what was Duff's reaction to Hemingway's
fictionalizing her? She was not so much angry as hurt; she resented
his portrait of her. She thought he had played a mean trick on the
other characters too. The book itself, she believed, belonged to the
realm of cheap reporting. I was interested to know how Duff's reaction
compared to that of some of the other fictionalized characters. Cody,
King's friend, had heard that Loeb was going to beat up Hemingway
and that Loeb shortly thereafter went to an analyst. King's reply dealt

with the general reaction. Of course, many of the fictionalized were
embittered by Hemingway's treatment of themselves as well as of their
friends who had been fictionalized.

There is more to say about Duff—her relationship to Pat Guthrie,
the Mike Campbell of the novel, a final word on her relationship to
Loeb, an estimate of Hemingway's knowledge of her and the use he
made of it in writing *The Sun Also Rises*, and the reaction of Aileen
Twysden to certain of King's statements.

After Sir William Twysden died in the winter of 1970, I regarded
Aileen Twysden as spokesman for the family. When we met again, she
remarked that she was glad to hear that Duff had made Mr. King a
good wife and that they had had a happy marriage. But she was
shocked beyond words to hear of Duff's claim to link with the royal
family; she reminded me about clan structure of Scotland. As for the
friendship of Duff's aunts with Chopin, that, she said, could be
checked in any biography of the composer. There remained, however,
certain incontrovertible facts. Duff had been twice divorced by her
husbands; she had abandoned her child when the boy was still quite
young. Sir Roger's mother had to seek out the child and take care of
him for many years. Miss Twysden disqualified herself from speaking
about any other problems Duff might have involved herself and others
in. She agreed with her brother William. My inquiries ought to be
turned in the direction of Scotland Yard. The references to her brother
Roger in *The Sun Also Rises* were, in her opinion, provided to Hemingway by Duff whom she considered untrustworthy. No doubt Duff
must have fascinated Hemingway, but Lady Brett was the product of
imagination. He accepted some of Duff's fictions and let himself be
swayed by her manners and her looks.[167]

Scotland Yard represented a dead-end. Clinton King wished no further inquiries. Any further information about Duff's character and
background had to come, therefore, from other sources—some such information will be provided. All that could be checked out immediately
was the friendship of Duff's aunts with Chopin. The listing of his dedi-
cations in Grove's *History* shows that Opus 55, one part in F minor
and another in E flat major, was dedicated in 1843 to Jane Stirling. Apparently, she had acquired all the French first editions of Chopin's
works. These were sold in 1933 and became the basis for the "Oxford
Original" edition of Chopin.[168] It was not that easy to verify Duff's
Stuart lineage, and, in the long run, not much would be accomplished
by doing so. She might have been told of her descent by her mother
who had, in turn, been so informed by hers. Even if the Stuart descent

were mythical, Duff could have been telling what she thought to be the truth, as certainly Clinton King was. Morrill Cody, who has known King for forty-five years, said that the information he gave me was trustworthy. He had never in all the years he had known King ever remembered his telling a lie.[169] Some comments of Mr. Lett-Haines are in place here. He had known Duff's family before 1920. The mother was known to him as Mrs. Duff-Stirling and her daughters as Jean and Mary respectively. Jean was at one time engaged to Brigadier-General Eric Rudin, A.D.C. to King George V. Haines recalled his own parents as having referred to Duff's mother as Miss Duff-Stirling. He speculated that she abandoned her marriage name altogether and that she might have assumed her original name by Deed Poll at Somerset House, London. Were that so, the children too would have had their name changed. Whatever the explanation, Haines was certain that everything was proper and legal, particularly since Duff's family were part of a distinguished social circle. Their home at Bridge of Allan, Stirlingshire, Scotland, was made of granite. Though modest, it conveyed an aristocratic air. The door was answered by a maid in appropriate livery. Haines could not recall Duff's ever having pretended to be other than what she was. Some of her friends may have exaggerated her status, and unquestionably some of her male friends used her title to get credit.[170]

No doubt, one of those friends, was Pat Guthrie.

Moreover, Cody told me, Duff was not the kind to keep secrets from her husband; presumably, she would not have lied to him. For example, if she had had an affair with Hemingway, King would have known about it. Cody, who knew Duff and most of *The Sun* set in Paris remembered her as "gay, good fun, partyish." He thought that Hemingway was attracted to that side of her personality, and apparently, Cody's opinions about her were shared by the late Hilaire Hiler who was one of the best informed persons about the Paris of the 1920's.[171] Although there were rumors of an affair with Hemingway, Cody himself had no knowledge of it. But he could understand Hemingway's being fascinated by Duff. Cody was not sure that Harold Loeb's account of an affair was true, but if true, it was not quite so idyllic as Loeb made it out to be in *The Way It Was*. He had found Loeb to be vain and he did stupid things. He was said to have been rude to Joyce and he incurred the hostility of Sylvia Beach. But he did like Jimmy Charters. However, there is no doubt that he had been a close friend of Hemingway whom Cody classified as nobody's close friend. After *The Sun Also Rises* was published, Loeb was going to beat up Hemingway when he saw him—the other rumor was that Loeb afterwards went to an analyst. Cody also heard that Loeb had a gun. He believed that Loeb had a guilt complex about being Jewish. At any rate, in Cody's opinion, Hemingway did draw Loeb accurately but none of the other characters.[172]   Loeb had no recollection of offending Joyce. He remembered Sylvia Beach as someone who had helped the sales of *Broom*, and, of course, he regarded the tales of analysts, fisticuffs and gun-play as ridiculous. Cody's attitude, Loeb told me, was colored by Loeb's having made a play for his girl-friend.[173]

Neither Cody nor Loeb thought Duff an alcoholic. "Not compared to some of the others," Cody said. "She drank a lot but she was not a serious drinker. She'd get gay and then collapse." It might have been true that Pat Guthrie was hooked on drugs; in *This Must Be the Place* Cody and Charters suggested that Guthrie might have taken his life through an overdose.[174]   Cody was now quite sure he had. But Duff had nothing to do with drugs, and she was not sexually promiscuous. Clinton King sometimes reminisced to Cody about their happy days in Mexico. King was very devoted to her. But their marriage had surprised Cody; he never expected Duff to fall in love with King. He had not heard the rumor that King knocked out Hemingway. To be sure, Hemingway's ring prowess was imaginary. Jimmy Charters, who had boxed professionally, avoided fighting him because he could knock him out easily. On the one or two occasions when they boxed, Charters had to hold himself in check. Hemingway was not much of a boxer and he wouldn't have been much of a husband. A man of that conceit, Cody added, would have been impossible to live with. His literary intelligence was likewise limited. Once Cody showed Hemingway some literary reviews from a French newspaper. Hemingway simply muttered, "Crap." He couldn't understand Joyce either. Years later when Hemingway and Cody met again the novelist told him about the projected *A Moveable Feast*. It was going to be "a big book," Hemingway said. Cody doubts if the book as published is anywhere near complete. Hemingway had advised him how to write *This Must Be the Place*, which reminded Cody that Hemingway had taken one-third of the notes for the book and never returned them. (That book has recently been reissued as *Hemingway's Paris*).

When they met in Pamplona in the 1950's, Hemingway called Cody "my oldest friend." They had known each other since 1923 when English Walling had introduced them. But it is evident that Cody is neither spokesman for Hemingway or Loeb. He impressed me as having been impartial about Duff, recalling her as a woman without pretenses.[175]

Something of the impression communicated by Cody of Duff's gay spirit (and her drinking habits) was also conveyed to me in a note from Stuart Chase. The Chases had met King and Duff in 1933 when they were vacationing at Lake Chapala, Mexico where the Kings had a home. The banks had just closed and they were all stranded. "...As stranded foreigners we met together every night for conversation and altogether too many drinks. I became quite expert in pouring tequilla out of the window and into potted plants. One night Clinton insisted on giving me perhaps his finest painting. It was of a little Mexican girl and a very beautiful and valuable thing.... I had to stagger back (due to the size of painting not to alcohol) to our inn with this large painting at midnight because he angrily refused to keep it." Moreover, it was carried off to prevent King from painting in Chase's name on the canvas.[176] The next day in the afternoon—the Kings were in the habit of starting life in the afternoon—Chase insisted on returning the picture and agreed to take instead a small oil of the beach of Lake Chapala, "a witty scene of bathers by the lakeside." He gave King "a strict, tough, economic reason" why he would not take the larger one. "I said that the depression might clean out the family business in Texas, and these paintings might be all he had to live on....I shall never forget Duff, at the close of my lecture on economics, saying with her nice British accent, 'Perfect bilge!'"[177] And a year or so later, when the Kings were in New York and short of funds, the Chases gave them their check for the painting.[178]

Mrs. Marian Chase told me that they had met the Kings at a café. Duff arrived wearing a big Spanish hat. Liqueurs were ordered, and they all drank but Duff. After a while she had before her several unconsumed glasses of liqueur when suddenly she drank them down one after another with no visible after-effect. A very attractive woman, Mrs. Chase thought, gay and sophisticated. But she also gave the impression of being quite snobbish. At any rate, she was making constant disdainful remarks about people. Perhaps, Mrs. Chase said, "we were on different wave lengths." The only painting Duff talked about was her husband's. The only songs she sang (on one occasion in a boat) were sea shanties. But once she broke down. It was her son's birthday, Duff said, and she began to cry. "They don't let me see him." That was all Mrs. Chase remembered her saying and we must suppose that Duff was referring to those in charge of her son's upbringing.

It would be impossible to judge how much Hemingway knew about Duff and how accurately he drew her as Lady Brett Ashley without considering her relationship to Pat Guthrie, the model for Mike Campbell. Not much has appeared in print about Guthrie—nor about Duff, for that matter—other than the accounts of the two in *This Must Be the Place.* They were known to authors Cody and Charters in a fairly limited way. Cody had some acquaintanceship with each of them; Charters knew Duff and Pat from the other side of this bar and that. When he served drinks, more often than not, Pat charged them; when by herself, Duff did too. Charters, who liked them near the point of idealization, has preserved an image of Duff as an ornament to British aristocracy and an image of Pat as the once upon a time inspiring officer of England's military.[179] In Paris, they were generally without a sou, and Charters laid out money for their drinks and cigarettes from his own pocket.[180] When they could, they repaid him. Stories have come down of Duff and Pat splurging when they had money only to leave themselves destitute at the end of a week. Such stories, I suspect, are part of the Duff Twysden myth.[181] In fact, Duff and Pat were very poor. Contrary to Hemingway's fictional account, they were deeply in love but their poverty precluded Duff's thinking in terms of anything so practical as marriage. In Chapter V Jake speaks of their counterparts, Brett and Mike, as being in love—actually he says that Brett is in love—only to add a bit of smudge to the effect that some day Mike will be extremely rich. At that point in the novel Mike has not yet made a personal appearance. He is supposed to be in Scotland. Hemingway, of course, had to keep him offstage to allow for the action between Jake and Brett as well as between Cohn and Brett to develop. Guthrie probably was there; Duff told Loeb he was.[182] The allusion to Pat's being in Scotland is reported without his location there or without the purpose of his being there. In real life Pat Guthrie had lived in Scotland where, Clinton King said, Pat's mother had a castle.[183] Pat's mother did have money and she was very devoted to Duff. She hoped they would be married.[184] How much of that actual background Hemingway knew, it is difficult to say. From the novel itself one cannot tell just how limited Hemingway's knowledge of Guthrie was. There is much ambiguity as to Mike's comings and goings, much ambiguity about his finances. The information we think we get from *The Sun Also Rises* is that Mike was a remittance man, and this is the reputation that Pat Guthrie earned.[185] In Chapter VIII, when Mike has just returned from Scotland having had, according to his account, just a drink a day with his mother, he gives evidence of having been on a binge. A wound on the upper part of his nose is suggestive, and his explanation that some old woman's luggage fell on him comes across as an obvious lie. The day of his arrival, June 20th—

that date is given to us immediately in the next chapter—is but five days off from the proposed trip to Pamplona. Brett has already announced that with Mike's arrival they are once again in the money only to have Mike slip and say that their coming to Pamplona is contingent on his receiving funds from home. It is Brett who guarantees that they will have money (Chapter IX). Quite clearly, Mike has returned with nothing; he makes a further slip by saying that he and Brett are living in a hotel which was probably a bordello. Not until the concluding chapter are we made aware that Brett has some sort of meager income and that whatever she had she had given to Mike before her leaving Pamplona to go away with Pedro Romero. In brief, Mike had all the time been penniless and Brett had been covering for his lies as well as providing, as best she could, for his needs.

This discussion about Brett and Mike's finances has to be seen in the perspective of the realities of Duff and Pat. If, as Clinton King said, Pat's mother adored Duff and wanted to see him married to her, why were they unable to plan a future, why were they living on credit? The answer is provided by Lett-Haines who knew Guthrie's past. He had been an extreme alcoholic and had to be institutionalized. Guthrie made his escape from the "dypso home," as Haines called it, and at once his mother cut him off without a cent.[186] Apparently, he had been in all sorts of difficulties and, up to this time, according to Cody, his family had seen him through. Cody saw him as one in rebellion against his family and against prevailing conventions. Guthrie had no special creed; he was not on a soapbox. Duff joined him in rebellion; she took everything as a lark.[187] Probably, by the time he and Duff were in Paris he had lost his family's support. It would appear that Hemingway knew this, although it is by no means certain that Hemingway knew he had been in a "dypso home." In deleted Chapter I the word "dipsomaniac" occurs; it is applied not to Mike but to Lord Ashley. Mike is alluded to as nice, weak, charming, and drunk. His drinking and that of Brett is accounted for by Hemingway's giving us a brief summary of their lives. This novel, we are told, is to be about a lady born Elizabeth Brett Murray. Her first divorce was obtained by mutual consent. Her husband had found her too expensive. The second husband, a dipsomaniac, would not divorce because they had had a son. Therefore, at the start of the novel the lady was merely separated. She would have liked to marry Jake Barnes but she couldn't; we who have read the completed novel understand why. Meeting Mike Campbell, she took up with him as an alternative and with him went to Paris. Her future was uncertain, her present a bore. She took to drink as a result. But,

Hemingway noted, nothing about her was typical of the real alcoholic
—a comment spared the readers of the published novel. Another significant deletion was the statement that Brett had verve and exhuber-
ance. Those traits would evanesce as she took one drink after another.
She might lose her senses but she never acted drunk. Apparently, she
entrusted Mike to expedite her divorce. He would sometimes return to
England for that purpose—also, to persuade his own family not to stop
the remittances he had been getting. Quite clearly, Hemingway had
started out by drawing Duff in the role of Brett more realistically than
the final published portrait. It is also evident that Hemingway knew
about Mike's personal difficulties with his family. It would appear that
the original for Ashley was being credited with Guthrie's dipsomaniac
traits. One cannot say for certain if Hemingway was crossing attributes
over. In this deleted chapter he refers to Ashley as having become
alcoholic during maritime rather than during matrimonial experience.
    The original portrait of Mike is simply that of a bibulous com-
panion. Neither in the deleted section nor in the completed novel is
Mike given any depth of character—depth that would suggest a capacity for love or a capacity for deep feeling. Nor did Hemingway anticipate that his own model for Pat Guthrie was a potential suicide.
(Haines confirmed that Guthrie did take his life).   Donald Ogden
Stewart, Harold Loeb, and Kitty Cannell had not heard that Guthrie
took his life; Hemingway too might have been unaware.   But the
strange thing is that when Hemingway gave Herbert Gorman a key to
some of the characters in *The Sun Also Rises*, he identified Mike Campbell as "Duff Gordon."[188] There was such a person, Kitty Cannell
told me, but he had nothing to do with *The Sun* set or with the novel.
    Guthrie did not make much of an impression on Kitty Cannell. As
we might expect, Loeb disliked him.   Cody's impression was that
Guthrie had the good manners of the British upper classes and the education they generally had, although he doubted if Guthrie went to college. Cody thought him to be sweet, gentle, aimiable, and friendly[189]—
some of these qualities come through on his meeting Jake at the Select
(Chapter VIII). Clinton King conceded that he had charm but no character and certainly, not sufficient strength of character to lead a responsible life.[190] It is not clear if Guthrie was the person for whom
Duff ended her marriage to Sir Roger Twysden. Haines in stating that
Duff was sincerely in love with Guthrie and that, indeed, she was not a
woman of loose morals, said that she sacrificed everything at the time
of leaving Sir Roger Twysden.[191] Part of this statement was confirmed
by Clinton King. He recalled that she was profoundly in love with Pat

and that it took her a considerable time to realize how meaningless a marriage to him would have been.[192] The depths of her romance and its agonies were contemporary with Hemingway's writing *The Sun Also Rises.* By the time the book was published Duff and Pat were probably finished; he had left her for a Lorna "Lindsay" (the spelling of her surname is in doubt—she was the daughter of a U.S. ambassador to Latin-America).[193] A great many people knew Pat and Duff; you met Pat and Duff at bars, Cody said. The romance between them was a matter of public knowledge in the Quarter. Many people there knew about them, and their love for each other was looked on as something ideal. When they had a real falling out, Cody recalled, all their friends tried to patch it up. One day at the Trois et As bar, there was Duff at one end and Pat at the other—she in tears, he glum. Attempts to get them to speak to each other failed. It rocked Duff. She fell apart. The breakup was almost a public calamity.[194]

In July 1927, Duff was still miserable. She had had nothing but bad luck, Sir Cedric Morris told Haines.[195] They therefore invited her to join them at Tréboul to visit a fellow artist, the New Zealand painter, Frances Hodgkins. Haines, who had met Clinton King (he looked like 17 but was all of 23) mentioned the plan, and King asked to be included. That was the night of 11 July 1927; Haines had a record of the date because he had gone to see his actress friend Marie Spinelli in what turned out to be a dull bedroom farce. He became acquainted with King—he recognized him as a fellow artist—during the intermission of the play. King had wanted to come along as soon as he heard that Duff would be in the group.[196] Evidently, by the early summer of 1927, he had already met her. The communion in the mirrors, it would be a good guess, must have taken place in the spring and Guthrie's forsaking Duff for the ambassador's daughter probably in the winter of that year. Perhaps those events followed even more closely than that, for when it became evident that King and Duff were courting, or whatever the equivalent terms for going steady was on the Rive Gauche, there was much indignation. Partisans of the Pat-Duff romance accused King of indecency. A good many at the Trois et As bar criticized him.[197]

By that time *The Sun Also Rises* had been published so that Hemingway did not know, while he was writing and revising it, of the terrible anguish through which Duff was to go in the next year or so. But, had he taken her romance in the same light as some of the Parisians who shared in her delight and sorrows, he would never have reduced her love affair to the crass level of the Brett-Mike liaison. One might say that his final judgment of Brett, if not redemptive, allowed for generosity. But that is a matter to be considered later. However, in the first two books of *The Sun Also Rises*, Brett established herself in the minds of readers of more than one generation as a libidinous lush. That is the impression of her character, or the lack of it, that lasts; and that is the reputation which was transferred gratuitously to her model, Duff Twysden. Around Paris, Cody pointed out, before publication of *The Sun Also Rises*, she was not reputed to be promiscuous.[198] Loeb had never heard that she was,[199] and Haines thought the charge ridiculous.[200] She once boasted to Haines' friend, Sir Cedric Morris, that she could charm him into a marriage proposal within ten days. A fantasy, Haines thought, which showed how really naive she was.[201]

Hemingway credited her with two intimacies she never had and ridiculed one she had briefly. She never had an affair with the author, as the author's equivalent, Jake Barnes, would have had were he able; and she never had an affair with Cayetano,[202] the model for Pedro Romero. The comment is attributed to Duff that she facetiously lamented not having enjoyed the bullfighter in reality. She told Hemingway that.[203] As we have seen, she was actually quite hurt by Hemingway's cruelty to those whom she knew. The affair with Loeb did occur, and it did have its romantic moments. I have seen the letter written to Loeb in Duff's handwriting just after their tryst at St. Jean-de-Luz and just before her setting out with Pat to join Hemingway and the others in Pamplona, and I can testify to her expressions of love and longing for Loeb. I cannot, however, understand her having had that liaison while presumably in love with Pat Guthrie. Perhaps she sensed the futility of that love; perhaps out of a desire for escape, she was sincere in wishing Loeb to take her to South America.[204] Loeb had more than once talked of having missed the chance to marry Duff; I was misled in thinking that she wished that[205] and, after Loeb's refusal, had reverted to Pat. But Clinton King assured me she never planned or hoped to marry Loeb.[206] He, in turn, may have been misled because in the summer of 1926 Duff talked of wishing to be married. Loeb when he was seeing her furtively—the Dutch girl whom he was later to marry was very possessive—thought that Duff's talk of marriage was intended for him.[207] What she apparently meant was that her relationship with Guthrie ought to be legalized or that she would have to seek elsewhere. But she was still with Guthrie. Charles Norman, biographer and critic of E. E. Cummings and Ezra Pound, met them in Paris at that time. He remembered Guthrie's having a bad eye but looking handsome and elegant. Duff made little impression on him.[208]

Sir Cedric Morris, portrait by Berenice Abbott. *Collection of Berenice Abbott.*

Some indication has been given to show that Hemingway knew the broad outlines of Duff's past and the high points of her present. He knew of her liaison with Loeb, her involvement with Guthrie, and her two marriages. Seemingly he is aware that there is no father in her current biography, but mention is made of her mother (Chapter VII) and of her brother (Chapter V). The toast to royalty offered by Brett (Chapter VII) suggests that Hemingway may have been told of her Stuart lineage. There is no doubt that Brett's close relationship to Jake is an exaggeration of that of their living counterparts. Yet, Hemingway would not have known as much as he did about Duff had there not been a close friendship between them. Said to have been introduced to her by Michael Arlen,[209] Hemingway soon found out about her and Mike's financial difficulties. A note from Duff to Hemingway written in Paris asks him for a loan.[210] Assumedly, they were friendly enough for her to have asked such a favor. She was also friendly enough with Hadley Hemingway to have balked at Ernest's desire for an affair. Clinton King said that her unwillingness was partly owing for her consideration for Hadley;[211] Kitty Cannell knew that she held Hemingway at arm's length for the same reason, although, Mrs. Cannell added, that was also an excuse for rejecting Hemingway politely.[212] Loeb thinks that Hemingway was jealous of his success with Duff and that caused him to create Robert Cohn as an outlet for his rage.[213] The contempt expressed by Jake against Robert, increasingly so from Chapter X onwards, need not have arisen from the author's personal motives; but the contempt might well have given the author some satisfaction.

A good deal of the account of Duff and Pat at the fiesta is drawn from Hemingway's imagination. Loeb did not knock out Pat; they snarled at each other merely. Nor did Loeb knock out Hemingway, although they almost came to blows. Cayetano, the toreador, appeared in their lives for only a moment, not long enough for an affair or a knockout; yet, it was believed that some scuffle took place between him and Loeb.[214] Duff and Pat did not pay their bill at the hotel, as Mike says they did in Chapter XIX. Evidently, in real life, Pat and Duff arrived penniless, or spent quickly that little they had; Donald Ogden Stewart rescued them. For that he was toasted, and he and Pat and Duff went off to Biarritz, not, as the concluding chapter has it, to St. Jean-de-Luz. Jake Barnes was said to have gone with the group as far as Hendaye; in reality Hemingway did not accompany them.[215] But if, on the whole, Hemingway captured the irresponsibility of Pat Guthrie in creating Mike Campbell—leaving out his good looks and whatever it was that induced Duff to make for him what sacrifices she did—he was

not that responsible in delineating Duff as Lady Brett Ashley. Nowhere
in the novel are her talents in music and painting in evidence. Her
kindness, suggested in the final chapter, comes there as a sudden grace
in the presence of accomplished degradation. The lugubrious Brett we
meet at the end of Chapter III and the flip and bantering Brett we meet
thereafter does not correspond to the gay, vivacious, spirited Duff
Twysden who could electrify those who knew her (Charles Norman is
an exception).[216] She is cherished in memory by her husband, Clinton
King, and by her friend in adversity, Sir Cedric Morris. I have seen
her New York acquaintance, Mrs. John Rogers, confined by a stroke
to a wheel chair, seem to have an almost supernatural burst of energy
as she recalled Duff's brightness and gaiety. Millia Davenport (Mrs.
Edward Harkavy), when asked if she knew Duff, communicated the
feeling Duff's memory evoked with a "Jeeeeesus, yes." Donald Ogden
Stewart became so enraptured about her beauty that he had to explain
to me that he didn't mean to suggest that he had been madly in love
with her.[217] From Tokyo, Mr. Paul Blum, Duff's old friend, wrote
of her, "She was an extraordinarily vital person, an intensely human
being ...."[218] Blum had known Duff in Paris when he was a young
man "with problems." They met in the summer of 1927 and saw each
other on and off for the better part of a year until she married Clinton
King. Probably, one gathered from Blum's conversation (we met on
one of his frequent trips to the United States), she would have married
King sooner had she not been beset with qualms. There was an age
difference to consider; King was about ten years her junior. And the
transition to be made from Montparnasse to Texas, King's home! Duff
did not discuss these anxieties in detail or at length. She sometimes
sighed about them as a phrase escaped her. Blum had become friendly
with Duff at a bar. Later they had many chats at the Trois et As. She
impressed him as practical, a woman with both feet on the ground.
When they knew each other better, Duff suggested their meeting at the
Crillon. There they would talk past midnight, but Duff would never
permit him to accompany her home. She would listen patiently and
sympathetically to the woes of this young man then in his mid-twenties.
"Duff had a wet shoulder," Blum said. "Everyone cried on it." Did she
ever talk about Hemingway? Not directly, he explained, but she spoke
about *The Sun Also Rises*. She was indignant about the book. It had
hurt her deeply. She called it a cruel book, a terrible indiscretion. Did
she really wear a man's felt hat as Hemingway decked her out when we
first meet her in the novel? She always wore a beret, Blum recalled;
in fact, she was associated with the beret in Paris—she was really very
well known in Paris—so that Hemingway probably had to change her

headgear to conceal her identity the least bit. Did she become associated with the novel in people's minds? Absolutely, Blum said, and not
only Duff but the other characters as well. In Montparnasse you might
hear remarks when one of the characters stepped into a cafe. "He's in
Hemingway's novel or she's in Hemingway's novel."

Blum had seen Pat Guthrie on occasion—much of a drunk, a bit of a
nuisance, but genial and friendly. He saw him sometimes in the company of Lorna, the ambassador's daughter. Blum also noted Harold
Stearns at the Select where Stearns would give out tips on the horses
to anyone who asked him. He did not know Loeb but he had heard
that Loeb exposed himself to suffering. Duff was the one whom he
knew best, and she was an extremely compassionate woman. Her
charm was incredible. Her personality was such that you forgot to
observe whether or not she was beautiful.[219]

The portrait Blum gives us is neither Hemingway's nor that of the
Twysden family. That was impressed upon me again on receipt of
another letter from Mrs. Anne Fellowes. She kindly provided me with
what details she could about Duff's alleged smuggling and Duff's
alleged affair with a Black man. She recalled that Duff had once given
a package to one of the Twysden family (a cousin of Mrs. Fellowes),
and on his arrival in England he was detained by the police. The package contained drugs. The Black man she dimly remembered as a possible bit of evidence to be brought in to bolster Sir Roger Twysden's
suit for divorce.[220] I then called Aileen Twysden in New York to
explain to her that there was much conflicting evidence about Duff.
My obligation, I said, was to put it all down. There was, for example,
a Miss Stirling who had been a friend of Chopin. Miss Twysden
pointed out that the similarity of names did not guarantee that that
particular Miss Stirling was a blood relative of Duff. There was the
matter of the clans which she had already explained to me. But Duff's
mother had an impressive home in Scotland, I told her, recalling Lett-
Haines's statement to that effect. Miss Twysden only knew of an un-
pretentious residence in Westminster; she remembered Duff's mother
as a person quite ordinary, somewhat vulgar, in fact, and with no outward signs of aristocratic bearing. Was it true that Duff ran away
from Luttrell Byrom after having been married two days? That
couldn't have happened, she said. They were together long enough for
Duff to have been introduced to country society. In fact, Roger met
her at a ball in Exeter. And did Sir Roger actually make her sleep
on the floor and did he threaten her with a revolver? Nonsense, Miss
Twysden said. He was ill for a while. He had been shellshocked in

the war and convalesced in a Greenwich hospital. But his so-called maltreatment of Duff was a fabrication.[221]

A far cry from Blum's recollection of "a woman of profound feeling" and remote too from that special enchantment that Hemingway's Robert Cohn felt. Harold Loeb talked of her often as having had some mysterious quality rarely found in women. He never looked at her as Robert Cohn did in Chapter V where he is likened to Moses beholding the promised land. Nor did he meet her through Hemingway at Mme. Lavigne's where, the reader gathers, Robert Cohn was introduced by Jake Barnes. Loeb had seen Duff around the Quarter and he searched this café and that until at last he encountered her one day. Then he introduced himself.[222] He was soon to find out that she was not the model for Iris March, the promiscuous woman of Michael Arlen's, *The Green Hat*.[223]

That was the moment, I suppose, when Duff was destined to become the subject of many more rumors. The most remarkable one, of course, was that she symbolized for a generation, or some good and sad part of it, the model of modernity. For it was not only the Smith College girls who allegedly imitated her; Josephson declared her to be the object of emulation in France as well, particularly, one would guess, on the Rive Gauche.[224] Josephson may be right, and those who say that Lady Brett Ashley was the inspiration here at home may be right too. But I never met those disciples, nor have I ever met anyone else who did, no more than I have ever met emulators of Jake Barnes. If, as Thornton Wilder said,[225] Yale undergraduates modeled themselves on Jake, it would be difficult to tell, unless one had a candid admission from such students. I am not sure that in those days—almost half a century ago—students were the darlings of the news media and the sociologist or psychologist, so that it would have been very difficult at that time to elicit from them their literary or personality allegiances. No doubt, there were a lot of hard-boiled looking kids around the Yale campus; but there always have been. And no doubt there were a lot of sad, attractive young women around Smith, or the haunts of Smith girls, and no doubt they threatened things which, in those days, sounded daring or desperate, say, an affair or a binge. And, no doubt, some of them had read *The Sun Also Rises*; some of them acted suspiciously like the female protagonist. A case for Duff's fame could be built on that. But, in fact, Duff had a romantic fame in the limited world of her Parisian milieu; you would never know that from reading Hemingway's novel. And after it was published, Duff became somewhat better known, in France, at any rate. One day Florence Gilliam, the dancer

and Kitty Cannell's friend, was sitting at a bar in Marseille. She had
a beret on and as this was associated with Hemingway's heroine, she
found herself being asked, "Ah, you resemble Duff Twysden?"[226] Even
if we grant that Hemingway launched Duff Twysden into fame, that
was not his intention and her fame resulted from the wrong and, it
should be asserted, specious reasons.

When we consider that Pat Guthrie, for all his irresponsibility, was
a very sick man, that Loeb was not the fool that Cohn was made out
to be, that Kitty Cannell was anything but a golddigger, and that Duff
Twysden was a remarkable person, déclassé for the moment, it must be
apparent that Hemingway was nothing less than cruel to those who
were his friends and whose anguish he used as grist for his mill. But
I think that two or three of the minor characters were treated with
even greater inconsiderateness. The reference in Chapter VI, for
example, to two homosexual friends of the heroine, one of whom was
called Lett, is a case in point. Hemingway carefully skirted the libel
laws in referring only to part of one such character's name and he could
always protest that he never had in mind any real person such as Duff's
acquaintance, Arthur Lett-Haines. He also eluded legal suit by not
giving any name to Lett's companion. Off the printed record, however,
Hemingway was calling those men homosexuals[227]—he did so to Loeb;
and, of course, since Haines and Morris were often seen together,[228]
it was assumed by readers in the Quarter that these were the men
Hemingway had in mind and that what he said about them was true.
He knew very well that there were persons in his and their coterie to
make such malicious assumptions. That they did I have verified by
some of the personnel of *The Sun* set and by a few Parisians who were
in Haines' and Morris' circle at the time. Yet, when I questioned such
persons, they admitted taking Hemingway's fiction for fact, although
every one of them recollected both Sir Cedric Morris and Haines as
having had girl friends.[229] Strangely enough, not one of them knew that
Morris and Haines were frequently together not because they were
inverts but because, since 1918, they had been business partners; and
that they have been for over 50 years.[230] There is not the slightest
hint given by Hemingway that each of these men was a successful
painter and that, in addition, Haines had published extensively both
poetry and prose in contemporary journals—and drawings as well.
These include the *Little Review, Rhythm, New Age*, and *Gargoyle*. His
appreciation of *Ulysses* in the March 1922 issue of the latter was one of
the earliest, if not the first, public tribute to Joyce's novel. The hard-
working, talented, man of many interests—friend of Pound and of

Loeb's cousin, Peggy Guggenheim[231]—is in no wise the frivolous friend of Lady Brett Ashley as Hemingway depicted him.

I would guess, however, that it was the unnamed companion of "Lett" that was Hemingway's real target. As indicated, gossip-mongers assumed him to be Sir Cedric Morris. Like "Lett," Hemingway (I should be saying Jake Barnes) represented him as having no absorbing interest but that of killing time. The one bit of accuracy to be found in their delineation is that they were friends of Duff. She was a casual friend of Haines, but, he said, Duff did not like him very much. Her best friend at the time was Sir Cedric Morris. Perhaps she turned to him, more than anyone else, to pour out her confidences. To this day, Sir Cedric Morris will not reveal any information about Duff. He honors her memory.[232] If we suppose there was some jealousy on Hemingway's part against Loeb, some rancor against Duff for her rejecting him in Loeb's favor, we may assume that Hemingway had a little jealousy to spare for Duff's friend and confidant, Sir Cedric Morris. It would seem that Hemingway was intent on aligning Duff with homosexuals by attributing to Brett a comraderie with them. A deleted passage in the novel (to which Baker has called attention) indicates that Mike Campbell was formerly homosexual until Brett set him to rights.[233] No one else who knew Guthrie thought him to be, or to have been, an invert. Charters had heard that Guthrie was buried in the same cemetery where Oscar Wilde was[234]—apparently at Guthrie's request; later his mother had his remains removed—but Charters thought that Guthrie, apart from his drinking, was otherwise normal, at least, in respect to being attracted towards women.[235]

Then again, it may be said that Hemingway seemed preoccupied with fictionalizing persons of his acquaintance into homosexuals. When asked point blank by Bill Hoffmann of Key West whether the Greek portrait painter, Duke Zizi (whom we first meet with Count Mip-pipopolous in Chapter IV) was based on a real person Hoffmann had known, Hemingway cooled at once. Hemingway resented the idea that his characters were based on real persons.[236] In real life "Zizi" had a reputation that would have embarrassed Hemingway were he linked in friendship with him. He was, of course, a Greek. He told Hoffmann many young Greeks of his class were brought up in the homosexual tradition.[237] Homosexuality was part of his upbringing. He had studied art in Munich where Hoffmann was a fellow-student. His father, he told Hoffmann, held a high post in the Greek government. He made no allusion to being a Duke; the assumption of a title came with his sojourn in Paris. Before going there, Hoffmann and "Demmie"

(as he was then nicknamed) went to Florence. Up to that moment
"Demmie"—or "Mitzie," as he was also called—appeared to have no
financial problems. These began in Florence. "Mitzie" daily expected
a remittance from home and went to the American Express office to get
it. No money arrived. Hoffmann helped him through this period. The
help was not substantial—something in the neighborhood of $80—but
it was enough to get him to Paris. The money was never repaid. His
name was Demetrius "Ziki."[238]

Hoffmann described him as "small and of slight build and
swarthy."[239] That description fits, in part, Jake Barnes's mention of
Zizi as being little. Barnes himself had his doubts about the noble
claims of that fictionalized character. In Chapter IV he asks Brett if
Zizi is a bonafide Duke. She thinks it quite possible that he is. The
person whom Hoffmann had financed to Paris appears to be the very
same mentioned in *This Must Be the Place*. In that book he is alluded
to as Mitzy, a well-known character of Montparnasse who was presumably the Duke of Mitzicus; and though a Greek, he often served as
guide and interpretor for many a recently arrived American and Englishman.[240] Hoffmann pointed out that he had been educated in
England and that he also spoke French and German. "I'm sure," he
said, "that while he was in Germany he received money from home but
when he was in Paris I believe he had to shift for himself, and the last
I knew of him he was drawing portraits of tourists in cafes...."[241]
The man mentioned by Hoffmann and by the collaborators of *This
Must Be the Place* is unquestionably the model for the fictive Duke
Zizi. He perhaps had homosexual friends (as indeed, Hemingway and
just about everyone in Parisian literary and artistic circles did), but that
relationship in itself would not seem to have been reason enough to
have earned him a place in the story. Hemingway was evidently aware
of his poverty; he is being supported in the novel by Count Mippipopolous.[242] But it would have been far more decent to have shown
the real Mitzie struggling to survive as he tried his luck with the vanity
of tourists. The man was poor (as was Duff), but here for Hemingway
was merely another opportunity to smother normal compassion.

That, it appears, was Hemingway's systematic aim as he presented
in fictional guise one unfortunate character after another. I do not say
this was his ultimate aim but it was the method he followed in achieving
his final effect. But one is still unsatisfied with the choice of someone
so obscure as Demetrius or Mitzy, however recognizable he may have
been to the Montparnassians of the mid-1920's. Hemingway was attempting to see through the characters he had fictionalized. "Mitzie,"

insignificant as he may have been in Hemingway's personal life, was a
good specimen for Hemingway's X-ray eye.

The other characters, too, were to be seen by him unfavorably in
depth. He was indifferent to the fact that some of those whom he
hoped to expose were the very ones who had been generous to him.
That may be difficult to understand. One can comprehend easily the
maxim that there is no one who hates you more than one that has done
you an injustice. Hemingway was to emend that to read that there is
no one who hates you more than one who has received a kindness.
On receiving the news in the spring of 1925 that Horace Liveright
agreed to publish an American edition of *in our time* Hemingway told
Loeb (the fact is beyond dispute) not that he was overjoyed but that
he felt as if he had been punched in the *cojones*.[243] Four persons who
had worked in the preceding months to get Hemingway an American
publisher were to receive their just desserts. Sherwood Anderson was
to be burlesqued in *The Torrents of Spring*, written between the first
and the revised drafts of *The Sun Also Rises*; Harold Loeb was to be
transformed into Robert Cohn; Donald Ogden Stewart (who, in addition, had sent Ernest and Hadley, a generous check for Christmas)[244]
became the model, in part, for the Jew-hating drunk, Bill Gorton; and
Harold Stearns was made into the loafer-chiseler, thinly disguised as
Harvey Stone.

Like Duff, Harold Stearns became a symbol of life in Montparnasse
and a symbol of the post-war generation; above all he was singled out
as the symbol of the heavy drinking expatriate who left America in
protest and settled in Paris only to go to seed.[245] His portrait in sloth
by Hemingway was taken as accurate, for Stearns was producing little
or nothing abroad. More often than not, in books about the period
he is connected with his pseudonym, "Peter Pickem," to emphasize
what had become of a once leading intellectual now turned tipster for
a local paper.[246] In justice to Hemingway one must point out that
others had singled out Stearns for inebriate leadership among the
expatriates. One was Sinclair Lewis, the other, Stearns himself. Lewis,
who met Stearns in London, invited him to go to Paris. The author of
Main Street financed the trip and gave Stearns about enough to stay
on for thirty days.[247] In Paris, and without funds or employment,
Stearns had his first taste of that Bohemian existence not unlike that
of Harvey Stone of *The Sun Also Rises*.[248] A year before Hemingway's
novel was published, Lewis satirized his former friend in the *American
Mercury* as the prototype of the pretentious expatriate. This monarch
of the Café Dome had promised the world a book, Lewis told his

readers, that would hold up to scorn all false idols, especially those who were no longer lending him money. The attack by Lewis came at the worst possible time.[249] In the summer and fall of 1925 Stearns was destitute. He thought that Lewis's piece had hurt his reputation so much that he could no longer be published in the *World* or *The New Yorker* despite the fact, he told Fitzgerald, that the editors of these periodicals had shown interest in his contributing.[250] Fitzgerald found him near collapse. But he did not know that money was not the only problem.

The year before had not been a bad one for Stearns. He was drawing an income from three different newspaper connections and he had a kind friend named Joan. One presumes that in mentioning that name in his autobiography Stearns was using a pseudonym. Loeb is certain she was Josephine Bennett whom he knew,[251] a woman of means although not a millionairess and apparently, according to Loeb, one of several women who tried to "rescue" Harold Stearns. The man they were trying to rescue was a graduate with honors of Harvard at its greatest, the Harvard of Kittredge, Royce, Santayana, Irving Babbitt, "Copey," Neilson, Barrett Wendell, Bliss Perry, and Yerkes. The man thought to be frittering his time away had edited *Civilization in the United States: An Inquiry by Thirty Americans*, a massive anthology published in 1922 and a reference book for those in protest against the crass values of the post-war period. Stearns, if he regarded himself as self-exiled in protest, and as a leader of the expatriates, had some right to the title; others regarded him in that role. Loeb, for example, had come under his influence;[252] and Malcolm Cowley distinguished him as exercising a tremendous influence on the then younger generation.[253] Stearns' friend Joan, about whom he writes in his memoir as the quintessence of kindness, was no doubt trying to get him to live up to his intelligence. But she intuited that his disorganized mode of existence was a symptom of something deeper. She asked him if he needed to see his son. If he did, she would provide the funds for his trip back to America.[254]

Stearns had left the United States about three years before her kind offer not merely in protest against intolerance there. His wife had died in bearing his son. She had gone to California to be with her parents—her doctor had warned her that childbirth might prove fatal—and Stearns never saw the child. The son was to be brought up by her parents; Stearns was shaken. He had never had much of a home. His own father had died just before he was born; his mother had to work. Marriage and the hope of a home had a profound meaning for him, and the death of his wife was also the death of a hope. He left the

United States without ever seeing his child. Now, in 1924, the child was five years old. Joan suggested that he was old enough so that Stearns might communicate with him face to face. Perhaps he could achieve a needed feeling of fatherhood. She gave him funds to see the boy in Carmel, California.[255]

The meeting with young Peter was another disaster. Stearns was a complete stranger to his son; no rapport appeared possible. He lingered for a while and then returned to New York.[256] There he saw Liveright and urged him (Stearns thought he was the one who persuaded him) to publish Hemingway's *in our time*.[257] Then Stearns was off to Paris. It had become his home.

He returned without a job.[258] Joan was out of his life. He felt that one of her motives for generosity had been to bring about a break without hurting him.[259] She was friendly to him on seeing him again in the spring of 1925. She said she had been to Switzerland to ski with the Hemingways.[260] Mention of her is made in Baker's careful and detailed biography of Hemingway and, of course, the Hemingways had gone to Austria in the winter of 1924–25. She evidently knew Hemingway quite well[261] and she may have been the source of his knowledge of Stearns' exodus and return. For Hemingway knew of his most recent whereabouts—and he could have known from Stearns himself or a dozen others whom Stearns had told. The clue is given in the very opening chapters where we are told that Robert Cohn moved his magazine (and his secretary) from Carmel, California to Provincetown. Neither Loeb nor his magazine had even been in Carmel. There never was a move to Provincetown. *Broom* was projected in Alfred Kreymborg's West Fourth Street apartment in New York City.[262] It was first issued from Rome. Its genesis in Carmel was pure invention. Hemingway took the name from Stearns' itinerary, just as Provincetown might have been on his mind as Bill Smith's destination in the fall of 1925 —his sister Kate was living there at the moment. Similarly, it was Duff Twysden who suggested to Loeb a trip to South America. That idea was then attributed to Loeb himself through his counterpart Robert Cohn.

The Harold Stearns who had run out of luck and money in the summer and fall of 1925—who was jumped on just at the wrong time by Sinclair Lewis—needed no such delineation as Hemingway's Harvey Stone. Only someone bent on saddism could have made him a target as Hemingway did.[263] Stearns is shown piling up plates for drink after drink,[264] making a touch from Jake Barnes, and lying about his need for the money (Chapter VI). The exchange of abuse between Robert Cohn and Harvey Stone (a little satiric touch about Harvard, perhaps?) never

took place in reality.[265] The two men had high respect for each other.
A year or so before Loeb had gone out of his way to speak favorably
about Stearns to an editor who had hired him.[266] He mentions Stearns
by name in a scene of *The Professors Liked Vodka*. The hero and
Stearns are at the Dingo bar where they discuss Prohibition and its
effect on the younger intellectuals.[267] Stearns and Loeb were on good
terms despite their representing polarities of opinion. The former had
turned his back on America. The latter, after publishing "The Mysticism of Money" in 1922, had rediscovered America (as Stearns himself
was to do in the thirties when he returned to the United States). But
their meeting in *The Sun Also Rises* is not that of two leaders of intellectual opinion. It is a confrontation of simians, one the product of
Princeton, the other of Harvard (Yale will get its due from Hemingway
in the person of Bill Gorton).

I once asked Loeb if it were possible that Stearns had abused him
behind his back to Hemingway. Loeb didn't think it likely. There
might have been the slightest animosity stemming from years before
when Stearns' wife was alive. She worked for Liveright then and one of
Liveright's employees, in attempting a play for Loeb's wife, was trying
to pair off Loeb with Stearns' wife. Loeb had indeed been friendly—
I gather it was no more than that—with Stearns' wife. But Stearns
might have borne a grudge. Yet, Loeb could not recall a time in Paris
when there had ever been hostility between them, despite their intellectual differences. Incidentally, Loeb did not know that Stearns too
had gone to Liveright in early 1925 to help Hemingway.

How did Stearns feel about being kicked when he was down? He was
able on several occasions to refer to Hemingway and even *The Sun Also
Rises* with remarkable equanimity. He thought it a good picture of
Montparnasse.[268] Years later, when the Depression of 1929 had
changed men's outlooks, he came to regard the novel as a period piece,
remote from the then present-day realities.[269] He could excuse traits of
violence in Hemingway, as, for example, his love of blood sports.[270]
Stearns interpreted that sort of primitivism as a natural reaction to
being brought up too overweening, as he thought American boys were
raised. His most significant comment, however, is that Hemingway was
to be understood not so much as a man that loved fighting but as a
man who was fighting himself.[271] He said that more than thirty years
before Hemingway's sister, Marcelline, was to quote the very same observation made by Hemingway's mother in 1919. And that comment is
perhaps the best insight into the obvious cruelty of the author of *The
Sun Also Rises*. In 1931 the two met again in Paris.[272] Stearns was

once more in desperate need; he had lost his job as "Peter Pickem" (which began after *The Sun Also Rises* was written) owing to a mysterious temporary blindness. Hemingway gave him money, possibly advice. Stearns said that Hemingway was always straightforward with him. His memory of Hemingway was that of gratitude.[273] When, years later, Stearns was dying of cancer, Hemingway received the news of his illness as another of Stearns' yarns. Stearns had suffered blindness because of infected teeth. He had the good fortune to recover his sight, but he had the bad fortune (even after productive years on his return to America) to earn in Hemingway's mind the reputation of a liar.[274]

In considering the fictive character Bill Gorton, one can readily anticipate the reason for Donald Ogden Stewart's providing for part of his role. Stewart had been generous to Hemingway in the Christmas of 1924. During his stay in New York about that time he had tried to "sell" Hemingway to publisher Doran.[275] Stewart was another whose generosity had to be set to rights. The situation of Bill Smith, who comprises the other part of Bill Gorton, is a bit more puzzling. Smith owed Hemingway a favor. Early in 1925 Hemingway was trying to get Smith a job as secretary-librarian to Sir William Johnston Gordon whose daughter, "Dossie," was a friend of Hemingway as well as of Josephine Bennett. "Dossie" joined "Jo" and the Hemingways for skiing in Schruns in the winter of 1924–1925.[276] Apparently, Hemingway's first efforts to help Bill Smith failed. He then tried to induce Ernest Walsh to make Smith editorial assistant on *This Quarter*. This negotiation was unsuccessful. Neither Walsh nor the financial backer of the magazine, Ethel Moorhead, was willing to replace Hemingway's gratuitous services with Bill Smith's at 1,000 francs a month.[277] But then, if Hemingway was bent on pushing meanness to its limits, we might consider that Bill Smith was his boyhood friend and Bill's brother, Y. K. Smith, had allowed Hemingway to share his elegant Chicago lodgings and through him was able to meet such friends as Sherwood Anderson.[278]

However, it is possible that Hemingway was nettled by a situation closer at hand. The falling out between Loeb and Hemingway at Pamplona which was almost climaxed in a fist fight did not result in Bill Smith's taking sides. At Pamplona, Loeb recalled, "Bill Smith and I were together most of the time."[279] Hemingway noticeably cooled at once towards Loeb after the quarrel at Pamplona. That coolness was still evident to Loeb in his meeting with Hemingway after his return from Spain to Paris in mid-August 1925.[280] In the meantime, Loeb and

Bill Smith were double-dating Princess Cleopatra and Countess Vera. The two men planned a bicycle trip to Loeb's ancestral home in Worms; they started out but bad weather forced them to return.[281]   Smith was also seeing much of Kitty Cannell.[282] He had been occupying the Hemingways' apartment during their absence and,[283] one would guess, that Smith thought his old friend Ernest the soul of kindness. To this day, in fact, he remembers with gratitude Hemingway's attempts to get him a job on his arrival in Europe.[284] He was not permanently affected by his portrait in *The Sun Also Rises*,[285] perhaps not even affected for the moment.   Provincetown his destination, he left Paris with Loeb in September 1925[286]—just after the first draft of *The Sun* had been completed[287]—and he heard from Hemingway that the new novel was to include portions about Ford Madox Ford.[288] It would seem that Hemingway did not tell Smith that the novel would also contain portions about him.   Nevertheless, there was a farewell party before Smith and Loeb left Paris. Loeb's relationship with Hemingway must by that time have been quite strained; he recalled the party only dimly,[289] although he did remember having played a lackadaisical game of tennis with Hemingway during that period.[290] Hemingway commemorated his victory over Loeb on the courts by having Robert Cohn lose to Jake Barnes in Chapter VI. Cohn's loss is explained as a consequence of his having fallen in love with Brett, and presumably Hemingway believed Loeb's loss at tennis to him was the result of his being broken up over Duff.[291] Here began the myth of Loeb's being ruined.[292] Hemingway was seeing the signs he wanted to see, but apparently Bill Smith was remaining neutral. And, not so neutral at that. He was not playing the role of one who ought to be in Hemingway's debt nor the role of one of Hemingway's old friends. He and Loeb had been socializing and now were returning to America together. Moreover, like Loeb, Smith was revolted at bullfighting.[293] Hemingway took them as one target when, at that farewell evening, he boasted to Kitty Cannell, after telling her that he was writing a novel that would, of course, exclude her, "I'm going to tear these two bastards apart." The Jew Loeb would be the villain, he told her. Yet he called Robert Cohn the hero in the two chapters he sent to Scribner's the following year, deleting them at the suggestion of Fitzgerald.[295]

Bill Smith knew that Hemingway was bitter at Loeb even before the entourage had assembled at Pamplona. Smith had witnessed Hemingway's fury when Josephine Bennett (don't be confused about gender; Loeb refers to her as "Joe Bennett")[296] had told him of Loeb's and Duff's departure for a rendezvous in the south of France. (In the novel

Barnes gets the news directly from Brett after her return to Paris in Chapter IX.) Smith's increased friendship for Loeb was enough to qualify him for Hemingway's scalpel, but Hemingway made the attack ambiguous by blending Smith with Donald Ogden Stewart. The person referred to as Bill Gorton in Chapter VIII whose last book had netted him a lot of money was obviously Stewart. He had done well with *Mr. and Mrs. Haddock Abroad.* The person letting off bibulous steam in Chapter XII where there is much talk of utilization is Bill Smith.[297] Obviously, the fishing scene near Burguete is all Bill Smith; Don Stewart was not there with Hemingway in 1925.[298]

Since both Stewart and Smith stayed at the Hemingway apartment,[299] either one would have been familiar with the "stuffed dog" owned by the landlady, Mme. Chautard.[300] Likewise, both men were in Pamplona. There the ambiguity begins if we ask who it was that indulged in the Jew-baiting epithet against Robert Cohn (Chapter XV). To be sure, Stewart had anti-Semitic attitudes in those days; he recalls them with deep regret.[301] But when *The Sun Also Rises* appeared either candidate for the role of Bill Gorton could have had the slur of bigotry imputed to him, and Hemingway could have denied that Bill Gorton was, after all, anyone in particular. Most of the dialogue credited to Gorton as Smith or Stewart was imaginary. The Englishman Wilson-Harris who appears in Chapter XIII was evidently the person with whom Smith and Hemingway had lunch in Burguete.[302] The part he played in their lives was not in fact anywhere equal to the role he is given as a fellow fishing enthusiast.

Nevertheless, Smith saw himself as Bill Gorton. "Hem gave me the impression," Smith wrote to me, "that Bill Gorton was a composite character."[303] When I visited Donald Ogden Stewart in London,[304] he made it clear that he did not want to enter into any competition with Smith for rights of identification. I told him that Hemingway himself had identified him with Bill Gorton. "I'm honored," he said. He thought Hemingway admired Bill Smith because he had once tried out for the St. Louis Cardinals ("Never," Smith said).[305] And then, over a small glass of vermouth—Stewart had cut down on drinking; I had cut it out altogether—he reminisced about the first trip to Pamplona in 1924. Some Spaniards had loaned him a blanket which he used to wave at a bull. He was frightened as the bull charged. But at the last minute as the bull came at him, he lost his fear. Two ribs were broken in the encounter. That was the last time he would go into the bullring.

The subject seemed a bit remote in Stewart's living room with its two inch deep powder blue oriental rug. Around the room were African art objects. Good paintings hung on the walls of the staircase leading from the foyer downstairs to the living room. The far end of it looked out on a garden thick with flowers. Stewart was tall; he seemed a bit over six feet. He was quite bald, his face and head flushed, his manner agreeable. In a moment he became serious. Hemingway's *A Moveable Feast* was more on his mind than the novel in which Stewart himself occasionally figured. "Hemingway's treatment of Fitzgerald in *A Moveable Feast* was inexcusable," he said, "and the scenes in the Louvre were absolutely cruel. That's the treatment he gave Sherwood Anderson too." Stewart meant, of course, the treatment Anderson had received in *The Torrents of Spring*. "I introduced Ernest to Scott and the Murphys, and he made Gerald Murphy into the 'pilot fish,' the villain of *A Moveable Feast*. Murphy felt very guilty when he found out Hemingway meant him to be 'the pilot fish,' but I assured him he was not.

Bill Smith dragged by a bull at Pamplona, from a contemporary Pamplona postcard. *Collection of Harold Loeb.*

I thought Hadley a lovely person and a good wife—the perfect wife,"
Stewart added. He remembered having given a party for Ernest and
Hadley just after meeting them. I gathered from Stewart's remarks
that he felt involved in the slur against Gerald Murphy, inasmuch as it
was Stewart who had introduced Hemingway to him. At a later date I
heard that Stewart had seen some fifty letters, friendly and affectionate,
written by Hemingway to Sara Murphy—they were written, from what
I could surmise, about twenty years after the period of *The Sun Also
Rises* and *A Moveable Feast*—the two books are almost contemporary
in their setting. Evidently, Stewart was pleased that these letters had
been found; they would discredit Hemingway's attack on the
Murphys.[306]

Stewart looked up Hemingway in Paris at the suggestion of Edmund
Wilson or John Peale Bishop—he could not recall which; but the suggestion was made when he was vacationing at Capri. He did that on his
next trip to Paris. Stewart was then living with his mother in Vienna;
they made that their headquarters because the cost of living there was
cheap. He said he was writing for Harper's at that time.

"That coincides somewhat with the novel. Hemingway has Bill
Gorton in Vienna. So I guess he had you in mind."

In rechecking the novel (Chapter VIII), I found that Bill Gorton first
arrived from New York, spends some time at the author's apartment,
goes off to Vienna, and then returns altogether drunk to Paris. He has
been to the fights in Vienna and has tried to help the Black boxer
who had failed to get himself knocked out.

"Had you been to the fights in Vienna? Was there any truth to the
story of the Black boxer? Were you that drunk when you came to
Paris?"

"I haven't read the novel for many years. I don't recall any such
fight in Vienna. I drank a lot in those days, but not that much. That
much of Bill Gorton wasn't me. There's some of Ernest in him.
Ernest could hold his liquor."

Had Hemingway completely imagined the story of the boxer? Could
Stewart have forgotten the entire incident? I tried to prod his memory
by alluding to Bill Gorton's comment that the Vienna prizefighter resembled Tiger Flowers. Stewart remembered having seen Tiger
Flowers, but he didn't associate him with Vienna. (Correctly so: Tiger
Flowers never fought in Europe.) Did he go to the fights with Hemingway as Bill and Jake do in Chapter IX? Yes, Stewart sometimes went
to the fights with Hemingway, and to bicycle races too. "I couldn't
stand the bike races," he said, "they were boring—like the bullfights.

But I would never let Hemingway know that. He wouldn't have stayed
friends, and I was afraid to stand up to him. I wanted him to like me.
I want people in general to like me." He explained that his autobiography was difficult to publish because there was not enough hate
in it. I mentioned that Harold Loeb felt Hemingway might have been
down on him because, like Robert Cohn (Chapter XV), he disliked
bullfights. "Ernest certainly would have been," Stewart agreed.

Stewart had explained to me that he started out as a humorist but
that his whole outlook changed when he became a Marxist. I wondered if some such leanings were already evident in 1925. Hemingway
had made Stewart as Bill Gorton concerned about the Black prizefighter in Chapter VIII. Did he do so because he sensed in Stewart the
future advocate of the proleteriat? Probably for other reasons, Stewart
observed. There was a long established tradition in the Stewart family
for aiding the Black cause. Stewart's grandfather had been the first
president of Fisk University. Hemingway most likely knew about that
background.

What did he think of Hemingway as a humorist? "Hem liked my
stories, I didn't like his. Meanness got into his humor. It went off the
track, therefore. He sent me two or three things for *Vanity Fair*." We
went back to the question of social justice. Did Hemingway have any
passion for it? "I would say he was on my side in those matters."
"And how about his alleged anti-Semitism?" "Not really," Stewart
said, "no more than anyone else. On principle, Hemingway would
have been against it."

I had spoken to Sir William Twysden just the day before and I was
interested to know what Stewart thought of the innuendo that Duff had
been engaged in smuggling dope.

"Great! That's Duff for you! Just what you'd expect!"

Stewart meant to be funny. Without realizing it, he was carrying on
the Brett-Duff myth set in being by *The Sun Also Rises*.

And what did he think of Duff?

"Beautiful! Just beautiful! Beautiful!" I guess he suddenly realized
that his wife, Ella Winter, who was in the next room, might have over-
heard him. He quickly added, "I don't mean I was in love with her.
But she was so attractive. Just beautiful!" He didn't know if Hemingway and Duff had had an affair. It seemed so to him at that time. But
he hadn't thought about it. He didn't want to think about it. Hem's
marriage to Hadley was something he looked on as holy. Hadley was
a lovely person. Well, was Hemingway in love with Duff? "It was
hard not to be. She played her cards so well. But I didn't understand
why Hem became angry with Harold Loeb at Pamplona. He may have

resented Harold's success with Duff. But then, we were all in love with her."

He could never account for Pat Guthrie's being at Pamplona. He had no idea that Guthrie and Duff had been having a love affair. At Pamplona he and Guthrie joined a line awaiting entrance to a brothel. Harold Loeb was always leaving to get a shave. I remembered mention of that in Chapter XIV.

Guthrie was a nice guy—that, and nothing more. Stewart had not heard of Guthrie's having committed suicide. Hemingway was fun to be with, especially in Pamplona. But the first trip in 1924 was better. That was like a class reunion. The second trip was spoiled by mixing sexes. The second trip was more like a prom. Duff was beautiful in a toreador's hat.

"What about Hemingway's insinuating that she had homosexual male friends?"

"Never realized that. But I was a Yale man. A Yale man was not supposed to know about such things. If you were a Yale man, you could hold your liquor. Scott Fitzgerald couldn't. He wouldn't have been a good Yale man. But if you were a Yale man, you didn't know about such things as fairies. Once one tried to make me. I didn't understand what he was doing." It never occurred to him—before and after reading insinuations about Hemingway in Morley Callaghan's book[307]—that Ernest had homosexual traits.

"Was Duff the character Hemingway portrayed?"

"I never thought of her as morbid. She used to laugh at all my jokes."

"Who was this Edna?" I was referring to the girlfriend Bill Gorton has in Chapter XVII. "Did you bring a girl along to Pamplona?"

"No, I don't remember any girlfriend in Pamplona. I had one in Paris: a Zelli girl. She was my mistress, my first mistress: Paulette, really Josephine. She was one of the dancing girls at Zelli's. We all went there, the Murphys and I. Not Hemingway. Paulette wanted to go honest. So I set her up in a grocery store. I told the Hemingways about her, and they bought there religiously, even though the store was quite a distance from their home." Stewart explained that Hemingway was not the kind to go to a night club such as Zelli's. If so, he seemed to know a good deal about it—or imagined a good deal about it; for, in Chapter VII, Jake Barnes accompanies Brett and Count Mippi-popolous there. Of course, the details—noise, smoke, drink, and dance—could have been applicable to any night club. But Hemingway, at least, knew one of the ex-dancing girls, Paulette, really Josephine.

Our conversation turned to Pamplona again. Stewart remembered

Quintana, the hotel keeper who is fictionalized as Montoya.   The
friendship indicated in Chapter XIII between Jake and Montoya corresponded to that between Hemingway and the real host.[308]   And that
was why Hemingway was angry when Pat and Duff could not pay their
bill.   The matter was not resolved in actuality as is reported in Chapter
XIX where Brett bails out Mike in paying the bill.   Neither Duff nor
Pat had any money.   Hemingway was embarrassed and incensed at
Duff and Pat.   "Ernest was sensitive about money, and he almost
turned on them," Stewart recalled.   "I paid the damn bill."   Later
(without Ernest) they went off to Biarritz with Stewart.   They toasted
him for his help.   All bitterness was forgotten.   "There were no reca-
pitulations, no post-mortems.   We had had a marvelous time, and we
were off to more marvelous times."   Even though Hemingway had
been wrought up against Harold Loeb in Pamplona—someone, perhaps Hadley, had mentioned Loeb's affair with Duff in Hemingway's
presence—Stewart remembered him as part of the marvelous time.
"He was really a wonderful person—especially in Pamplona—he was
fun to be with."

     "And did you have any idea that *The Sun Also Rises* was to come
out of all this?"

     No, Stewart had no idea.   When Hemingway returned to Paris, they
had dinner together on the Boulevard Montparnasse.   "Hemingway
threw a bottle of wine in the street.   It was 'a feeling good thing.'   We
were having a good time."

     "Then you were still good friends.   And what happened after the
novel was published?"

     They remained good friends. It wasn't the novel that caused a change
a few months later.   At the MacLeish's Ernest read a nasty poem about
Dorothy Parker.   Stewart was outraged.[309]   "That's a goddam thing to
do," he said.   Ernest turned on him.   You couldn't disagree with
Ernest.   That was the end of their friendship.   They stopped seeing
each other regularly.   They met in later years only occasionally and
sometimes by chance.   Then, Hemingway played the part of the famous
writer.   Yet, in the early 1940's, when they encountered each other at
the Club 21, "Hemingway couldn't have been nicer."

     That was the trouble.   He was, Stewart said, "a dangerous friend."
Ella Winter, Stewart's wife, agreed.   "You could never tell when he'd
turn on you, especially if he first trusted people."   Stewart added, "He
had that sudden suspiciousness about life and people."

     Stewart was in California when *The Sun Also Rises* was published.
He read the novel not long after publication date and he recognized

himself in Bill Gorton. Apparently, he was not resentful. He didn't
drink as much as Bill Gorton, but he did love to get drunk in those
days. At any rate, he felt himself superior to Hemingway's portrait.
He didn't recall Hemingway's questioning him prior to the writing in
order to get information. "Hemingway never asked questions," he
said. But the novel was mere reporting. It wasn't "writing," just reporting. And Stewart has never taken it as a serious piece of literature.
Nor, apparently, did Ford Madox Ford. Braddocks—the fictional
name of Ford Madox Ford—is among those who meets Mademoiselle
Hobin and who organized the dancing club to which the group goes. It
is at Braddocks' *bal musette* where they are visited by Brett and her
friends (Chapter III). Braddocks reappears for a moment in the next
chapter to praise Mlle. Hobin's idiom after having discovered her profession. Her diction weighs more heavily with him than her doings.
It was Braddocks who led the way to the civilities extended the
madamoiselle from Mrs. Braddocks and Frances Clyne. They take up
his cue when he shows good English manners by saying he has known
Mlle. Hobin for a long time. Mrs. Braddocks (Stella Bowen) is shown
so excited in talking French that she might well lose the trend of her
own thoughts; Frances Clyne is facile enough in the language to en-
gage in platitudes. Braddocks' greeting to Jake Barnes on first sighting
him ("I say") is that of the conventional Englishman. Presumably
Hemingway is showing him as pretty much of a stereotype and very
much in a fog.

It was not his intention to let Ford off that briefly. As Braddocks, he
occupied several pages in the first two deleted chapters. Some of this
material—for example, his confusing of Aleister Crowley with Belloc
—reappeared in *A Moveable Feast*.[310] Personal traits repugnant to
Hemingway—the asthmatic wheeze, the odd figure, the lustreless eyes
—were also salvaged for that book. But parts of the deleted chapters
were never reproduced. Those sections reflect both on Loeb and Ford.
We are told that Robert Cohn gave his new novel to Braddocks, his literary friend, for criticism. Braddocks, in turn, palmed the novel off to
Jake Barnes who found it lacking in organization. When Cohn asked
Braddocks for his reaction, Braddocks, who, of course, hadn't
bothered to read the book, muttered something about problems of organization. The novel Hemingway had in mind was Loeb's first, *Doodab*. But he never gave it to Ford to read; he had, in fact, asked William Carlos Williams for criticism.[311]

The attack on Ford began before *The Sun Also Rises*. In 1924
Hemingway did a slight story on Ford and Stella Bowen in which they

are shown arguing bitterly over wine.[312] (Morrill Cody recalls Ford's
having been devoted to Stella.)[313] Ford seems for Hemingway to have
been a case of contempt at first sight and persistent hate in retrospect.
A Moveable Feast was not the last of the attacks. Ford was again to be
cited for madness in *Island in the Stream*. James Joyce is brought in to
aid as young Tom, son of the hero of that novel, recalls Joyce's having
said that Ford had been out of his mind for a very long time.[314] Of all
the characters abused in *The Sun Also Rises* Ford remained Hemingway's obsession. Was the motive the usual one? Had Ford offended
Hemingway by some kindness? To be sure, he had praised the young
writer enthusiastically. He was sure that Hemingway would soon be
famous.[315] He made him editorial assistant on the *transatlantic review*
and, when he left for New York in the middle of 1924, he turned the
reins over to Hemingway. At once Hemingway used the July issue to
denigrate Cocteau and Tzara, both of whom were esteemed by Ford.[316]
The August issue was larded with Hemingway's choices, many of them
Americans, but Ford was able to delete some of these, which he did on
the grounds that the *transatlantic review* was an international journal.[317]
As Hemingway had also included many non-Americans, Ford was
somewhat unfair in his criticism.[318] Matters reached a climax when
Hemingway took the occasion for a special supplement devoted to
Conrad to attack T. S. Eliot. In the November issue Ford apologized
for Hemingway's attack; Hemingway was highly offended.[319] He told
Gertrude Stein that Ford was a crook and a liar.[320] One would guess
that anyone who was Ford's friend might well become fair game for
Hemingway. That would include Sir Cedric Morris, Loeb, and Kitty
Cannell. That would include any author admired by Ford, W. H. Hud-
son, for example.
  "The unapproachable master of the English tongue"—these were
Ford's words of praise for Hudson written in 1921.[321] The onslaught on
Hudson in the opening of Chapter II is also one against Robert Cohn,
because he admires *The Purple Land* by that author; it is also against
Ford. Actually, *The Purple Land* was not the favorite of Cohn's model,
Harold Loeb. Of all of Hudson's novels, he preferred *Green Mansions*.[322] It was Ford who valued *The Purple Land* as the greatest of all
Hudson's writings. The fact that both Loeb and Ford admired Hudson
was enough to condemn each of them. And Kitty Cannell, who incurred Hemingway's wrath for her being shocked at the shabby style of
life to which he had reduced Hadley, would likewise be on Hemingway's list of the ten most wanted for her friendship with these two
men. The *bal musette* scene in Chapter III provided Hemingway with

the means of showing us Ford through the company he kept: a fool, a golddigger, some fairies, and an inept young novelist named Robert Prentiss. Brief as the scenes are in which Braddocks appears, they are heavily charged with Hemingway's venom.

And Ford's reaction? He has told the story of the *transatlantic* days in *It Must Be the Nightingale*; he has summarized that story in his preface to the Modern Library edition of *A Farewell to Arms* (1932). The younger men, Hemingway among them, were generous in denouncing him as incompetent to write and to edit. Hemingway had cut his contributors to a snip and printed his extremist friends extensively. Ford was able to look back on all this with amusement.[324] He bore Hemingway no grudge, although, as we know from Burton Rascoe's account, Hemingway had publicly ordered Hadley under no circumstances to allow Ford to pay for her drinks.[325] Perhaps Ford knew that Hemingway regarded his *bal musette* as ridiculous—Cody had heard Hemingway make such a denunciation.[326] But Ford rose above Hemingway's insults. In his preface to *A Farewell to Arms*, he spoke of *in our time* as possessing great artistic ability. No, he did not care for two subsequent books—obvious references to *The Torrents of Spring* and *The Sun Also Rises*—but he wanted to think of them as trials towards a longer form than had been achieved in *in our time*. Quite calmly and quite candidly, Ford said that if he hadn't liked the two novels, he was quite sure he hadn't been expected to.[327] But he carried over no hostility as he appraised *A Farewell to Arms*. It was a great work, fresh and radiant. It placed Hemingway among the two other masters of English prose, Conrad and Hudson.[328] And then, six years later, in *The March of Literature from Confucius' Day to Our Own*, Ford spoke of Hemingway as he remembered him in Paris in the 1920's. He was among those, many of them American "Middle" Westerners, who rekindled the spirit of literature.[329]

Ford included Glenway Wescott among those "Middle" Westerners.[330] He is the Robert Prentiss of Chapter III (originally named Robert Prescott in the first deleted chapter).[331] Part of Ford's entourage in the *bal musette* scene, Prentiss, like Braddocks, has a code of manners. Offered a drink, he responds with a prompt genteel refusal; urged, he accepts. He is very nice and handles Barnes's anger with decorous tact. Hemingway introduces him as an up-and-coming novelist with an English accent. The accent was real; Margaret Anderson had noted it too.[332] I recall hearing Wescott years later and can testify to the accuracy of Hemingway's comment. But I could also understand Hemingway's instinctive dislike for the man. It was based, no doubt,

Glenway Wescott, a recent photograph. *Collection of*
Gale Research Company.

on grounds similar to his repugnance towards Ford. Neither was fit
company for landing a marlin or stalking a kudu or meeting any of
those tests by which Hemingway measured masculinity. Hemingway
had his private Stanford-Binet system. The painter, Gabor Peterdi,
told me that on meeting Hemingway in Paris, he had his arm muscles
felt by the writer. The muscles being adequate, he was qualified to
join Hemingway in punching wooden fences along a Paris street.
Another antic was told to me by Paul Blum: Hemingway's account of a
bicycle race down the Rue de la Paix at four o'clock in the morning.
Hemingway and friends borrowed some bicycles which had been left

unattended. They were used for bread deliveries and the boys who made them had evidently gone off nearby to do their chores. Hemingway and the other racers, in acting as their own cheerleaders, made enough noise to incite a protest heard from an upper story window. A woman leaned out and yelled, "Either make less noise so I can sleep, or more noise so I can keep awake." Hemingway and the others liked the wit. They decided to visit the woman to tell her so. Gendarmes arrived. Arrests were made. Hemingway said he was released on declaring to the officer in charge that he was a writer. He promised to send the officer one of his books. One can be certain that neither the eccentric Mr. Ford nor the staid Mr. Wescott ever joined Hemingway in smashing fences or swiping bikes.

But apart from showing up Ford as a ringleader of the retarded, Hemingway had a special dislike for Wescott himself. At the very time Ford was reproaching Hemingway for his tactics in the management of the *transatlantic review*, Ford had opened its columns to Wescott. "This Quarter's Books" (II, 446–448), a report on the literary situation in New York, was Wescott's contribution. In it he contrasted the "grand style" of Kenneth Burke with the "naturalistic" style of Hemingway.[333] The contrast was not intended to embarrass Hemingway, but he must have felt that coming from the author of the recently published *The Apple of the Eye*, this young critic-novelist was being a bit presumptuous. *The Apple of the Eye* in itself was enough to kindle fury in Hemingway. It had most of the faults of a first novel and all of the faults that Hemingway himself tried to avoid: fine writing, purple passages, pathetic fallacies, and echoes of Anderson's contrived simplicity. When Hemingway's mother, two years after the publication of *The Sun Also Rises*, proclaimed herself to an Oak Park reporter as cheerful about life and therefore, so unlike her terribly realistic son, Hemingway angrily suggested that her preference was for the Glenway Wescott type, a storybook prince given to books about grandmothers. Wescott had just won the Harper's Award for his novel, *The Grandmothers*.[334]

And then, Wescott had published a poem and some criticism in *The Dial*,[335] now considered by Hemingway one of his unforgiveable enemies. In March 1925 he received a rejection from *The Dial* for "The Undefeated."[336] His story had been turned down as being too strong for American readers. Thereafter, he waged unremitting war against that publication.[337] Evidently, Hemingway concluded, one had to be somewhat dainty, like Wescott, to be published in first-rate journals these days. Wescott had also been printed in *Broom*[338] and was now one of Ford's rising stars.

The mention of Wescott as Roger "Prescott" in the early deleted chapters suggests that Hemingway had originally more ambitious plans of devestation for that writer. I have not been able to get Mr. Wescott's reaction to even the brief treatment to which Hemingway finally limited himself. A reasonable guess would be that Mr. Wescott was not pleased. It would be safe to say at this point that of all the persons mentioned thus far who went into Hemingway's novel only Bill Smith, Harold Stearns, and Juanito Quintana remained on friendly terms with the author.

Juanito Quintana was the Montoya of the novel, the hotelkeeper in Pamplona between whom and Jake Barnes there existed some spiritual affinity. It is explained in the novel (Chapter XIII) as growing out of their being *aficionados*, passionate devotees of bullfighting. That was true in reality; the two men also liked each other as friends. On several occasions, when in Spain, Hemingway made it a point to see Quintana (sometimes with Hotchner along).[339] For Quintana, Hemingway was the incomparable Ernesto.[340] He appears to have taken no umbrage at the comment in Chapter XVI that prices were doubled at his hotel for the fiesta, and the remark in Chapter XIII that, as a fellow aficionado, Montoya tolerated Jake's friends is partially true. When the staff of the Hotel Quintana, finally having become disgusted with the drunken behavior of Pat Guthrie and Duff Twysden, served lobster water to them as if it were consommé, Quintana thought that was what Hemingway's friends deserved.[341]

Neither Loeb nor Smith could identify Krum and Woolsey, the two newspapermen in Chapter V. Robert McAlmon, who identified most of the major characters correctly, thought Krum to have been based on Krebs Friend, Hemingway's co-worker in Chicago on *The Co-operative Commonwealth*.[342] Krebs had come to Paris, married a wealthy woman, and looked worse than the Ancient Mariner before the reprieve.[343] He had now enough money to rescue the *translantic review* when, in the fall of 1924, Ford had run out of cash and patrons.[344] Hemingway brought him to Ford, but no sooner had Friend agreed to give cash and accept the presidency of the journal, than Hemingway turned on him too. Hem had become furious with Ford, disgusted with the review, and was now irate at the man he had brought around to save the enterprise. He accused Friend of trying to show off his talents as entrepreneur. He predicted imminent failure, and the prediction, as it happened, was correct. The review went out of existence at the beginning of 1925.[345]

The similarity of the beginnings of the names Krum and Krebs is about the only reason to lend substance to McAlmon's theory that the bearers are to be identified. Krum is, like Jake and Woolsey, a foreign correspondent, and with them has been to an unrewarding news conference at the Quai d'Orsay. He has been thinking of coming over to the Dingo or the Select some evening—if he can get away from his wife and children; the suggestion is that he'd like to be on the town. And maybe he might get himself a job with Saturdays off, a place in the country, and a car (Chapter V). None of this sounds like the Paris biography of the newly affluent Krebs Friend. Unfortunately, McAlmon didn't give his reason for making the identification, nor did he give his source for it. And he was not able to make another very obvious one. He had no idea who Mike Campbell was, although he knew Pat Guthrie. He thought Guthrie might be the model for Braddocks. Duff Twysden and Guthrie were not known to him as lovers; he thought they were merely cousins (some kinship was also suggested in *This Must Be the Place*.)[346] As for the mysterious Count Mippipopolous, McAlmon identified him and Duke Zizi as characters around the Quarter, the Count, a Spanish painter. Mippopopolous, as Baker has pointed out, was the subject of much speculation.[347] Hadley Hemingway, now Mrs. Hadley Mowrer, told Baker she thought that the Count was one of Ernest's inventions.[348]

The significant omission in McAlmon's list is the character Pedro Romero. He was, of course, the well-known matador who had adopted the name Niño de la Palma. Born Cayetano Ordóñez, he was spurred on by heroic dreams even in boyhood when he brandished wooden swords against imaginary bulls. So runs the account in Shay Oag's biography of Cayetano's more famous son, Antonio Ordóñez (*In the Presence of Death* [New York: Coward, 1969]). Hemingway, who saw Cayetano in Pamplona in 1925, extolled his artistry in those memorable passages in *The Sun Also Rises*; but Cayetano was not Hemingway's discovery. The Spanish public had discovered him at least a year before when the twenty-year-old bullfighter, hitherto hardly known—he had experienced a few encounters for novices of his age— came to be regarded as a messiah sent to revive the fallen sport (or art) of bullfighting (p. 64). A phrase coined by a Madrid critic was to accompany his fame: "He is from Ronda and his name is Cayetano." Hemingway seemed to know little of Cayetano's background and, in creating the fictive Pedro Romero, provided some palpable fictions. One was an affair with Brett, the other a fight with Cohn. According to Oag, Hemingway made it clear that, apart from the quite realistic descriptions of Cayetano's style in the bullring, Romero was the product of invention (p. 66). Depicted by Hemingway as a somewhat

morbid young master, he had, in real life, a great love of gaiety. He
loved flamenco parties and the manzanilla that heightened them (p. 68).
If money lured him (as Hemingway implied it did to Romero), the goad
was not avarice. Cayetano had been born in a poor family. When he
was thirteen his impoverished father had to sell his shoemaker's shop
in Ronda and the brothers had had to take menial jobs. Cayetano himself had become a waiter. When success brought him comparative
wealth, Cayetano restored his family to Ronda from which they had
had to move and he enabled father and brothers to pursue what goals
they wished. He was generous to friends and to news vendors whom
he knew (pp. 65–68). After his marriage in 1927 to Consuelo Araujo
de los Reyes, a half-gypsy dancer, there were signs of his faltering
which the critics were quick to notice, Hemingway among them. He
was to turn on Cayetano in *Death in the Afternoon* by predicting
an end to this career. Hemingway, it developed, was wrong. Cayetano
still had some good seasons ahead (pp. 73–79).

But not many. With increasing age Cayetano had to retire, and then
much began to be heard about a new star, his son Antonio. The father
faded into obscurity. One day a young American student in Madrid
was asked to share his pension bedroom with a pockmarked and somewhat unpleasant man who turned out to be the former Niño de la
Palma. He was broke at the moment, the lady who owned the pension
explained, and it would be nice if young Sam Adams would help him
out (p. 58). The student did for about three weeks. Afterwards, he
wrote an account of those days, "The Sun Also Sets," for *Sports Illustrated* (June 29, 1970).

Adams recognized his impoverished roommate as the character
whom Hemingway had fictionalized as Pedro Romero and whom he
had charged with cowardice and faltering in *Death in the Afternoon*.
The bullfighter did not dispute the charge. He told Adams that Hemingway probably could not conceive of the fear he experienced in those
days he fought. The bulls then were larger and fiercer, he insisted
(pp. 58–59). This talk was heightened by drink. Cayetano drank and
drank all afternoon and night when his check came. It was said the
family paid him to stay away (p. 58). One morning his remittance
arrived and Adams stayed with him to do a tour of the cafés. Bartenders would not serve him until he showed cash. He had the cash
that day and he drank his fill (pp. 62ff). In a moment of anger Cayetano tore down an advertisement for a performance of his son Antonio.
And then, at the end of a picaresque night, he turned to Adams and
pointed to a passing cab. There, he said, there was his famous son.
Adams looked at the cab. Except for the driver, it was empty (p. 64).

Cayetano died a few months after Hemingway. The once graceful and allegedly handsome young man (his face had none of the strength and less of the good looks of Antonio) had spent his last years in half squalor, in drunkenness, and ultimately, like Hemingway, in delusion. Three characters out of *The Sun* were afflicted. Ford had always been harmlessly tetched; Cayetano ended his days seeing what was not there; Hemingway, victim of imagined persecutions and unwilling to live merely to survive without purpose, took his own life. Duff excepted, most of the other characters lived on. Perhaps, as Jimmy Charters suggests in a later page, even the little Greek portrait painter, Zizi, is somewhere still alive.

Georgette Leblanc who died a generation ago, was not a character in the novel; one wonders why Hemingway used her name in introducing the prostitute, Mlle. Hobin. The former companion of Maeterlinck, she settled in Paris in the 1920's where she began a close friendship with Margaret Anderson—a friendship that lasted through the early years of World War II and ended with her death. Was the equating of Georgette Leblanc with Mlle. Hobin an indirect way of sniping at Margaret Anderson? I asked her this question in the Fall of 1970, and from her reply (January 9, 1971), I gather that Miss Anderson was somewhat bewildered. She said that Georgette Leblanc had never met Hemingway and that neither Georgette Leblanc nor she knew that the name had been mentioned in the book. Miss Anderson only became aware of the reference when she saw the film. Had Georgette Leblanc seen the film, Miss Anderson said, she would have regarded the use of her name as a bit of absurdity. Other persons who knew Georgette Leblanc might have felt astonished. Apparently, she did not feel that Hemingway was getting at either one of them. She always regarded Hemingway as a good friend.

It was Hemingway's intention to have included two more persons in the novel.[349] The first was John Dos Passos. The scene in which Bill Gorton and Jake visit Mme. Lecomte's restaurant in Chapter VIII is drawn from Dos Passos' biography. It was he who had "discovered" the restaurant.[350] The second character Hemingway had planned to include was one Flossie, a singer, the only jovial girl in the Quarter. That unquestionably was Flossie Martin, who sang at Zelli's, and it was at her apartment that Duff stayed before leaving for St. Jean-de-Luz with Harold Loeb.[351] Whether Hemingway knew of her part in bringing Loeb and Duff together is problematical. She had no use for Hemingway.[352]

And there is, finally, Jake Barnes, modelled on Hemingway himself. A brief background sketch of Jake Barnes in the original deleted

Hemingway, Key West, 1928. *Collection of William B. Smith.*

chapters helps give us an idea of the man Hemingway conceived his fictionalized version to be. Invalided home from a British hospital at the end of the war, he went to work for the *New York Mail*. With one Robert Gordon he moved over to the Continental Press and got an assignment in Paris. He is now a foreign correspondent writing his first novel—this one, *The Sun Also Rises*, is it. All this is suggestive of Hemingway's career as a correspondent for the Toronto *Star* and of his personal literary ambitions. But in fact, as Baker discovered, the journalistic background parallels that of Bill Bird and David Lawrence.[353] Jake is not married; he is unable to marry, although Brett loves him. Quite obviously, Hemingway has stepped out of his real role as husband to Hadley and father to Bumby to represent himself as single. We will want to see how much more extensive the fictionalizing becomes. How much was there really to the romance with Duff Twysden? Was she, like Brett, really in love with Hemingway, or he with her? I have already indicated that Hemingway knew a great deal about Duff, however he may have excluded certain virtues and talents in presenting her fictionally. He even knew that Sir Roger Twysden was the tenth baronet in the family line—the original text was changed from "tenth" to "ninth,"[354] one would assume for precautionary reasons (Chapter XVII). And Hemingway seems to have known that Duff was a middle name; he mentions her in the first deleted chapter as the former Elizabeth Brett Murray. The family name "Murray" contains a syllable of her family name, Smurthwaite: Hemingway seems to have known that name too. All this background could have been absorbed second-hand or directly in conversations over drinks at bars such as the Dingo where, we know, Hemingway sometimes met Duff— on one occasion, at least, in the company of Fitzgerald.[355] Some sort of friendship was indubitable. But Don Stewart, for example, didn't think the relationship ran much deeper. After all, everyone in his circle, himself included, was fascinated by Duff. Nor did Loeb know of Hemingway and Duff carrying on a romance. His questioning Duff when they were at St. Jean-de-Luz as to whether she liked Hemingway and as to whether she would have an affair with him were mere conversational items, perhaps items through which Loeb was testing Duff's character.[356] It was not until Duff wrote to him from Paris, after her return there, that she was coming down to Pamplona with Hemingway who, she said, promised to behave, that Loeb had any inkling that their relationship might have had some depth. But even then he just entertained a mild suspicion.[357]

At the very time she was writing a love letter to Loeb, she was

seeking out Hemingway. She wrote to him that she was in trouble.[358]
In the latter part of the year, after the Pamplona business and the
completion of the first draft of *The Sun Also Rises*, Duff again wrote
Hemingway begging for a loan. She and all her friends were broke.
Would he please lend her 3000 francs? She was certain she could
repay him.[359] Obviously, Duff and Hemingway were more than mere
casual friends. He had recorded some fragments of her conversation
suggestive of a passionate relationship which had to be foregone and
which was driving her to desperation. These remarks,[360] without
being quoted in the novel verbatim, provide the background for the
conclusion of Chapter III and the dialogue between Jake and Brett in
Chapter VII. One of Duff's statements to the effect that one must not
hurt people, that our sense of decency is our substitute for believing
in God, does find its place in the book.[361] It is the redemptive note for
Brett in the final chapter of the novel. She has given up the young
bullfighter rather than selfishly ruin him. She feels damned good having decided not to be a bitch. Of course, the entire episode between
Brett and the young bullfighter is pure fiction. Quite obviously, in
real life, the vow not to hurt people had to do with not hurting
Hadley; and the idea that our sense of decency is what we have in
place of supernatural belief is something Duff told Hemingway when
she refused to have an affair with him.

And *that* is not the language of a mystic, as Duff represented herself
to have been when in St. Jean-de-Luz with Harold Loeb.[362] Another
of her tall stories to Loeb was that of running off with the best man
and marrying Sir Roger Twysden instead.[363] The Twysden family
would not have been reluctant to confirm that story as evidence of
Duff's wilfulness. Aileen Twysden said that Duff pursued Roger for a
considerable time. Finally, without notifying the Twysden family, he
went off to Edinburgh with her to be married. There had been something of a courtship and there were the formalities of a wedding.[364]
Duff and Roger were the best looking bride and groom that he had
ever seen, one of those who attended told Lett-Haines. That was
Brigadier Ray Buller, O.B.E. (6th Hussars).[365] Let us keep in mind that
when a male fabricates, he is a liar; when a female does, she is merely
a woman. Duff was assuming the prerogatives of her sex in lying to
Loeb. She had to justify to him (perhaps to herself) her running away
from Pat Guthrie. Oh! That Wedding! She was so impetuous! And
then there were those inner voices whose dictates she blindly obeyed.
No wonder she did things on the spur of impulse. She might have even
thought that Loeb himself was a mystic. He frequently talked to people
about "The Mysticism of Money." Duff might have been misled into

thinking he would like a mystical friend. She certainly had things clarified for her when, in the midst of the romantic interlude, Loeb gave her his monetary treatise to read.[366] At any rate, it's clear that she was drawing on her defenses to allay any suspicions that Loeb might have had regarding her character. And she sensed rightly, on first talking to Loeb in Paris at the bar where they met, that he would respond to some mysterious (and expeditious) approach. A "miracle," she called their encounter.[367] That sort of bolt from the blue was exactly what Loeb needed in his condition. He had broken with Kitty Cannell and was down in the dumps.[368] He was still somewhat timid about women[369] (Hemingway's remark in Chapter I that Cohn was married *by* his first wife had some appropriateness for Loeb himself). Duff led him to believe she was in love with him and appeared duly startled when he suggested he was.[370] All of this was playacting. Loeb himself now sees that his suspicions at the time (he was not so naive as Hemingway made him out to be) were probably justified.[371]

To Hemingway, as I have indicated, she was anything but a mystic; Paul Blum found her a down-to-earth, practical woman. She was also, he said, a man's woman. That too, was the opinion of Duff's New York friend, Mrs. John Rogers.[372] In brief, she knew how to handle men. Something of a self-assurance was in her boast that she could get Sir Cedric Morris to marry her within ten days. I think Lett-Haines missed the point in thinking her naive;[373] he was not wrong in thinking her anything but sensual. (Dr. Edward Harkavy guessed that she was probably frigid.[374]) Her expertise was in fulfilling the fantasy or the need of the particular man of the moment. Something like that must have happened in her relationship with Hemingway.

From his records of her remarks, it is apparent that she gave him the idea that his sexual attractiveness put her beyond the limits of self-control.[375] To Hemingway, for whom muscularity was the measure of manhood, that was the right approach. It served a two-fold purpose, and the technique is at least as old as women's colleges. The lady rejects without offending, flatters while withdrawing. "I wouldn't trust myself alone with you" is by now a commonplace technique of extrication, and Duff used it. Nevertheless, there seems to have been some sort of romantic encouragement on her part. She enjoyed being captivating and Hemingway was at some stage of the game naive enough to believe that her feelings, which were merely dramatic, were sincere. "He was fascinated by her old world charm," Berenice Abbott told me. McAlmon, who said that he introduced Hemingway to Duff, remembered his having been carried away by her title.[376] After he met her, he spent weeks with her and Guthrie in Montmarte. Hemingway

Hemingway, Key West, 1928. *Collection of William B. Smith.*

also spent money. He paid for Duff's and Pat's drinks. Hadley came along, and McAlmon describes her as being in tears. Hemingway sometimes asked him, sometimes Josephine Bennett, to take Hadley home so that he could stay on with Duff. McAlmon was impressed with Hemingway's new attachment. If it wasn't the real thing, he said, it was a deep involvement. He thought Hem was about to break with Hadley. Therefore, neither Josephine Bennett nor McAlmon felt obliged to take her home nights. Let Hemingway do it himself. And when the break with Hadley came, McAlmon was startled to find Ernest marrying Pauline Pfeiffer. He had expected the new wife to be Duff Twysden.[377] Prejudiced though McAlmon was against Hemingway, his report of this period does not sound contrived.

Up to the present time we were not certain as to whether Hemingway was exaggerating completely his involvement with Duff. From McAlmon's testimony it is now clear that he was seeing her often, that he was very much taken with her, and that he was quite callous about Hadley, who, it appears, was somewhat of an intruder. If Duff had not told Clinton King that Hemingway was not her "type,"[378] one could assume that Duff was as deeply involved with him as he with her. It would seem, however, that she stirred up his romantic emotions without feeling anything more for him than friendship. Her concern for Hadley would have provided a good and a right excuse for keeping him at a distance. Kitty Cannell thought it no more than a mere excuse although it is unquestionably true that she did have a concern for Hadley's feelings.[379] But it is also possible that she enjoyed Hemingway's passion for her. In a deleted passage (originally Chapter IX) Brett and Jake indulge in an exchange of vows of the most sentimental kind. One cannot be certain whether this deleted section is a transcript of what really was once said, but it is worth mentioning. I will not quote it verbatim but will give, as it were, the essence of it.

"You are my dearest love," she said, "and I will love you forever. And you are the only man I ever told that to."

"And I will love you forever. I must. I know I must love you forever." And so on. The deletion was out of character for Jake and Brett, but it gives us some idea of the possibility of a real sentimental exchange having taken place. In still another deleted section Jake Barnes insists to the reader that he is recording accurately what took place. He is telling us what Brett's actions actually were and what her words actually were. Should they seem unconvincing, it is because he is avoiding the usual literary tricks. These days, lovers in novels are presented intellectually from the point of view of the psychoanalyst, or, alternatively, they are represented as merely having an affair. True love has come to be regarded cynically, but Jake had true love for Brett. He was aroused passionately when with her; when away from her, he lived an untroubled life. Such is a summary of this section. It is conceivable that some of the love scenes, including the one deleted, were based on reality. There is an outside chance that Duff fell in love with Hemingway. But then, there was Pat Guthrie with whom she was most certainly in love, and Loeb, with whom she most certainly was not.[380] Most likely, she was enjoying a role with Hemingway as with Loeb and enjoying also the drinks he bought for her and Pat.

Jake Barnes, Hemingway had planned to tell us, did not wish a mere casual affair nor did he have mere materialistic, that is to say, Freudian views about love. And he was to have been shown as somewhat sentimental and altogether a romantic lover. If Hemingway cut out such scenes, it was because presumably the reader is to infer all this from Jake's constancy to Brett, from Jake's attempts, however imperfect, to be religious, and from his little acts of generosity in the initial parts of the novel. Hemingway had attempted to depict a man who, despite some limitations of character, had essayed a spiritual view of life and love. Dedicated to his craft, Jake might have been novelist; Hemingway had intended to inform us of that in the deleted first chapter. But we are left to infer that too as we read Jake's beautiful descriptions of the Spanish countryside and his clean, sharp delineation of the bullfight spectacle. The man could write.

Last scene of all is Jake Barnes grown bitter and cynical. By the middle of the story he has ceased to care about life; he wants to learn only how to live it (Chapter XIV). What is it he learns? That you wait for the fifth serving on the train bound south from Paris, unless you are a well-to-do pilgrim from Dayton, Ohio en route to Lourdes by way of (please observe) Biarritz. That you go to the fiesta of San Fermin to find the prices doubled for the saint's festival. That you go to Burguete, the monastery of Roncesvalles overlooking it from the mountainside, and you are made to pay an exorbitant price for your room, outfitted, of course, with a picture of Our Lady of Roncesvalles. Even where God is, the dollar is almighty.

And if you turn to the world of artifacts, as we already have, there are those idiotic toys, crass advertisements, and dreary pictures—all produced with an eye to return and heedless of taste. Turn to the social world and you discover that a Lady may be your companion if you own (as Count Mippipopolous does) a chain of sweet shops across the Atlantic. For two hundred francs a concierge will revise her opinion of your being a *poule* and will designate you to be genteel. Everywhere you turn—in the hotel, the restaurant, the train—someone expects a

tip. Your friend Bill Gorton has made a mint on his last book and
hopes to duplicate the success on his next (Chapter VIII). The handsome young bullfighter, Romero, who handles himself with perfect
artistry, handles himself so with the hope of being a millionaire (Chapter XVI). Harvey Stone has ceased to work and has become an object
of charity. Mike Campbell doesn't work either; he charges, he bor-
rows, he makes demands on his rich mother. Usurers nip Brett's small
income (Chapter XIX), and Cohn gets a bounty from his mother.
Sports used to be above scandal. Now fights are fixed.[381] The French,
at least, are clear about money. If you want to be liked, you have only
to spend. Jake plans to spend (Chapter XIX).

Hemingway, Don Stewart said, was sensitive about money. Loeb
thought him to be quite honorable about it in daily life. He paid
his share, was fair about tips. If we try to impute to Hemingway
Jake's ultimate concern for the dollar, it is because we have the benefit
of hindsight from having read *A Moveable Feast*, one of "the short
and simple annals of the poor" whose protagonist allows himself at last
to be bought. The conclusion of *The Sun Also Rises* presents us with
a dubious hero whose world, if he is to live in it, as he had proposed
to do, requires a putting away of all spiritual ideals and romantic
aspirations. His future is left for us to imagine. It is there in *A Moveable Feast*. But Jake Barnes has not been presented to us as a poverty-
ridden man, as Hemingway thought himself to be in his later account of
the mid-1920's. Not discontent with his $1800 bank balance, Jake
would have had no trouble if it hadn't been for Brett (Chapter IV).
The Sun Also Rises is no tale of nagging poverty—not for Barnes, at
any rate—but it is suggestive of a still unwritten tale of a nagging
desire for wealth. Perhaps, in saying that, one is influenced by one's
knowledge of *A Moveable Feast*. But the question is whether or not
there are high points of similarity, other than those that have already
been noted in considering the members of *The Sun* set, between Jake
Barnes and Hemingway. All that can be said with certainty is that the
author had one-third less in cash than his character, seemed, to those
who knew him, not preoccupied any more or less with money than
Jake in the early part of the book, had much more charm than the
character, certainly made far more trouble for people than Jake who
said he gave them none (Chapter III), was married and had a child,
loved bullfighting, as Jake did, and fishing too, as Jake did. Unknown
to his friends, Hemingway might have been deteriorating inwardly as
Jake was. One cannot prove that the inner life of Jake Barnes corresponded to that of Ernest Hemingway. It is presumptuous to make
such an analogy; it is also irresistible.

But the externals are only in part based on reality. Hemingway
never overtly treated Loeb with the contempt he attributed to his fictional counterpart There was no final scene in Madrid with Duff as
there was with Jake and Brett. Such scenes were drawn from Hemingway's imagination, and he imagined situations for the other characters
too, fist-fighting in Pamplona, Duff running off with a toreador, Harold
Stearns insulting Loeb to his face. The book was not mere reporting
as Loeb, Stewart, and Duff Twysden said of it. Yet much of it was
drawn from actual events, actual conversations, actual relationships.
This is saying no more than one would expect from a *roman à clef*,
although there are degrees of invention even in that genre which
permit either a close adherence to or a wide divergence from fact.
Hemingway clung close enough to fact to make his characters instantly
recognizable to those that knew the real persons. Some accepted their
fictionalization with good humor or with supportable indifference.
Others, like Loeb and Duff Twysden, were quite hurt. Few could enjoy
the novel. But it would be best to hear them with their own voices
or to hear about them vicariously from those who knew them well.
The following pages will permit the reader to judge of the accuracy of
Hemingway's portraits and to judge also, if imitating Pedro Romero,
who liked the very bulls he killed,[382] Hemingway found writing a sport
in which destructiveness was part of the game.[383]

NOTES

1 Leah R. Koontz, "'Montoya' Remembers *The Sun Also Rises*," below, p. 210.
2 Harold Loeb, "Hemingway's Bitterness," below, p. 125.
3 George Wickes. *Americans in Paris* (New York: Doubleday, 1969), pp. 149 ff. The
  symposium on American exiles sponsored by *transition* in the Fall of 1928 is apropros
  to this question. In an unpublished letter to Professor Norman Holmes Pearson of
  March 31, 1951, Robert McAlmon said, among many unpleasant things about Hemingway, that he did portray the younger generation of the time with accuracy.
  The concept of Montparnasse as one vast and continuous party is given by Clinton
  King (below, p. 43) and by Morrill Cody ("*The Sun Also Rises* Revisited," *Connecticut
  Review*, IV, 2 [1971].)
4 This is apparent from such memoirs as Matthew Josephson's *Life among the Sur-
  realists* (New York: Holt, Rinehart and Winston, 1962), John Dos Passos' *The Best
  Times* (New York: New American Library, 1966), James Charters' *This Must Be
  the Place: Memoirs of Montparnasse*, ed. Morrill Cody with an introduction by

Ernest Hemingway (London: H. Joseph, 1934), and Kay Boyle's *Being Geniuses Together* (New York: Doubleday, 1968), a revision of and a supplement to McAlmon's *Being Geniuses Together* (London: Secker and Warburg, 1938). A first-hand account of the notoriety of the characters of *The Sun Also Rises* is given by Paul Blum (below, p. 56). Morrill Cody who was in Paris at the time recalled "everyone in Paris talking about it from the beginning and eventually the news spread to England and America by word of mouth and through the literary press" ("*The Sun Also Rises* Revisited").

5 "Out of Little, Much," III (December 11, 1926), 420–421. The passage cited here is quoted from William White, *Studies in The Sun Also Rises* (Columbus: Charles E. Merrill, 1969), p. 9.

6 "Readers and Writers," *The Independent*, CXVII (November 20, 1926), 594. Quoted from White, p. 5.

7 Harold Loeb, *The Way It Was* (New York: Criterion, 1959), p. 14.

8 Idem.

9 Ibid, p. 292. "The photographers caught Bill as he was being butted, and me at the moment I was born aloft on the bull's head, and sent the photographs to New York, where they appeared in the rotogravure sections of the *Times* and *Tribune* a few Sundays later, much to the excitement of my family." Mr. Loeb, in conversation, said that Smith's picture never appeared in these rotogravure sections.

10 Malcolm Cowley, *Exile's Return* (New York: Viking Press, 1951), pp. 3 ff., 225–226.

11 *The Letters of F. Scott Fitzgerald*, ed. Andrew Turnbull (New York: Scribners, 1963), p. 229. The letter was postmarked December 23, 1926.

12 Charters, p. 98. Cf. Morrill Cody, "*The Sun Also Rises* Revisited." For Hemingway's awareness of this myth, see Carlos Baker, *Hemingway, The Writer as Artist* (Princeton: Princeton University Press, 1956), p. 78.

13 Morrill Cody as told to author, October 11, 1969.

14 Morrill Cody as told to author, October 11, 1969.

15 Mrs. John Rogers Jr. as told to author, September 12, 1968.

16 Josephson, p. 319.

17 Mrs. Dana Suess Burr as told to author, April 5, 1969.

18 A. E. Hotchner, *Papa Hemingway* (New York: Random House, 1966), pp. 47–48. Hotchner reported having met Loeb at a cocktail party and having been asked by him if he looked like the type who would commit murder. Hotchner did not report his answer, if there was any, nor did he make it evident that he accepted Loeb's denial of a plot to murder over Hemingway's report of the alleged plot (CBC May 26, 1970).

19 Ibid, p. 48.

20 Clinton King to author, February 6, 1970.

21 Donald Ogden Stewart as told to author, October 5, 1969.

22 Donald St. John, "Interview with Hemingway's 'Bill Gorton,'" below, p. 188.

23 Cowley, pp. 14–15.

24 Hotchner, pp. 49–50.

25 An attempt at reminding such critics has been made by Donald Torchiana, "*The Sun Also Rises*: A Reconsideration," *Fitzgerald/Hemingway Annual, 1969*, pp. 83–84. Cf. *Hemingway, The Writer as Artist*, pp. 80–82.

26 Cowley, pp. 225–226.

27 Carlos Baker, *Ernest Hemingway, A Life Story* (New York: Scribners, 1969), p. 180. Baker's source is a letter from Wilder to Hemingway (February 15, 1927).

28 Ibid. The source here is Cowley, loc. cit.

29 From Cowley's introduction to *The Sun Also Rises* (New York: Scribners, 1962), quoted in White, p. 104.

30 *The Flowers of Friendship, Letters Written to Gertrude Stein* (New York: Knopf, 1953), ed. Donald Gallup, from William Cook, March 27, 1938. The charge is that people were in no way as Hemingway had depicted them. Another writer concedes that some of "the bitter young men and women" were lost, but not as much as "the tourists and wealthy Americans..." (Carlos Drake, *Mr. Aladdin* [New York: Putnam, 1947], p. 116).

31 "*The Sun Also Rises*," *The New York Times* (August 1, 1943), quoted in White, p. 54. Farrell also made Cowley's point that college students were acting like Hemingway characters—not merely Smith alumnae and Yale undergraduates, but students throughout the country! (pp. 54–55). The germ of Farrell's thesis is to be found in Frederick L. Allen's *Only Yesterday*, rev. ed. (New York: Harper, 1957), pp. 120 ff. The original edition was published in 1931.

32 Below, p. 126.

33 Below, p. 117.

34 Below, p. 118. Loeb's account has it that he stopped the return of Hemingway's *in our time* just as Beatrice Kaufman, Horace Liverwright's reader, was about to send it back as a rejected manuscript. According to a recent publication, Liverwright and editors T. R. Smith and Edith Stern approved of Hemingway's proposed book. It is conceded that the copy they had was probably the one Loeb had Hemingway give Leon Fleischman in Paris (Walker Gilmer, *Horace Liverwright, Publisher of the Twenties* [New York: D. Lewis, 1970], pp. 120–121).

35 Loeb to author.

36 Baker, p. 179. Loeb says there is no substance to the story of his developing an ulcer (Loeb to author). The story of his requiring seven years of psychoanalysis is not from Baker. It was told to me in the mid-1950's by a member of the circle of the late Charles Fenton. Loeb likewise denies this legend.

37 Jacques Baron as told to author, October 9, 1969.

38 Loeb to author.

39 Morrill Cody as told to author, October 11, 1969.

40 Baker lists five persons who knew of the work in progress: Hemingway's father, Sylvia Beach, Barklie Henry, Howell Jenkins, and Gertrude Stein (p. 589). Bill Smith was also aware that Hemingway was writing the novel (below, p. 66), likewise Morley Callaghan. Vide his *That Summer in Paris* (New York: Coward-McCann, 1963), p. 49.

41 Kathleen Cannell, "Scenes with a Hero," below, p. 149.

42 Baker, p. 179. Baker's remark that Kitty Cannell took to bed out of anger was clarified by her to mean that she was angry at what Hemingway had done to the other characters (Cannell to author.) She was not surprised at his treatment of her because she never trusted him to begin with (below, p. 150). This statement was confirmed by Kitty Cannell's friend, Florence Gilliam, who was in Paris with her at the time *The Sun Also Rises* was published (Gilliam as told to author, October 9, 1969).

43 *The Way it Was*, p. 257; Kitty Cannell to author.

44 Loeb to Cannell, unpublished correspondence.

45 Cannell to Loeb, unpublished correspondence.

46 Loeb to author.

47 Cannell to author.

48 Cannell to author.

49 Loeb to author. Cf. *The Way it Was*, p. 229.

50 Loeb to author.

51 Loeb to author.

52 Loeb to author.

53 This was stated and implied in several letters during the Fall of 1925. This part of the Loeb-Twysden correspondence is unpublished.

54 Loeb to author.

55 Below, pp. 125–126.

56 Below, pp. 110–117.

57 Mrs. Paul Scott Mowrer to author, postmarked December 29, 1967.

58 William Horne to author, December 17, 1967, excerpted in the *Connecticut Review*, I, 2 (1968), 144.

59 Baker to author, summarized in the *Connecticut Review*, I, 2 (1968), 144.

60 Loeb to author. He discussed the possibility of a lawsuit with Dwight Fanton of Westport.

61 Lady Castle Stewart as told to author, October 3, 1969. Lady Stewart was under the impression that Loeb had wanted to sue Hemingway for libel for *The Sun Also Rises*.

62 Loeb to author. Kitty Cannell had heard that Loeb's writings on economics were those of a genius (Cannell to author).

63 Baker, p. 552.

64 Loeb to author. Baker points out (ibid.) that there was no connection in Hemingway's mind between *A Moveable Feast* and Loeb's biography which he had been reading.

65 Loeb to author.

66 Loeb to author.

67 Loeb to author.

68 Loeb to author. Cf. Baker, pp. 145, 150.

69 It was Loeb who was kicked under the table by Kitty Cannell (Loeb to author).

70 Loeb to author. Loeb felt a bit uncomfortable because Kitty Cannell's blonde hair and floppy red hat made for a combination a bit too garish for him. He did not know, however, that Kitty Cannell's mother who lived on the Boulevard Raspail, objected to her daughter's choice. The Cannells had as much right as the Loebs to indulge their tastes. On her mother's side Kitty Cannell was first in line to claim title to an Irish castle; on her father's side (Eaton), she could trace her ancestry back to the Mayflower (Cannell to author).

71 Loeb to author. In *The Way it Was* she is given the pseudonym, "Betsy Stanwick," and is described as the daughter of one of Loeb's old friends (p. 210).

72 Loeb to author. At one point Loeb said that Barbara intimated marriage; at another point that she suggested intimacy. At any rate, his version in *The Way it Was* leads one to believe that Barbara and Loeb's mother had at least discussed breaking up the relationship with Kitty Cannell (p. 212).

73 Loeb to author.

74 Horne to author, December 14, 1969. Loeb insists that once Horne apologized to him for having mentioned the name Spider Kelly to Hemingway. The apology, in Loeb's opinion, implied that Horne had said a good deal more to Hemingway about his Princeton days.

75 Horne to author, December 14, 1969.

76 Hemingway was reported by Cowley in his introduction to the novel (n. 10) as working to the point of exhaustion. It was supposedly begun on July 21, 1925,

Hemingway's birthday, and completed on September 6 (quoted in White, p. 103). Baker dismisses the birthday date of composition as part of Hemingway's myth-making. The Ms. notebooks show July 23 as the inceptory date, and Baker has found a fragment that might have been written as early as the second week in July (p. 589). Hemingway told Hotchner (p. 52) he did the first draft in six weeks, certainly a little short of the truth since that draft was not completed until September 21, 1925 (Baker, idem.). At any rate, Hemingway did work fast and undoubtedly put himself under pressure.

77 Samuel Putnam, *Paris Was Our Mistress: Memoirs of a Lost and Found Generation* (New York: Viking Press, 1947), p. 129.

78 Leicester Hemingway, *My Brother, Ernest Hemingway* (Cleveland: World, 1967), p. 249.

79 Loc. cit.

80 Hemingway told Cody the following when they met in 1933. " 'I was writing a novel,' he said, 'not a biography.' He was annoyed, he told me, at all the fuss that had been made about 'the six characters in search of an author-with a gun.' Even seven years after the publication of the book he was still threatening to punch Harold Loeb in the nose if he ever met him again because he was the one, he thought, who was complaining the loudest" (*"The Sun Also Rises* Revisited").

81 Below, p. 128.

82 For example, Nicholas Joost, *Ernest Hemingway and the Little Magazines* (Barre: Barre Publishers, 1968), pp. 72–73 and by Josephson, pp. 317–320.

83 Hotchner, loc. cit.

84 Loeb to author.

85 Loeb to author.

86 Loeb to author.

87 Cannell to author.

88 Baker, pp. 183, 595–596. Hemingway's attending church coincides with his involvement with Pauline Pfeiffer. Evidently, few knew of Hemingway's having been converted in 1918; it is not surprising, therefore, that Loeb had no knowledge of Hemingway's turn of faith. Hemingway, in fact, led people to believe that his conversion took place circa 1926. That becomes clear in Callaghan's account, p. 94.

89 Baker, p. 584.

90 Loeb to author.

91 Letters addressed care of her publisher failed to elicit a response. Ultimately, I was able to get her address and I received a promise that information would be forthcoming. None ever came.

92 Loeb insisted in conversations with me that he gave Frances no money at all because he was not obliged to. She was not an employee of *Broom*, he said; she came from New York to Paris with the understanding that she might have a job with the magazine. At one point Loeb gave her four letters—no, they were really just notes—and when she failed to do them, he informed her that any possible opportunity to work on *Broom* would be closed to her. However, I have assumed the account in *The Way It Was* to be more likely. In that account Loeb mentions his willingness to undertake the extra expense of a secretary and he recalls a dozen letters to be done that he gave to Frances—her pseudonym is "Lorraine" (pp. 15, 65). Dorothy Kreymborg said that Loeb contracted with Frances in New York, telling her that no written agreement was necessary (Mrs. Kreymborg as told to author, November 3, 1970). Kitty Cannell recalls that at that time of Frances' dismissal Loeb told her that he had given Frances adequate money (Cannell to author).

93 "Robert had a little secretary on the magazine," Frances Clyne tells Jake Barnes in Chapter VI, "Just the sweetest little thing .... So I made him get rid of her, and he had brought her to Provincetown from Carmel where he moved the magazine, and he didn't even pay her fare back to the coast." McAlmon does not mention the story of Frances specifically, but he does allude to incredible intrigues going on at the Hotel Jacob at the time that Loeb and the Kreymborgs settled there (p. 34).

94 Mrs. Kreymborg as told to author, July 6, 1970.

95 *The Way It Was*, loc. cit.

96 Ibid., p. 64; Mrs. Kreymborg as told to author, July 6, 1970.

97 In *The Way It Was* Loeb recalls "*Dial* made a jocular comment about its unborn rival that ... there was unlimited money behind the project..." (p. 11). He heard that he had as much as $1,000,000, ten times the amount mentioned above and in Alfred Kreymborg's account of his association with *Broom* (below, n. 101).

98 Loeb to author.

99 Mrs. Kreymborg as told to author, July 6, 1970.

100 Mrs. Kreymborg as told to author, July 6, 1970.

101 Alfred Kreymborg, *Troubadour* (New York: Boni & Liveright, 1925), p. 380. The previous pages give the history of Kreymborg's partnership with Loeb in the publishing of *Broom* and refer to the figure of $100,000 which *The Dial* credited Loeb with having behind the project.

102 Cannell to author.

103 At first, Loeb insisted that this gift was another of Mrs. Cannell's fictions. Subsequently, he remembered buying her a squirrel coat.

104 Cannell to author.

105 Cannell to author.

106 Cannell to author. Morrill Cody thought Kitty Cannell to have been grossly misrepresented by Hemingway. Cody thought her to have been one of the stable characters in Paris ("*The Sun Also Rises* Revisited"). Mrs. Cannell believed the novel to have been—from an aesthetic point of view—"an awful book" (Cannell to author). Cf. below, p. 149.

107 Cannell to author.

108 Loeb to author. However, he insisted, she did want him to marry her, thereby confirming an aspect of the relationship as drawn in *The Sun Also Rises*.

109 Cannell to author.

110 Harold E. Stearns, *The Street I Know* (New York: Lee Furnam, 1935), p. 256; Baker, p. 587.

111 Josephson, loc. cit.

112 Cannell to author.

113 Cannell to author.

114 The Red Indian came from the Eaton side of the family (Cannell to author).

115 Kreymborg, pp. 313 ff.

116 Ibid., p. 264.

117 Cannell to author. Frances Clyne alludes to having gotten her divorce in Chapter VI.

118 Cannell to author.

119 "They came to Europe where the lady had been educated, and stayed three years" (Chapter I).

120 Kreymborg describes her as "A Frenchwoman even to the perfect accent" (p. 365).

121 Cannell to author.

122 Loeb to author.

123 Cannell to author; Loeb to author. In *The Way It Was* Loeb gives her a somewhat

different career. "She was a professional singer and had given several acclaimed concerts" (p. 64). I assume Loeb was trying to hide the identity of Mrs. Cannell and modified her career just as he modified her name to Lily Lubow.

124 Cannell to author. Cf. Mrs. Cannell's review of Jacques Baron's *L'an I du Surrealisme suivi de l' an Derniere* (Paris: Denoël, 1969) in the *Connecticut Review*, IV, 1 (1970).

125 Cannell to author.

126 Loeb to author.

127 Loeb to author.

128 "Robert Cohn was once middleweight boxing champion of Princeton .... He was Spider Kelly's star pupil" (Chapter I).

129 Loeb to author.

130 Hemingway does not say that he took up boxing to beat up specific persons but to take out his hostilities "in boxing" (Chapter I).

131 Cannell to author; Loeb to author.

132 Harold Loeb, "*Broom:* Beginning and Revival," *Connecticut Review*, IV, 1, (1970), 11-12.

133 Loeb to author.

134 Kreymborg, loc. cit.

135 "*Broom:* Beginning and Revival," 10.

136 Ibid, 9.

137 Idem.

138 Loeb to author.

139 Above, n. 88.

140 Josephson, pp. 317, 320-321; Dos Passos remembered Duff as "hardboiled" (p. 154). Author Jerome Bahr, for whose book, *All Good Americans*, Hemingway wrote an introduction, said he was astonished when speaking to Duff. They saw each other a few times during the mid-1930's, and on these occasions Bahr heard with his own ears Brett's dialogue in *The Sun Also Rises* (Jerome Bahr to author, November 10, 1970). Novelist Edward Fisher wrote, "She is perfectly evoked in SUN" (Edward Fisher to author, November 1, 1970).

141 Loeb to author. Cf. *The Way It Was*, p. 274. Cody, who knew Duff, said that the idea of her being a mystic was ridiculous (Morrill Cody to author, November 6, 1970). In *Being Geniuses Together* McAlmon records that the phrase, "one of us," was used by Duff to indicate that someone belonged to her social class. "He or she is not one of us" meant to McAlmon that Duff was indulging in snobbery (p. 306).

142 Clinton King to author, February 6, 1970.

143 Aileen Twysden as told to author, August 6, 1970.

144 Loeb to author.

145 Below, p. 45.

146 Clinton King said that he gave the correct information to the hospital but that it was erroneously recorded (below, p. 42). Duff was listed as "Mrs. Duff Stirling King," occupation: "housewife," employer: "artist," religion: Episcopalian, birthplace: "London," name and birthplace of father: "Smurthwaite Sterling, London," name and birthplace of mother: "Mrs. C. L. Stirling, London" (Sister Mary Joachim to author, November 15, 1968).

147 *Burke's Genealogical and Heraldic History of the Peerage, Baronetage, and Knightage* (London: Burke's Peerage, 1967).

148 Aileen Twysden to author, May 5, 1969.

149 Unpublished correspondence, October 25, 1925, written from Stirlingshire, Scotland.

Edward Fisher recalled Duff's carrying with her a snapshot of her son (Edward Fisher to author, November 10, 1970).

150 Mrs. Anne Fellowes to author, April 26, 1969. Most of the information had been conveyed from her through Mrs. Peter Dickens on April 17, 1969. Mrs. Dickens had communicated with Mrs. Fellowes and passed the information on to me. In addition to what has already been mentioned in the text, the following data were sent. Duff had been christened "Mary Duff Stirling." Her mother, having dropped the name Smurthwaite, appeared to have changed her name to Stirling; the younger daughter, Jean, also took this name. Mrs. Fellowes did not think Duff did. She recalled Duff's having married Luttrell Byrom, who divorced her. She then married Roger Twysden in Edinburgh in 1917. She couldn't understand why Duff might have been christened Stirling, when her name was Smurthwaite unless, possibly, she was Mary Duff Stirling Smurthwaite.

151 Cannell to author. Miss Abbott wrote to me that Duff was upset but merely tried to remove the book from the local library near her family (Berenice Abbott to author, circa November 7, 1970).

152 This meeting took place in New York, July 10, 1969.

153 Through the courtesy of Malcolm Tooze, Town Clerk of Richmond, and His Worship, the Mayor of Richmond, an inquiry regarding B. Smurthwaite was referred to Leslie P. Wenham, Head of the Department of History, St. John's College of Education, York. Mr. Wenham replied, "The Smurthwaite family certainly owned a wine shop in Richmond. At one time this was in the pit of the converted Georgian Theatre Royal.... Later they moved from this place to another wine shop only thirty yards away. Both of these places are in Victoria Road, Richmond." However, Mr. Wenham was not able to say that a B. Smurthwaite owned either of these stores. He added that although Smurthwaites lived in Richmond from 1788 to 1922, there is no B. Smurthwaite buried in the Richmond Churchyard (Wenham to author, October 14, 1970). This evidence is suggestive rather than conclusive. For example, there are many Smurthwaites listed in the London telephone directory. Duff's hospital records indicate her father to have been born there. Were it alleged that he owned a wine shop in London, and were it shown that some member of the Smurthwaite family did indeed own a wine shop there, no concrete proof would have been demonstrated thereby.

154 Mrs. John Rogers Jr. as told to author, September 10, 1968.

155 Loeb to author. Cf. *The Way It Was*, pp. 219–220: "She was an English girl," Hemingway told him on that occasion, "who had served in the Red Cross in Italy. She had taken care of him when he was brought to the hospital." Agnes von Kurowsky, who attended Hemingway in Italy was not, of course, an English girl. Hemingway interwove this fantasy into Chapter V of *The Sun Also Rises* and into a *Farewell To Arms*. Agnes was reared in Washington, D. C. (Baker, p. 47), but she was born in Philadelphia (Baker to author, December 18, 1967). Loeb had believed her to have been born in Milwaukee because, he told me, he had been so informed by Bill Horne (below, p. 133).

156 Josephson, loc. cit.

157 "Lady Brett and Lady Duff," *Connecticut Review,* II, 2 (1969), 5–13; below, pp. 228–240.

158 Hotchner, loc. cit.

159 I believe I first heard this story thirty years ago at New York University.

160 King was slightly incorrect about the date of Duff's death. He believed it was in May 1938. He was also slightly incorrect as to the place of her cremation. Recalling that she died in a hospital in Sante Fe, New Mexico, he believed he had her cremated

there in accordance with her wishes. The director of the hospital told me that Duff died on June 27, 1938 and that she could not have been cremated at the hospital. Nor were there then facilities for cremation in Santa Fe. The probability is that she was cremated in Albuquerque (sister Mary Joachim to author November 15, 1968). However, there is no reason to doubt King's memory as to other details. He is certain that, under the circumstances, there was no funeral and, therefore, neither pallbearers nor final rites. Consequently, he insists Hemingway's account to Hotchner is without foundation (Clinton King to author October 28, 1968).

161 Duff apparently told Clinton King that Hemingway did not interest her sexually and that there was no sexual relationship between them (Clinton King to author October 28, 1968).

162 Clinton King to author, February 6, 1970. The information consisted of answers to a questionnaire and to comments made on my article referred to above (n. 157).

163 Mrs. John Rogers Jr. as told to author, September 12, 1968; below, p. 240.

164 Mrs. John Rogers as told to author, September 12, 1968; below, p. 236. The reader should not get the impression that Mrs. Rogers intended any malice. Much as she admired Duff, she succumbed to Hemingway's fictive impression of her.

165 Mrs. John Rogers Jr. as told to author, September 12, 1968; below, p. 236.

166 Above, n. 17.

167 Aileen Twysden to author, August 6, 1970.

168 *Grove's Dictionary of Music and Musicians*, ed. Eric Blom, 5th ed. (London: St. Martin's Press, 1954), II, 262, 266.

169 Morrill Cody to author, April 14, 1970.

170 Arthur Lett-Haines to author, September 12, 1969.

171 Morrill Cody to author, April 14, 1970; also interview October 11, 1969. Cody's printed account of Loeb is somewhat more generous than his comments to me! "Harold ... was a far more intellectual, sensitive, understanding person than the fictional character ..." (*"The Sun Also Rises* Revisited"). Some of the unfavorable reaction to Loeb by those who met him in Paris in the 1920's may have resulted from a mere superficial reaction. The late L. B. Kreitner recalled Loeb at that time as having been "pompous" (L. B. Kreitner as told to author October 16, 1969).

172 Idem.

173 Loeb to author. Among the things Loeb disputed was Cody's statement that at St. Jean-de-Luz and nearby Ascain, where Loeb had gone with Duff, the tryst could not have been as idyllic as Loeb had made it out to be in *The Way It Was* because Loeb was suffering from an abcessed tooth. Loeb said the ailment was cleared up in two days.

174 P. 228.

175 Cf. Arthur Lett-Haines, above, p. 45. Edward Fisher, who knew Duff in Paris not long after the publication of *The Sun Also Rises*, also praised her naturalness and unpretentiousness: "She was truly real, intuitive, gentle, and of course doomed" (Edward Fisher to author, November 1, 1970). The quotation from Fisher does not, however, tell the whole story (below, n. 204).

176 Stuart Chase to author, August 15, 1969, September 21, 1970.

177 Stuart Chase to author, August 15, 1969.

178 Stuart Chase to author, September 21, 1970. The passage that follows is a summary of a telephone conversation with Mrs. Chase on September 16, 1970.

179 Below, p. 243. The portrait of Pat Guthrie in *This Must Be the Place* is less flattering. Allegedly, he fleeced friends in Capetown of two thousand pounds and absconded to England (p. 226). Charters' eulogy on Duff should be compared with

the unpleasant remarks recorded from him by Callaghan (p. 127). Guthrie was reported to have been indifferent to his portrait in *The Sun Also Rises* ("*The Sun Also Rises* Revisited").

180 Below, p. 244.

181 *The Way It Was*, p. 270.

182 Loeb to Author; *The Way It Was*, p. 271.

183 Clinton King to author, February 6, 1970.

184 Idem.

185 Baker, p. 145.

186 Arthur Lett-Haines to author, September 12, 1969.

187 Morrill Cody as told to author, October 11, 1969.

188 The exact date of the conversation between Hemingway and Gorman is unknown, but it probably was not many years after publication date. Gorman's entry is in a first edition of the novel (identified by "stripped" on p. 181). "This is the list given me by Hemingway," Gorman wrote on the flyleaf. Only nine characters are mentioned. Some of the minor ones and Bill Smith are omitted altogether. Cf. James B. Meriwether, "The Text of Ernest Hemingway," *Papers of the Bibliographical Society of America*, LVII (1963), 412. Subsequent printings of the major characters include Sheridan Baker, *Ernest Hemingway* (New York: Holt, Rinehart and Winston, 1967), pp. 42 ff., Carlos Baker, pp. 147 ff., and Philip Young and Charles W. Mann, "Fitzgerald's *Sun Also Rises:* Notes and Comments," *Fitzgerald/Hemingway Annual 1970*. The essay by Young and Mann is a scholarly analysis of the deleted chapters which Hemingway cut following Fitzgerald's criticism of them. The discovery of Fitzgerald's letter to Hemingway was reported in *The Washington Post*, November 30, 1969. An account of the deleted chapters is to be found there, in Young's and Mann's essay, and in Baker, p. 153.

189 Morrill Cody as told to author, October 11, 1969.

190 Clinton King to author, February 6, 1970.

191 Arthur Lett-Haines to author, September 12, 1969.

192 Clinton King to author, February 6, 1970.

193 Charters, p. 224; Loeb to author. The identity of the American girl must remain in question. No listing for "Lindsay" or a comparable name is to be found in *Foreign Service of the United States, Diplomatic and Consular* (Washington, D.C.: U. S. Government Printing Office, 1926). The name is given as Lindsley in some Hemingway correspondence comprising part of the Fitzgerald papers at Princeton. From these we learn that Miss Lindsley saved Pat Guthrie from a bad check rap. We are also told that Pat broke with Duff on learning that it was her intention to take custody of her child even if she had to kidnap him. This correspondence apparently belongs to the early part of 1927. It suggests the approximate time when Pat broke with Duff and turned to Lorna.

194 Morrill Cody as told to author, October 11, 1969.

195 Arthur Lett-Haines to author, September 12, 1969.

196 Arthur Lett-Haines to author, September 12, 1969.

197 Morrill Cody as told to author, October 11, 1969.

198 Morrill Cody as told to author, October 11, 1969. However, after the publication of *The Sun Also Rises*, her reputation was affected by Hemingway's portrayal. Fisher, who met her in the late 1920's, recalled, "I'd never have known her reputation from her manner" (Edward Fisher to author, November 1, 1970).

199 Loeb to author.

200 Arthur Lett-Haines to author, September 12, 1969.

201 Arthur Lett-Haines to author, September 12, 1960.
202 Cayetano Ordóñez was reputed to be extremely handsome. His prowess, described
    by Baker (p. 149), made him into a hero for Hemingway who saw his performances
    in the following weeks in Madrid and Valencia (Ibid. pp. 151–152). Hadley too was
    fascinated by his work, and Cayetano gave her (not Duff, as we are told in Chapter
    XVIII), the bull's ear. Hotchner noted the detail (p. 176). Hemingway also told
    Hotchner that Hadley had fallen in love with Cayetano (Idem), which assertion,
    along with many others told to Hotchner, one is at liberty to doubt.
203 Baker, p. 179. Duff was supposed to have told this to Hemingway when they met
    one evening at the Dingo. Hemingway recounted her quip to Fitzgerald in a letter
    circa September 15, 1927. Even if Hemingway did not make up the conversation it
    is clear that Duff was not telling him her true feelings (above, p. 43). Similarly,
    she told Loeb that she was indifferent to her treatment in the novel (Loeb to author).
    She even defended Hemingway's writing the novel ("*The Sun Also Rises* Revisited").
    But she told others, as we have seen, that she was highly offended. Indeed,
    Hemingway had put in jeopardy her chances of seeing her child again because of
    his malicious aliusions to Sir Roger Twysden. It is also quite clear that Duff was
    in the habit of giving different persons different impressions. Note her comment to
    Edward Fisher on her being teamed up with Romero in *The Sun Also Rises:* "One
    thing I do know: Duff felt quite horrible about being ganged up with those bloody
    little bullfighters in SUN..... Duff said it would have been like being up to the
    arse in midgets" (Edward Fisher to author, November 1, 1970). I asked Fisher if he
    was quoting Duff verbatim in the last phrase. He said he was (Edward Fisher
    to author, November 10, 1970). Duff's dislikes apparently were even more extensive
    than those just cited. Writing to Loeb from St. Jean de Luz on August 25, 1925, she
    complained of the influx of "Spanish bastards" (Unpublished correspondence).
204 Edward Fisher, who admired Duff (above, n. 175), nevertheless did not put it past
    her to get an all expenses paid trip around the world, and, when Loeb refused, to rid
    herself of him.
205 Below, p. 234.
206 Clinton King to author, February 6, 1970. Either Duff felt more deeply about
    Loeb than she was willing to admit, or she felt deeply the need to protect her
    reputation against having gone off with him. Edward Fisher, who knew her between
    June 1928 and April 1929, heard her berate Loeb three years after their romantic
    episode, as one who was "always running off at the mouth" (Edward Fisher to
    author November 1, 1970). In the early 1930's Duff told her New York friend, Mrs.
    Rogers, that she disliked Loeb enough to say, "C'est une vache" (Mrs. John Rogers Jr.
    as told to author, September 12, 1968).
207 Loeb to author.
208 Charles Norman as told to author, October 10, 1970. Norman's attitude is the
    exception to the rule. Most people who met Duff shared the reaction of Fisher
    (n. 175). Jerome Bahr, Waldo Pierce's brother-in-law, was enchanted by her ability
    to establish immediate rapport. "A rare woman," he though her to have been
    (Jerome Bahr to author, November 10, 1970). To be sure, there were some who
    disliked Duff altogether—I refer to those outside the Twysden family. McAlmon
    remembered her as boozy, disorganized, and too fearful to face life (Robert McAlmon
    to Norman Holmes Pearson, March 31, 1951). A young Canadian friend of
    McAlmon, perhaps influenced by his aversion to Duff, stigmatized her as unspeakable.
    (John Glassco, *Memoirs of Montparnasse* [Toronto & New York: Oxford University
    Press, 1970], pp. 48–49). Fitzgerald told Perkins that he did not like the model

for Lady Brett Ashley (*The Letters of F. Scott Fitzgerald*, circa June 25, 1926, p. 205). However, Zelda and Scott used to dine with Duff. Cody thought Scott liked Duff but was persuaded by Zelda to a change of heart ("*The Sun Also Rises* Revisited").

209 Michael J. Arlen, *Exiles* (New York: Farrar, Straus and Giroux, 1970), p. 226. However, McAlmon says that he introduced Duff to Hemingway (below, p. 227).

210 Below, n. 359

211 Clinton King to author, February 6, 1970.

212 Cannell to author.

213 Loeb to author. Cf. Baker, p. 145.

214 Above, n. 1.

215 Below, p. 72.

216 Above, n. 208.

217 Donald Ogden Stewart as told to author, October 5, 1969.

218 Paul Blum to author, August 8, 1970.

219 Paul Blum as told to author, October 2, 1970.

220 Mrs. Anne Fellowes to author, October 15, 1970.

221 Aileen Twysden to author, November 2, 1970. The story of Sir Roger's alleged cruelty was passed on to Jerome Bahr from Waldo Pierce who evidently had it from Hemingway. In this somewhat modified account Sir Roger was supposed to have slept with a sword between him and Duff (Jerome Bahr to author, November 10, 1970). Also of interest is Duff's having told Edward Fisher that her line of descent went way back to Banquo (Edward Fisher to author, November 10, 1970).

222 Loeb saw Duff at one of Josephine Bennett's parties (*The Way it Was*, pp. 247–248), but he did not then make her acquaintance. His recollection at one time was that they became known to each other on his encountering Duff at the Select (Baker, p. 144). In subsequent conversations he said he was not certain of that; but he did meet her at some cafe or the other (Loeb to author).

223 There were evidently rumors that Duff was the model for Iris March. Duff told Loeb that she was not. He still believes that she is in part the model for Arlen's heroine (Loeb to author). Cf. "Fitzgerald's *Sun Also Rises:* Notes and Comments." Young and Mann are impressed by the fact that Edward Fisher used to see Duff wearing a green hat. Likewise, Cowley associated her with a green hat and mentioned the belief that she was the heroine of *The Green Hat* (quoted in White, p. 103). It is good to keep in mind that Cowley, having left Paris in 1923, never met Duff abroad, Indeed, his first meeting with Hemingway known to us is in 1948 (Baker, p. 464). McAlmon maintained that Nancy Cunard was the original of Iris March (p. 339).

224 Josephson, pp. 312 ff.

225 Above, n. 27.

226 Florence Gilliam as told to author, October 12, 1969.

227 Loeb to author.

228 *This Must Be the Place*, p. 179; *Being Geniuses Together*, p. 109. McAlmon mentions Thelma Wood as being constantly in their company, but he shares Hemingway's view in *The Sun Also Rises* that the two painters would rather frequent cafes than work (Idem). At one time, Morris was much involved with Mary Reynolds (Cannell to author). Both men were said to have had a lifelong friendship with Frances Hodgkins (E. H. McCormick, *The Expatriate, a Study of Frances Hodgkins* [Wellington: New Zealand University Press, 1954], p. 221).

229 Above, n. 228; also Harold Loeb and Florence Gilliam.

230 Arthur Lett-Haines to author, September 12, 1969.

231 Arthur Lett-Haines to author, September 12, 1969; Cannell to author.

232 Arthur Lett-Haines to author, September 12, 1969.

233 Baker, p. 153.

234 James Charters to author, May 20, 1970.

235 James Charters to author, May 20, 1970.

236 William Hoffmann, quoted in Donald St. John to author, December 7, 1968 and September 14, 1970.

237 William Hoffmann to author, October 19, 1970.

238 William Hoffman to author, October 19, 1970. The pseudonym "Ziki" represents two actual syllables from the real name. I have selected those particularly to indicate how close to the original name the fictive one, Zizi, was in fact.

239 William Hoffmann, quoted by Donald St. John to author, September 14, 1970.

240 *This Must Be the Place*, p. 120. "Mitzie" never told Hoffmann that he was the Duke of Mitzicus. Hoffman was quite sure he was not, but he did believe him when told that his father "had been a minister in the Royal Court of Greece" (William Hoffmann to author, September 28, 1970).

241 William Hoffmann, quoted in Donald St. John to author, September 14, 1970; William Hoffmann to author, September 28, 1970.

242 "He's putting up for Zizi..." (Chapter IV). Mitzie's poverty is described by Charters, below, p. 271.

243 Hemingway to Loeb, unpublished correspondence, circa the end of February, 1925. Cf. Baker, p. 140.

244 Baker, p. 139; below, p. 200.

245 *This Must Be the Place*, p. 131; *Being Geniuses Together*, pp. 328–330; Baker, p. 179; and especially Wickes, pp. 151–154.

246 Wickes, p. 153.

247 Stearns, pp. 206–207.

248 Ibid, pp. 207 ff.

249 Wickes, pp. 152–153; Stearns, p. 225.

250 *The Letters of F. Scott Fitzgerald,* Fitzgerald to Alexander Woohlcott, Fall 1925, pp. 486–487.

251 Loeb to author; Cannell to author. Cf. *The Way It Was*, p. 131. Here the genuine kindness of Jo Bennett is praised. Loeb remembered Jo Bennett as always wearing a turban. Kitty Cannell recalled her as having two grown daughters, a car, and a friendship with Larry Murphy who pretended to be jealous in order to flatter her. The descriptions of Loeb, Cannell, and Charters correspond to those of "Joan" given by Stearns, pp. 222–223.

252 Loeb to author.

253 *Exile's Return*, p. 79. However, Cowley thought that Stearns' anthology, *Civilization in the United States*, had serious limitations. That was his judgment, however, on rereading it and at a later date (p. 74).

254 Stearns, p. 225.

255 Ibid, pp. 224–225.

256 Ibid, pp. 247–248.

257 Ibid, pp. 251, 301.

258 Stearns, loc. cit.

259 Ibid, pp. 239–240.

260 Ibid, p. 256.

261 Baker, p. 587. Below, p. 227.

262 "*Broom:* Beginning and Revival," *Connecticut Review* IV, 1, 5.

263 Sinclair Lewis and Stearns are referred to in *The Torrents of Spring*.
264 Stearns admitted that he used to do that (Stearns, p. 358).
265 Loeb to author.
266 Loeb to author.
267 p. 62.
268 Stearns, p. 277.
269 *America: a Re-Appraisal* (New York: Hillman-Curl, 1937), p. 81. Stearns put *The Great Gatsby* and *Manhattan Transfer* in the same class as *The Sun Also Rises*.
270 Stearns, p. 164.
271 Idem. Cf. Baker, p. 62 for Grace Hemingway's similar observation.
272 Stearns, pp. 367–368.
273 Idem.
274 Baker, p. 383.
275 Baker, p. 139.
276 Ibid, p. 587.
277 Ibid, p. 588.
278 Ibid, pp. 77 ff.
279 Loeb to author.
280 Loeb to author.
281 Baker, p. 154.
282 Cannell to author.
283 Loeb to author. Cf. Baker, p. 144.
284 Below, p. 156.
285 Below, p. 155.
286 Loeb to author.
287 Above, n. 76.
288 Below, p. 187.
289 Loeb to author.
290 Loeb to author.
291 Below, p. 125.
292 Hotchner, loc. cit.
293 Baker, pp. 149–150.
294 Ibid, p. 154.
295 "Fitzgerald's *Sun Also Rises:* Notes and Comments."
296 Below, p. 119.
297 Below, p. 151. However, the words of Bill Gorton's song in Chapter XI, "Oh, Give them Irony and Give them Pity," were probably the words of Stewart. He commented on the frustration of Smith and Hemingway on their finding the Irati log-jammed so that fishing plans had to be cancelled. The pity and irony of it were his sentiments (Baker, p. 149). Cf. Matthew J. Bruccoli, "Oh, Give Them Irony and Give Them Pity," *Fitzgerald/Hemingway Annual 1970*, p. 236.
298 Stewart as told to author, October 5, 1969. Before setting out for Burguete and Pamplona, Hemingway told Bill Smith that he had been in touch with the bullfighters whom they were to see and that the bullfighters had promised to lend them their capes (CBC, May 26, 1970).
299 Stewart as told to author, October 5, 1969; above, n. 283.
300 Baker, p. 131. The reference to the taxidermist in Chapter VIII has its origin in Chautard's having had the body of her dead dog taken to one in order to preserve the animal for her. Baker comments that she, of course, never visualized the dog achieving fame in American letters (Idem) any more than Loeb and Cannell dreamed

that their cat, Feather Puss, would find his way into Hemingway's posthumous novel, *Islands in the Stream.*

301 Below, p. 201.

302 "Harris may have been the name of a chap who joined Ernest and myself when we were having lunch near Burguete" (William B. Smith to author, September 29, 1970).

303 William B. Smith to author, October 10, 1970.

304 Below, p. 67ff.

305 William B. Smith to author, October 10, 1970.

306 Donald St. John to author, June 11, 1970. St. John had interviewed Stewart a few months before this time.

307 Callaghan, pp. 55–56, 134. Actually, Callaghan quotes McAlmon to point out that Hemingway, by wearing three sweaters and by his treatment of homosexuals in *The Sun Also Rises*, was probably overcompensating for sentimental, if not effeminate traits with himself. This rumor was current long before publication of Callaghan's memoirs and *Zelda*. Fitzgerald reported that McAlmon had told Hemingway that Fitzgerald was a fairy: McAlmon then told Callaghan that Hemingway was one also (*The Letters of F. Scott Fitzgerald*) Fitzgerald to Perkins, circa November 15, 1929, p. 216.

308 Below, pp. 209–210.

309 Stewart did not recall the title. Cf. Baker, p. 176.

310 The section, in fact, is called "Ford Madox Ford and the Devil's Disciple." Vide "Fitzgerald's *Sun Also Rises:* Notes and Comments."

311 Loeb to author.

312 Mentioned by Baker, p. 135.

313 Morrill Cody as told to author, October 11, 1969.

314 Ford's eccentricities, his aristocratic contempt for facts, did not alienate him from others. A sympathetic account is found in Harold Loeb's, "Ford Madox Ford's *The Good Soldier:* A Critical Reminiscence," *The Carlton Miscellany*, VII, 2 (1965), 29–34.

315 Baker, p. 126.

316 Joost, pp. 100–101; Baker, p. 128.

317 Baker, p. 131.

318 Idem.

319 Ibid, p. 136.

320 Idem.

321 Ford Madox Ford, *Thus to Revisit, Some Reminiscences* (London: Chapman & Hall, 1921), p. 69.

322 Loeb to author; Baker, p. 588.

323 Baker, p. 124.

324 Not only in *It Was the Nightingale*, fictionalized as it is and as Joost says (p. 67), corrected painstakingly by Bernard Poli's *Ford Madox Ford and the Transatlantic Review* but also in Ford's introduction to the Modern Library edition of *A Farewell to Arms* (1932).

325 The anecdote, originally from Burton Rascoe, *We Were Interrupted* (New York: Doubleday, 1947), pp. 184–186, has been retold many times: Joost, p. 125, Wickes, p. 180, and Baker, p. 136. Drake found Hadley alone at one of Ford's parties (p. 33).

326 Morrill Cody as told to author, October 11, 1969.

327 p. xviii.

328 Ibid, p. ix.
329 *The March of Literature from Confucius' Day to Our Own* (New York: Dial Press, 1938), p. 828.
330 Idem.
331 The name was changed at the suggestion of Perkins (Baker, p. 594).
332 Margaret Anderson, *My Thirty Years' War* (New York: Covici, Friede, 1930), p. 140.
333 The remainder of the article was ephemera: troubles about censorship and other topics of the day.
334 Baker, pp. 188–189; William H. Rueckert, *Glenway Wescott* (New York: Twayne, 1965), p. 18.
335 Rueckert, p. 30.
336 Baker, p. 143; Joost, p. 146.
337 Baker, pp. 143, 587–588. The treatment of Hemingway and others by *The Dial* broke out into a paper war between that publication, the *New Republic*, and other journals (Joost, pp. 157 ff).
338 *The Way It Was*, p. 198. Hemingway had expressed his contempt for Wescott to Alfred Harcourt in February 1926 (Baker, p. 164).
339 Below, p. 210.
340 Below, p. 211.
341 Below, pp. 209–210.
342 Robert McAlmon to Norman Holmes Pearson, March 31, 1951, unpublished correspondence. The acquaintanceship of Hemingway and Krebs Friend is found in Baker, p. 77.
343 Baker, p. 131.
344 Idem.
345 Ibid., p. 136.
346 Robert McAlmon to Norman Holmes Pearson, March 31, 1951, unpublished correspondence. Charters said that both Pat and Duff were distantly related to Captain Patterson, himself said to be a descendant of one of the Kings of Scotland (*This Must Be the Place*, p. 135). Apropos of that line of descent, Duff told Edward Fisher that she could trace her ancestry back to Banquo (Edward Fisher to author, n. 221); and Morrill Cody recalls Duff and Pat referring to each other as distant cousins (November 6, 1970). That relationship was also familiar to Loeb (Loeb to author).
347 Baker, p. 179. Morrill Cody had just the vaguest recollection of the Count as having been drawn from a Spanish painter, but nothing definite (Morrill Cody to author, November 6, 1970).
348 Baker to author, September 15, 1970.
349 These are mentioned in the deleted first two chapters.
350 Baker, p. 594.
351 Loeb to author; Cf. *The Way It Was*, pp. 256–257 where Loeb refers to her as "Flossie Barton." It was a phrase of Florence Martin that gave Charters the title for his book.
352 Cannell to author.
353 Baker, p. 589. Baker here is drawing from Bill Bird's unpublished autobiography.
354 It was suggested, however, that Hemingway might have looked up Debrett from whom he got this information and the idea for the name Brett (Edward Fisher to author, November 1, 1970).
355 Baker, p. 145.

356 *The Way It Was*, pp. 260, 274.
357 Loeb to author.
358 Baker, p. 148.
359 Ibid, p. 156.
360 Ibid, pp. 156–157.
361 Ibid, p. 156.
362 Above, p. 32.
363 *The Way It Was*, p. 260.
364 Below, p. 240.
365 Arthur Lett-Haines to author, September 12, 1969.
366 *The Way It Was*, pp. 272–273.
367 Ibid, p. 253. And in New York, a decade later, Duff could assume just the opposite persona. On meeting Jerome Bahr at the Midtown Gallery where Waldo Pierce was having a show, she said to Bahr, on their being introduced, "Don't come near me. I have tertiary syphillis" (Jerome Bahr to author, November 10, 1970).
368 Loeb to author.
369 Loeb to author.
370 *The Way It Was*, pp. 262–263. Loeb did not tell the readers of his biography that by next year he found his new girl, the Dutch "waif," far more attractive than Duff (Loeb to author).
371 *The Way It Was*, pp. 260 ff.
372 Mrs. John Rogers, Jr. as told to author, September 12, 1968.
373 Loc. cit.
374 Dr. Edward Harkavy as told to author, September 16, 1968.
375 Loc. cit.
376 Robert McAlmon to Norman Holmes Pearson, March 31, 1951, below, p. 227.
377 Robert McAlmon to Norman Holmes Pearson, March 31, 1951, ibid.
378 Loc. cit.
379 Cannell to author.
380 Clinton King to author, February 9, 1970.
381 However, in Chapter XIX, in what is the first thrust toward that irony and pity which Bill Gorton had earlier said Jake Barnes lacked, the narrator presents the following situation. He has met some bicycle racers who are joking among themselves and with some of their girl friends. The racers are quite relaxed and "did not take the race seriously except among themselves. They had raced among themselves so often that it did not make much difference who won." The seeming unconcern with money and the evident honesty of these sportsmen is at odds with Barnes' conviction that money rules even sport. He is unable (ironically) to see the shortcoming of his cynical views and passes off the contradictory evidence by saying that even in a foreign country they could be sure of their money: "The money could be arranged." The very obvious contradiction of his views takes place a few pages later when he learns that Romero puts concern for Brett above money, as she too refuses to take money from the young man. And then she shows pity for Jake, tries to stop him from drinking too much. Brett comes off better than we anticipated, but Hemingway later decided that Duff was an "alcoholic nymphomaniac," contrary to the view of her he had taken in the first deleted chapter (*Death in the Afternoon* [New York: Scribners, 1932], pp. 497–498).
382 Chapter XVI. The analogy suggested here is not to be understood as my being in agreement with Torchiana's thesis that the entirety of the novel is to be construed

in terms of a bullfight (above, n. 25). Hemingway himself disliked some of the gratuitous analogies drawn between snatches of the text and larger interpretations ("The
Art of Fiction XXI" Ernest Hemingway," *Paris Review*, XVIII [1958].)

383 Hemingway had a need, Stewart wrote to me, to destroy the love that many of his
friends felt for him. Stewart listed Dos Passos, F. Scott Fitzgerald, Gerald Murphy,
and himself among those friends. Finally, Stewart said, there was no one left for
Hemingway to obliterate but himself. (Donald Ogden Stewart to author, June 14,
1971).

Part II   FROM THE CHARACTERS
THEMSELVES

Hemingway's Bitterness

IN *A Moveable Feast*, written shortly before his death, Ernest Hemingway chose to denigrate several of those who had assisted him generously when he needed help most. Indignant at his ungraciousness, at his spiteful descriptions of Ford Madox Ford, Scott Fitzgerald, Edward [Ernest] Walsh and Gertrude Stein, each of whom, back in the nineteen twenties, had done what he or she could—and it was considerable—for the young, unpublished author, I started to write an article drawing on my own experience of Hem's early bitterness. I supposed that his use of Lady Duff Twysden and myself, or, at least, of our backgrounds, in his novel, *The Sun Also Rises*, had been the first instance of his propensity to assign disagreeable fictive characters and unpleasant behavior to the people he knew best. But I was mistaken. I soon discovered that *The Sun Also Rises*, was not the earliest example of this propensity, or the last either.

As the work proceeded, I came to feel that there was little reason to dredge from the past episodes probably of interest only to the original participants. And of these but four, so far as I know, were alive: Bill Smith, Hemingway's early friend, Donald Ogden Stewart, Hadley, Hem's first wife, and myself. Who else cared about what really happened in Paris and Pamplona in 1925? What did it matter that the

Reprinted from the *Connecticut Review* I, 1 (1967), pp. 7–24, by permission of the editor acting in behalf of the Board of Trustees for the Connecticut State Colleges.

events of a long past holiday were not as represented in Hemingway's
first novel? So I dropped the project.

But again I was mistaken. *The Saturday Evening Post* had published
—first installment March 12, 1966—an account by A. E. Hotchner of
Papa Hemingway's recollections of the period. [1] Since *The Saturday
Evening Post* appeals to a large, unspecialized audience, I concluded
that some interest must persist in those distant events. Furthermore,
Hotchner's quotations from Hemingway give, as I propose to show, a
false and at times scurrilous account of our various doings. Many of
the incidents described are either distorted or fabricated. And Hotchner has Hemingway give the real names, including my own, of the
individuals whom Hemingway travestied in *The Sun Also Rises*. Consequently, I feel released from the reticence, or whatever the emotion

Harold Loeb, 75, at home in Weston, Connecticut. *Collection
of Harold Loeb.*

was, which made me hesitate to rehash once again our old confusions. I shall therefore put down the story of that period as I remember it, citing examples in Hemingway's writings of his bitter animosity toward those who had helped him, and accounting, insofar as I can, for what appears to be his gratuitous bitterness.

I quite realize that no two witnesses of an event ever see or remember quite the same things and that in *The Sun Also Rises* Hemingway was writing fiction. But Hemingway, by giving the real names of those at the Pamplona fiesta during which most of the action took place, has implied that the fiction was based on fact. This seems to me verging on the libelous: libelous or not, it is false. Though some bias no doubt is unavoidable under the circumstances, I shall endeavor to be truthful and objective. I am satisfied that the account which follows, certainly that part of it directly experienced, is substantially accurate.

In describing the goings on at Pamplona and what came before and after, I shall not always use my own name or that of Duff Twysden or Ernest Hemingway. Sometimes, the names that Hemingway used in his story, *The Sun Also Rises*, are more convenient. This is not because I am particularly keen on the name Robert Cohn, though I have known several pleasant Cohns whose company I enjoyed. And certainly I prefer the name Duff Twysden to that of Brett Ashley, and Ernest Hemingway to that of Jacob or Jake Barnes. But by making use of the names so generously supplied by "Papa," I shall tie my story more closely to Hemingway's fiction and thereby enable the reader to compare more easily the fiction and the actuality.

Hemingway had that quality which it is fashionable at the moment to call "charisma." Myths circled in the dust behind him. Even in the early days before he had been published, exaggerated stories of his prowess were current. Latterly, books have been written about him which read, to those who knew him, like fantasy. I am not against myth. It may well be that Americans are better citizens because of the stories, like those of Abraham Lincoln, which keep alive the memories of favored historical figures. But such myths should be in character, should delineate with reasonable accuracy the actual man. Falsehoods, however glamorous, add little and may even detract from a man's stature.

Hem was a great writer. He developed a style which has affected, I believe beneficially, nearly all the better American writers that came after him. His life was filled with action. To some extent he overcame his fears. But I see no point in crediting him with virtues in excess of those which he abundantly possessed, nor in concealing weaknesses of which, like the rest of us, he had an appreciable share. So I shall to the best of my ability picture Hemingway as I knew him, crediting him with what he had but not suppressing the qualities which flaw the image.

Our first encounter was delightful. We met in the late spring of 1924 at one of Ford Madox Ford's tea parties in the gallery above the press where the *transatlantic review* was being printed. Hemingway was assisting Ford to get out the magazine. People were coming in, going out, rumbling around. But I best remember young Ernest, eyes and mouth smiling, white, regular teeth, hearty manner and slightly clumsy movements. He was twenty-five at the time and in good condition. He knew of *Broom*, my recently folded magazine of the arts, and I was aware of his stories even though at the time they had been published only in two small Parisian editions.

We got to talking, not about writing, painting or politics, but about fishing and hunting. Hem liked to fish and had done a lot of it in Michigan. I had gone after brook trout in the Canadian Rockies and in Maine, and had shot duck and prairie chicken in Alberta, quail and one deer in South Carolina. It was pleasant chatting about fishing with a writer. Hem invited me to play tennis on the public courts near the prison which harbored the guillotine. He and some of his friends worked out there several times a week. I turned up on the following Monday. He was no tennis player; a bad eye, damaged in a street brawl, and a weak leg injured by shrapnel, hampered his control. His back court drives were erratic and his net game non-existent. Nevertheless, he put so much gusto into the play and got so much pleasure out of his good shots and such misery from his misses, that the games in which he participated were never lackadaisical. Also, we usually played doubles, and by assigning the best player to Hem, a close match could sometimes be achieved. The tennis was fun, especially for me as old skills returned.

After tennis Hem suggested that we box. He kept a set of gloves in the locker room by the courts. I was not eager to take him on. He must have weighed over 190 pounds and I was still light in 1924, weighing perhaps 135 pounds. Also I was not a good boxer. Though I had devoted a month or two to boxing at Princeton in Freshman year, I had soon deserted it for cane spreeing, and then wrestling. In sophomore year, I made the wrestling team and did no more boxing. I did not feel I could hold my own with this big, eager, broad-shouldered fellow who talked like a pro. However, unable to think up an adequate excuse, I put the gloves on and we sparred awhile on the soft turf.

Though I feared that Hem would use his greater strength, reach, and weight to smash through my defenses and make me look foolish, it turned out otherwise. I noticed he was signalling his punches by a jiggling of the pupil and I was enabled thereby to forestall most of his swings by jabbing my left at his chin. In all the months we boxed together Hem never exerted himself fully. And he was generous with his praise and made me out to be a better boxer than I really was.

Through the spring and fall of 1924 our boxing and tennis continued, friendly and enjoyable. We visited each other's homes, learned contract bridge—the game was just being introduced—at Ford Madox Ford's, dined at the Nègre du Toulouse, Le Trianon and L'Avenue— Michaud's had long since folded, though Hem in his last book mentions eating there later with Scott Fitzgerald—and spent a weekend at Senlis where, after walking along the ancient moats and walls, we played poker in a hotel room.

I liked Hadley, Hem's wife, and Bumby the baby was cute and cheerful. I do not know why Hemingway told Hotchner he was so poor that he often fed the family on pigeons captured in the park. I don't know why Hotchner relates the story as if it were true. With corn or bread for bait and tremendous patience, it might be possible now and again to grab and hold a city pigeon. But then to wring its neck and kill it in the Luxembourg Gardens with hundreds of people walking around, and to do this repeatedly without being noticed seems to me quite incredible. Pigeons, like chickens, make an awful fuss when grabbed. Feathers fly and birds do not die easily. To my mind, Hem was clearly spoofing. Yet Hotchner repeats the anecdote in all seriousness. I do not remember that Hem was much of a spoofer as a young man. Perhaps he developed a taste for it as age overtook him.

Actually, Hemingway was not as poor, in my opinion, as he makes himself out to be in *A Moveable Feast*. Before I knew him, during his early years in Europe, he wrote for the *Toronto Star* as well as for a Hearst Agency. Then he returned to Toronto in 1923 where he received (according to biographers Aronowitz and Hamill) some $125 dollars a week. He returned to Paris in January 1924. I met him some months afterwards, as mentioned above, when he was already legman and associate editor of Ford Madox Ford's *transatlantic review*. Though the pay there may have been small and irregular, Ford was short of money nearly always, I believe the Hemingways had a supplementary income from Hadley or her family.[2] For Hem in those days did not stint himself except in the matter of clothes. On one occasion he bought and paid for a Miro, and on many others we drank *Pouilly Fuisse* and ate oysters, *Portugaises* when we felt poor, *Marennes* when we were flush. Hem always paid for his share or tried to. *Pouilly Fuisse* is a costly wine and French oysters even then were more expensive than their American counterparts.

When one considers that the Hemingways in those years went to Pamplona, Madrid, San Sebastian, Valencia, Northern Italy, and to Austria for skiing in 1924 and 1925, it seems improbable that Hem ever went without food because he was too poor to buy it. I imagine he went without food from time to time as I did, largely to find out what it felt like. Marcelline Hemingway says when her brother "became a bit too heavy for the lightweight football team, he used to starve himself before weighing-in for the Saturday games. Often toward the end of the week, Ernest would stick to a diet of lettuce and a little water to keep his weight down." I do not believe he was often, if ever, too poor to buy a croissant. Certainly, he never made himself out to be penniless. We always ate well when out together. And he never borrowed money from me, or tried to. Possibly he thought of himself as having been poor in his twenties, just as he thought of himself as being poor in his early sixties when, as Hotchner relates, he believed the Revenue Agents were after him.

We made plans to go skiing in the Austrian Alps. Hem knew a place where the food was good, the wine and beer excellent. The Bertram Hartmans, old friends of ours, planned to come along, as well as Bob Benchley. Later, in June, we would go to Pamplona to see the bullfights, but before that to a village in Spain where Hem had fished the year before and found the trout plentiful. Though Hem thought bullfighting wonderful, I did not expect to enjoy it. Yet I was curious about it. When I was a child, my uncles had given my father a collection of Mexican artifacts, among which was a set of pictures made of feathers, brilliantly colored, depicting various facets of bull running. I could still call them to mind, and wanted to compare my mental image to the reality.

However, a complication caused a change of plans. A month earlier, Horace Liveright had accepted for publication my first novel, *Doodab*, on the condition that I put back the "a"s and "the"s which I had left out of the text whenever I thought they did not contribute to the meaning,—that is to say, whenever their subject did not have to be marked as definite of indefinite. I was torn between going skiing with Hem in Austria or returning to New York to argue with Horace Liveright. Meanwhile, Malcolm Cowley, who was in America, offered to go see Liveright and check up on the situation. Isadore Schneider, a friend of Malcolm's and a former contributor to *Broom*, worked in the Liveright office.

While I was waiting to hear from Cowley, the date for our departure arrived. After some hesitation, I stayed on in Paris when the Hemingways, the Hartmans, and Bob Benchley set off in late December for Austria. I was unhappy about it though I hoped to join them later. However, on the first of January, I took a ship for New York.

From here on for a space I shall use the names so generously provided by Papa. As it becomes clear that in actual life Jake and Robert were good and close friends, one should be able to see clearly the difference between an author's attitude toward a friend and his attitude to one of his fictive creations even when the fictive character was based, as Jake Barnes told Hotchner, on the live friend. Jake, in real life, was assuring Robert how much he would be missed if he could not join him in Austria. And if he could come, he must not forget Jake's MS. Jake's reference to his book was the manuscript of *in our time* that he had left with Leon Fleischman and which was eventually published by Horace Liveright. I brought Hem to see Leon Fleischman in Paris somewhat earlier in the fall. Fleischman, an old friend of mine had been a partner of Liveright's and had become his European representative when he moved to Paris with his wife and child. He had not seen my manuscript which had been sent somewhat earlier to Liveright by Harold Stearns, Liveright's former representative. By the autumn, however, Fleischman had been deputised to find manuscripts suitable for American publication.

Leon and his wife, Helen, had received Hem and Kitty, a friend of mine, pleasantly, and without reading Hem's stories offered to send them to Liveright with his recommendation. Possibly he had looked over the limited paper edition of *in our time*, published by Bill Bird earlier in the year. During the conversation, Leon may have appeared officious, perhaps slightly patronizing. I did not notice it, having known Fleischman a long while, and being quite used to his assumption that he was a literary "aficiendo" as well as a tennis player. Leon was a great admirer of Turgenev and George Moore. I preferred Dostoevski and Bernard Shaw. But no controversial subject came up during tea and highballs, and Hem left his stories with Fleischman for submission to Liveright.

Afterwards, as we were walking away from the apartment, Hem muttered: "That damned kike." Kitty was outraged. When alone with me, she accused him of anti-Semitism. "Nonsense," I said. "He used the word as I might say mick or dago. It doesn't mean a thing."

By now Jake knew that Robert was not coming to Austria. He had gone to New York. Don Stewart had written Jake that Doran would not publish his short stories. They might be turned over to Mencken for a reading at Knopf, but Mencken did not like Jake's work—that might explain the snide reference to Mencken in *The Sun Also Rises*. Feeling guilty for having done nothing about the MS of *in our time*, I went over to Liveright's office and asked Schneider what had happened to it. Schneider told me that Beatrice Kaufman (the playwright, George Kaufman's wife) who was reading for Liveright had it. I knew Beatrice. I went to her office and told her about Hemingway and his work. "I know books of short stories are hard to sell, but Hem will surely write a novel and it will be a sensation. You can take my word for it."

After I had spoken, Beatrice said: "This is very odd. I was just about to mail the stories back." And she reached out and picked up a package addressed to Fleischman in Paris.

I said: "Hold it. Give it another reading. I know what I am talking about." Slowly she unwrapped the package. Beatrice and others gave it further reading. I do not know what their verdict would have been because Sherwood Anderson, then at the peak of his reputation and Liveright's star author, phoned Liveright. It was not difficult for Sherwood to convince Horace of the book's importance. Since Liveright was anxious to hold Anderson, his best-selling literary author, *in our time* was accepted. Schneider phoned to tell me. Cohn wired the news to Jacob. Jake's elation, it turned out, was embittered by the difficulty in convincing Liveright. Jake felt that he had been pummeled. Perhaps, back in 1925, when Hemingway was 26 years old, the news that at long last he was about to have a book published commercially was too overwhelming. Perhaps it was then that he felt one shouldn't wish for too much because one is likely to get it. That, in any case, is the best I could do towards understanding his reaction.

I returned to Paris in March. It was a busy, delightful spring. Bill Smith—Bill Gorton in the novel, Hemingway's friend from Horton Bay—was already in Paris when I arrived. Ernest had often spoken of Bill with whom he had spent happy summers. Bill was, as Hem put it, "one swell guy," and I was recommended to Bill for virtues that included wrestling, boxing, and tennis playing. After a moment of mutual sniffing, we accepted each other and became long-time friends.

Bill played tennis about as well as I did and we were more than able to hold off Hem and Paul Fisher, quite the best player on the court. There were many good matches. Hem and Bill and Paul largely filled the gap left by the departure for America some months earlier of Matthew Josephson and Malcolm Cowley. These two and other associates and contributors to *Broom* had kept me from being homesick for the United States.

Now everybody seemed to be coming to Paris. My mother and her new husband were already there. My cousins, Edmond and Peggy Guggenheim turned up unexpectedly. Beatrice Kaufman and Peggy Leach arrived from New York. Pauline Pfeiffer and her sister Jinny were working in Paris for *Vogue*. Kitty met them there and had them over to the apartment, where they met Hemingway. Scott Fitzgerald arrived with Zelda. (I knew him slightly from the Sunwise Turn Book Shop—I had found a rare book for him). Scott admired Hem and presented him with a copy of *The Great Gatsby*, hoping he would like it. And Hem was felicitous about my novel which he read in manuscript. He didn't say much about his own reactions, which did not surprise me. I suppose it wasn't his kind of writing, but he told me that Hadley had liked it, particularly the last part with its touch of sentiment.

I tended at that time to ignore the gossip, current in "The Quarter," about Hem's temper. It was told that friends had had to hold him back from knocking down an old man, an American architect, who had inadvertently brushed the cafe table at which Hem was sitting. Also Hem had beaten up Paul Fisher for no apparent reason. He said he just felt like it. I discounted these and similar stories not having seen the episodes myself. I was aware that people exaggerated.

Early in June, Robert Cohn and Brett Ashley spoke to each other at the bar of the Select. Cohn had been aware of Brett before he had left for America. He had liked to watch her face and listen to her voice even from a distance. But he had never spoken to her, not even at Joe Bennett's party where she and Mike had arrived together. Instead, he had drunk too much and left. But there is no need to tell once again the true story of Brett and Cohn. It was gone into at some length in my book of recollections, *The Way It Was* (New York: Criterion Books, 1959).

Brett's friend, Mike Campbell, was about to leave for England to visit his mother. Cohn's friend, Kitty, intended to go to London when Cohn, Jake and Bill went fishing. Cohn and Brett waited until they had gone and then took the train to St. Jean-de-Luz, a resort by the sea near Biarritz. After two weeks, Brett returned to Mike and Paris, as had been planned from the beginning. It was hard for Cohn to let her go but he felt it advisable under the circumstances. Something within him had said "no" when Brett had suggested that they go off together to South America. If only she had said Africa or Asia, he sometimes mused when a sinking in his stomach made him feel empty, everything might have been different. But he had let Brett go and stayed on at St. Jean-de-Luz.

Some days after her departure, a letter came from Brett. It went as follows: "I don't quite know what to say to you except that I'm miserable without you and things don't seem to improve at all with time. I had almost hoped they would. That glorious little dream we lived together seems ever more incredible and wonderful from a distance of a thousand years.

"Now for a doubtful glad tidings. I am coming on the Pamplona trip with 'Jake' and your lot. Can you bear it? With 'Mike' of course. If this appears impossible for you, let me know and I'll try and get out of it. But I'm dying to come and feel that even seeing and being able to talk to you will be better than nothing.

"I love you, dearest one, with all my forces. Have you missed me?" "By all means come," Cohn wired. He felt that if Brett could stand it, he could stand it, too. But he was not happy about it.

Yet he still felt his or their decision to separate had been sound. Brett was romantic, like Arlen's woman in *The Green Hat* who was partly based on her. She lived for love, or, perhaps, for the transfiguration of the outside world which being in love effected. When the enchantment faded, and Cohn felt it would fade sooner or later, Brett would fade, too. She wanted more than affection, security, friendship. Or so Cohn thought. But he did not convince himself, not fully.

It was towards the end of June that Cohn first sensed a coolness in his friend Barnes. There were allusions to Brett's friends, Cedric and Lett, which Cohn thought uncalled for. Cohn thought it best to stay in St. Jean-de-Luz. Brett had written him she would be coming there as soon as she and Mike could get organized.

Brett and Mike arrived on schedule. Brett looked the same except that instead of a floppy felt hat, she wore a beret. I did not like her in a beret. Hem usually wore a beret. I wondered if the two were more intimate than she let on. But I couldn't ask Brett about Hem before Mike. So we spent an evening at the Casino, taking my friend Ruth along to make the party even. The next day, we hired a car to go to Pamplona. The long ride went all right, a little boring at times. Mike was not a scintillating conversationalist. But I enjoyed the nearness of Brett, even under unfavorable circumstances. She was different, however. I gathered that the spell, as she called it, had definitely been broken. I was hurt by its loss but not acutely. It had been my own choice, I told myself, and perhaps I had been right to make it. I did not approve of the way Brett drank at the Casino. When she had been with me, she had drunk as I had, neither more nor less. Now she kept up with Mike.

Eventually—the ride taking a good part of the day—we reached Pamplona and the hotel on the square where Hemingway (to use real names again) had reserved rooms. Things were better now. New towns interested me, and I was not reminded, as I had been at St. Jean, of poignant moments that were to have no sequel.

On the following day, Hem, Bill, Don and Hadley came in by bus from their fishing trip. The idyllic scenes of *The Sun Also Rises* were purely imaginary. Hem was in a black mood. None of them had had as much as a strike. Apparently, an irrigation project had wrecked the fishing by diverting water into the stream, or out of it. It wasn't clear which, and they didn't want to talk about it. After a shave and a drink, Bill was himself again and Don seemed to be a delightful chap. Don, however, was not going into the bull ring because he had broken two ribs there the year before. It seemed that early in the morning, the town riffraff were permitted to go into the arena where they were pursued by a series of bulls, steers, and heifers with padded horns trained to chase one and all but not to single out an individual for special treatment. Bill and I decided to go into the ring with Hem, and the others intended to get up to see the fun although it started early in the morning with the running of the fighting bulls through the streets.

I had to force myself to climb over the barrier. The arena looked enormous and I had never had anything to do with cattle except in Alberta when sitting on a horse, a safer location. However, Hem climbed over the barrier followed by Bill, and I felt I had to follow. The next morning I went into the arena again but this time with one of the hotel's bath towels. No one told me that bulls are relatively indifferent to the color white. For a while I just stood around. Then a dark, well-horned young animal came along at a lope. I held the towel in front of me, waving it slightly. As the bull got nearer, I noticed that its mean little eyes were not looking at the towel which I flaunted before it, but over the towel at my head. Probably this bull was not going to be turned aside by the movement of a towel it was not looking at. There was no time to think. Reflexively, as one twists when lifted by a wrestler, I turned my back. When the bull lowered his head to butt, I dropped the towel and sat on its head, grasping the horns for support. Three long strides followed, slower than the rise and fall of a galloping horse, and the bull tossed its head. I was thrown into the air but had the good fortune to land on my feet. "One would have thought he had done it on purpose," Cayetano, the Pedro Romero of the novel, said, according to Hem when he and the matador talked over the feat later that evening.

Harold Loeb borne aloft in the Pamplona bull ring, from a contemporary postcard sold in Pamplona. *Collection of Harold Loeb.*

The better feeling which followed the amateur morning did not last long. The trouble started with Mike. He baited me whenever he got tight and he was nearly always tight. I had no notion how to handle insults from a drunk. If you knock one down, you're a brute for hitting a helpless man. If you ignore the remarks, which I usually did, the drunk doesn't notice it but keeps right on, more and more convinced that he's being terribly funny. Furthermore, Mike had an excuse for being nasty, an excuse of some validity. So I did nothing but keep out of his way as much as I reasonably could.

I was more troubled by Hem's attitude than by Mike's. Nothing overt had occurred but the old warm feeling was gone, and I had no adequate explanation to account for its disappearance. I asked Bill about it. With Bill I still felt at ease and increasingly friendly. Bill hadn't changed and the situation was throwing us closer together.

"What's wrong with Hem?" I asked. "You've known him longer than I have."

"Hem has moods," said Bill, who sometimes was more terse than meaningful.

"Sure," I said, "but they didn't use to last."

"It's the *wagon lits*," said Bill. "Hem doesn't like *wagon lits*."

"What do you mean?" I asked, bristling a little for I suspected what was coming.

Bill said: "When Joe Bennett told Hem that you and Brett had gone South together in a *wagon lit*, Hem went off muttering the foulest curses I'd ever heard."

"But why?"

"Hem doesn't like *wagon lits*," said Bill.

I mulled this over. Hem may have disapproved of my going off with Brett. He probably did. I had always felt that Hem was something of a Puritan. Though he had tried to slough off his Oak Park conditioning, I suspected that it still affected his actions and reactions. I had never seen Hem out with a woman other than his wife. Even at parties, he seemed uninterested in other women. Despite his writing about a compliant girl, I suspected that he had had little experience with women until he fell in love with Luz, the girl in "A Very Short Story" who, some years later was to rise again and die as Catherine Barkley. Actually, Luz was a nice though not beautiful American girl from Milwaukee who had left him for an Italian officer.

It was possible that Hem had changed toward me because I refused to be enthusiastic about bullfighting. There was still another possibility. Perhaps Hem had been annoyed because I had not gone fishing and instead had stayed in St. Jean-de-Luz to wait for Brett and Mike. This could have and no doubt did annoy him but surely not enough to account for the drastic change in his attitude. Or it could be that something had happened when Brett got back to Paris. Perhaps Mike had been late in returning from England and Brett had run into Hem. They may have gone dancing, though Hem was not keen on dancing. I suspected he felt dancing was not quite masculine. It was possible that back in Paris she had fallen for Hem shortly after she had written me that letter. Or perhaps he had fallen for her. She would have liked that, I suspected, even if she didn't accept it. Probably, I concluded, some such causes had combined to transform Hem's feelings toward me.

On the next to last evening of the Fiesta, Cohn,—if I may return to Hem's nomenclature—made another blunder. He met Brett on the town square coming from the hotel and asked her to have a drink with him. She tried to get out of it, said they shouldn't, it would cause trouble. But he insisted.

They were sipping an absinthe at the café—or what passed for absinthe in Pamplona—Cohn never discovered if the claim was authentic—when a Spaniard whom they had recently met came up to their table and asked if they would do him the honor of accepting the hospitality of his club. He tempted them with an offer of champagne. Since Brett was uneasy sitting there with Cohn, afraid no doubt that Mike would find them together and make a scene, she accepted and they went to the club which was located on the second floor in a spacious apartment overlooking the square. A piano stood in the corner of the main room. A monocled man with a grey goatee began to play popular tunes. Then Brett took over with French songs which she sang in a sweet, low voice. Cohn enjoyed her singing but soon had another worry. A crowd gathered. Champagne flowed freely. Cohn could not find a way to separate Brett from the piano, the champagne and the admiration. He could not get her away until the crowd dispersed in the small hours.

The next afternoon she appeared at the cafe with a swollen black eye. When Cohn started to ask what had happened, Jake cut him off by saying she had fallen down the stairs. Cohn said nothing further. In the evening, they were sitting around their usual table sipping drinks, and Mike started baiting him again. Cohn was used to that but Jake joined in. They intimated that he didn't know when he wasn't wanted. This made him furious because he and Jake had organized the expedition and had invited the others. He felt like throwing his drink into Jake's face. Instead he got up slowly and asked his former friend to walk out with him.

What happened was described as follows in *The Way It Was* (pp. 295 ff):

"I was scared—not shaken or panicky, but just plain scared. I had boxed enough with Hem to know that he could lick me easily; his forty-pound advantage was just too much. And the edge I sometimes had because of Hem's tendency to telegraph his punches would be lost in the dark. I could not hope to outbox him. My little jabs would miss their mark and Hem's swings would smash my face in. I considered clinching, but Hem would think it dirty fighting and react by gouging or strangling. Exchanging punches was the lesser danger. I would simply have to stand up and take it.

"We reached the last café, the last illuminated shop front. We went down a few steps. Now there were only street lamps. The small street carried on in semi-darkness.

"I took my glasses off and, after considering the safest place, put them in the side pocket of my jacket. Then I stopped, faced Hem, and took my jacket off.

" 'My glasses,' I said, 'are in the side pocket. If they're broken I couldn't get them fixed here.'

"Feeling ridiculous, I looked around for some place to put my jacket.

"Shall I hold it for you?' he asked.

"I smiled. There was just enough light for me to see that Hem was smiling too, the boyish, contagious, smile that made it so hard not to like him.

" 'If I may hold yours,' I said.

"We stood hesitantly looking at each other.

" 'I don't want to hit you,' I said.

" 'Me either,' said Hem.

"We put on our jackets and started back."

Later Jake apologized. But when the fiesta was over, Cohn knew that the friendship would never be the same.

At the close of the fiesta, the party broke up. Hem and Hadley went on to Madrid; Brett, Mike, Bill and I returned to St. Jean-de-Luz. I do not remember what happened to Don but have the impression he left earlier. On our way out with our bags, Hem introduced us on the hotel stairs to a young Spaniard in an undistinguished business suit who, he said, was the matador whose work he admired so much. That was the only contract Brett had with the bull fighter, a single handshake. Immediately afterwards, we got into the cab waiting downstairs and drove across the border. No doubt Hem's account makes a better story.

We saw Hemingway again, after his return from Spain. Bill remembers a dinner with Kitty and Hem at which a duck was consumed. However, our friendship was over and showed no sign of revival. Hem and I played tennis once, and for once I tried appeasement. I don't mean that I deliberately hit the ball out, but I didn't exert myself to win. So I lost, though I could hardly believe it. Hem put it in his book. He had Cohn lose to Jake at tennis because Cohn, supposedly was still upset by Lady Brett. The things one imagines!

In September Bill and I boarded the S.S. *Suffren*, an old tub with rats behind the radiators. I wanted to be in New York when my book came out. In June 1926, after Liveright accepted my new MS, I returned to Paris. I saw Duff at the Select the night I arrived. She was with Lett, Cedric's boyfriend, and had been drinking too much. I walked away after a few words of greeting. Then I joined up with a beautiful blond Dutch waif who knew no English and had, so she said, run away from home. Gradually my French improved, as it was our only verbal means of communication. And in the midst of this Duff came to the hotel. I went downstairs to speak to her. What had been was no longer there, or at least, I thought so. I saw her quite often a year later just before she met a young Texan at the seashore and fell in love with him and married him. I think it was Cedric who introduced them to each other. Shortly afterwards, the Texan brought her back to America and I believe she made him a good wife, though perhaps she drank too much. Nearly ten years later in 1935 or 1936, I saw her for the last time at a cocktail party. She looked terrible and died shortly afterwards.

But in the fall of 1926 I went south to St. Paul with the Dutch girl and rented a little farmhouse in a great field of artichokes and set about writing my third novel, *Tumbling Mustard*. I was still there when someone sent me a copy of *The Sun Also Rises*.

The book hit like an upper-cut. At first I had difficulty getting into it. I confined my reading to the passages that had to do with Cohn, seeking to discover if I talked like Cohn. Evidently I didn't act like Cohn, never having knocked anyone down or even hit anyone except with gloves on. I didn't seem to talk like Cohn either. But it is difficult to see oneself as another sees you; so I couldn't be sure. Then, having read the book, I tried to understand what had led my one-time friend to transform me into an insensitive, patronizing, uncontrolled drag. At the time I did not have the benefit of reading Hemingway's *To Have And Have Not*, which was not written for another eight years so that I lacked the illumination, such as there was, in the following passage: "... an ability to make people like him without ever liking or trusting them in return, while at the same time convincing them warmly and heartily of his friendship; not a disinterested friendship, but a friendship so interested in their success that it automatically made accomplices; and an incapacity for either remorse or pity, had carried him to where he was now." Not that I believe that Hemingway was consciously depicting himself when he wrote this. But I do think that was how Ernest saw our and other friendships ten years later, or perhaps one year later. So many of us rewrite history in the light of later feelings. Even governments.... Forty years later, after studying Hem's writing, it seems to me that Mr. A. E. Hotchner's term "persecutory"[3] is the key to much that happened, not only in Hem's later years, but also to what happened much, much earlier. I shall return to this thought later.

But when *The Sun Also Rises* first appeared, I had no clue to the cause of Hemingway's *unnecessary* nastiness, or to the bitterness which induced it. It would have been just as easy, or nearly as easy for him to have changed his protagonists' backgrounds as well as their characters. There seemed to be no purpose in making their identity recognizable to everyone acquainted with the seven who had gone to Pamplona. I was not the only one travestied. Duff, the Lady Brett of the story, was given a character that encouraged later commentators to put her down as a repugnant tramp. Duff didn't realize the book would hurt her at the time, and didn't, or at least pretended, not to mind much. This was in part because the Lady Brett described in the novel had redeeming qualities though not always those of the real Duff. Since anything I might say about her would be suspect, let me quote Hadley Hemingway. For Hadley had no reason to like Duff and may have had reasons to dislike her. As Hadley put it to Aronowitz or Hamill, "Duff, she was lovely, a very fine lady, and very much of a man's woman. She was very, very popular and very nice to women too. She was fair and square ... but she really was a lady and nothing could stop that ..." (p. 91).

And something of what Hadley was trying to convey shows up in the fictive Lady Brett of the novel.

In Hem's mind, Cohn, too, probably had redeeming qualities. For one thing, Cohn was supposed to have been middleweight boxing champion at Princeton. In my opinion Hem never got over his disappointment at not going to college. And he wanted to be champion of everything. So we may reasonably suppose, despite his disclaimer, that he himself would have liked to have been champion of Princeton. Hem had mixed feelings for the Ivy League and the Rich. My guess is that it was his combination of envy, suspicion and admiration for these categories that complicated his relations with Scott Fitzgerald and perhaps myself. It is even possible that Hem believed or hoped that making Cohn middleweight boxing champion of Princeton would take some of the sting out of his offensive characterization.

In the spring of 1927, I returned to Paris and stayed long enough for the incident which provided Hem's imagination with the basis for the following: He is reported by Hotchner as saying that: "The day after *The Sun Also Rises* was published, I got word that Harold Loeb who was the Robert Cohn of the book, had announced that he would kill me on sight. I sent him a telegram to the effect that I would be here in the Hole in the Wall for three consecutive evenings so he'd have no trouble finding me. As you can see I chose this joint because it is all mirrors. . . . I waited out the three days but Harold didn't show. About a week later, I was eating dinner at Lipp's in Saint Germain, which is also heavily mirrored, when I spotted Harold coming in. I went over and put out my hand and Harold started to shake hands before he remembered we were mortal enemies. He yanked his hand away and put it behind his back" (pp. 48–49).

Actually I never threatened to kill anyone, not even Hemingway, on sight or otherwise. Nor did I get a telegram to meet him at the "Hole in the Wall" or elsewhere. Possibly someone told Hem that I had threatened to kill him. It may have seemed funny. However, it was not the day or the week after the book was published that I met Hem in the restaurant, the episode which probably gave him the idea for his distorted account of what happened, but months later in the spring. I was sitting alone, in what may have been Lipps—I just don't remember,—reading a newspaper and drinking a Pernod. Hem came in and looked at me. He smiled, as I remember it. He did not come nearer but went directly to the bar where he sat down on a stool and ordered a drink. His back was turned and I continued looking at it. I distinctly remember being amazed at the color of his neck. Red gradually suffused it—and then his ears, right up to their tips.

Though mildly diverted, I was not tempted to go to the bar. I wanted nothing more to do with him. After a while, he got up, paid for his drink and walked out. He did not look around.

I saw him once again some years later. We were in the Stadium at Princeton, walking in opposite directions beneath the seats when we recognized each other at a distance. This time, more or less inadvertently, we both smiled. I felt sad afterwards.

It was the earlier meeting in the restaurant which supplied the basis for the story about my not "showing."

Hem's motive for this distortion may have been due in part to annoyance at my book, *The Way It Was*, which attempted to recount what actually happened at Pamplona in 1925. I don't expect Hem liked it. And he had the book on his desk, his last secretary tells me, while writing *A Moveable Feast*. At any rate, he told Hotchner that "those days with Lady Duff ruined poor Loeb for the rest of his life" (p. 48). It gave me an odd feeling to read in print that I had been "ruined" some forty years earlier, not an unpleasant feeling, for here I was not feeling ruined at all. I daresay Hem had a similar feeling after reading the obituaries which followed his aeroplane accidents.

Hemingway's belief that I threatened to kill him probably was due, I would guess, to something more deeply felt than annoyance at my book. His recalling the grievance after so long an interval may have been owing in part to irritation at its contents. However, there is a long history of similar delusions going back to his boyhood and culminating in his last illness.

These delusions must have had their source in Hemingway's earliest experiences. At the dawn of memory, Hemingway went through an ordeal from which he may never have recovered. His mother, by a not unusual quirk or fancy, treated him as the twin of his slightly older sister. Marcelline wrote about it in her book. "Mother," she reports, "often told me she had always wanted twins, and that though I was a little over a year older than Ernest (he was born July 21, 1899), she was determined to have us be as much like twins as possible. When we were little, Ernest and I were dressed alike in various outfits, in Oak Park in gingham dresses and in little fluffy lace tucked dresses with picture hats, and in overalls at the summer cottage on Walloon Lake .... Mother was doing her best to make us feel like twins by having everything alike" (pp. 61–62).

Marcelline included in her book a photograph of Ernest in a girl's dress and hat.

Though Hem, in the years I knew him, did no more than mention Marcelline and his other sisters, and never spoke of having been dressed in girl's clothes, it is my belief that this experience accounts in part for several of his more important characteristics. One day he must have waked up to what was happening to him. Possibly a playmate called him a sissy. Thenceforth he overstressed his masculinity and hardihood. Later, as his talk (to be quoted) with Gertrude Stein suggests, he was obsessed by fear of homosexuality and homosexuals, and the fear of homosexuality is often linked by psychiatrists with paranoia.

There are only a few mentions of his behavior as a child. Marcelline slights his early years though she describes at some length the personalities of their parents. However, in writing of the period, she does drop several hints that her brother was already "playing tough." One summer, for example, he refused to put on shoes. And he chose "the old Brute" as a nickname for himself.

The first hint of a delusion appears as a boy, when, according to Hemingway, his father, "was very strict about shooting only on the wing. He had his spies around so I never tried to cheat" (Hotchner, p. 179). In his teens, Hem sometimes felt his friends were out to get him. An example is given in *Chosen Country*, a novel by John Dos Passos. The author was trying to recapture the life of the young people in and about Horton Bay and Walloon Lake, Michigan, early in the century. The main characters, barely disguised, were Ernest Hemingway, YK, Bill, and Kate Smith to whom Dos Passos was married.

Evidently, Dos's information on life up in Michigan was provided largely by Kate, since he did not visit the neighborhood until many years later when the young people had grown up and departed.

It is not a good novel, probably one of Dos Passos' weakest, but it is of interest because of the light it throws on young Ernest Hemingway who is assigned the name George, or Georgie Warner.

Early in the narrative the young people go sailing. Joe, the steersman, swung the boat around to avoid a log, and the boom caught George (Ernest), knocking him overboard. Quickly the steersman reversed direction, and they went back and pulled George out of the water by his shirt, "dripping" as Dos put it, "like a wet dog." Then they disentangled the hooks of his spoon from the seat of his pants. George, scowling, teeth chattering from cold and rage, muttered, "Tried to drown me." Joe said he was sorry and went to get George some dry clothes.

Obviously, Dos Passos' report—if that was his source—of Kate Smith's memories of her summer vacation is not convincing testimony of Ernest's state of mind. Memories are erratic and change with the passage of time. However, Kate, a sweet young woman, had no ax to grind and her portrait, as transcribed by Dos, makes Hem into a sultry, difficult adolescent already in battle with the powers to be.

Despite the relative innocuousness of this description of the young Hemingway during his awkward age, Hem was furious when the book came out and had nothing more to do with Dos Passos although Dos had been one of his boon and respected companions. And when Dos tried to make it up by suggesting a visit, Hem warned him off in a brutal letter.

Marcelline Hemingway's description of her brother supports Kate's picture. She has their mother say, "When Ernest gets through this period ... of fighting himself and everybody else ... he will be a fine man" (p. 198). This was in 1919 after his return from the war.

Other examples of Hemingway's early fears may be found in his book, *A Moveable Feast*. He was discussing homosexuality with Gertrude Stein. He reports himself as saying, "I knew it was why you carried a knife and would use it ... when you were in the company of tramps when you were a boy...." And a little further on he adds: "When you were a boy and moved in the company of men, you had to be prepared to kill a man, know how to do it and really know that you would do it in order not to be interfered with" (p. 18).

Did the teenage Hemingway carry a knife? Did he know how to kill? Was he prepared to kill?

I do not know the answers. My guess—these memories had no basis in fact but were compensatory inventions to mitigate the shame he felt from having in his youth imagined deadly perils, among brutes and perverts, a delusion he finally succumbed to in his old age. Perhaps I am wrong. Perhaps Hem actually carried a knife and would have used it. Still, the import is much the same. At the end, his sense of being pursued by imaginary enemies became a conviction.

That Hem, some ten years after the event, if he really had this conversation with Gertrude, and again, some forty years after the event when he was writing his last book, remembered that as a boy "you had to be prepared to kill," may have been, in my opinion, a precursive symptom of the illness which finally overtook him.

A striking example of his trigger-happy distrust of even his most loyal friends comes from a later period, the year 1929, when Hem was 30 years old. Morley Callaghan tells about it in *That Summer in Paris* (pp. 213ff).

Hem and Morley were boxing and Scott Fitzgerald was keeping time. Either because the boxing fascinated him or because he was astonished that Morley was more than holding his own, Scott forgot to call time when the three minute round was up. "Right at the beginning of the round," as Morley tells it, "Ernest got careless; he came in too fast, his left down, and he got smacked on the mouth. His lip began to bleed. . . ." He charged Fitzgerald with complicity.

The following event must have happened when Hem was over forty because he had already written *For Whom the Bell Tolls*. He was with his son, probably one of Pauline's sons, since Bumby would have been about twenty years old by then. Edmund Wilson reports that Hem told him in all seriousness that on his recent trip through the Southern States in a car with his younger son, he had at one point suddenly become aware that he had entered Mississippi. Realizing he was in Faulkner Country, he let the boy go to bed at the hotel where they spent the night. Then he had sat up till morning with his gun on the table in front of him.

Since this event supposedly occurred in the 1940's before the recent Negro-White tension in Mississippi, the implication is that Hemingway feared that the low characters of Faulkner's fiction, presumably in the pay of or at the instigation of Faulkner, would attack him. But I believe further instances would be redundant. It seems to me that Hemingway during his life tended to imagine offenses where none were intended, a not unusual characteristic, but one which, in his case, grew and intensified until it destroyed his equilibrium.

In 1918, some years before the later examples cited above, Hemingway underwent the disaster which I suspect served to transform the jumbled youth into the dedicated writer, and to confirm the persecutory feelings which eventually wrecked him.

Turned down by the United States Army because of a bad eye, and reluctant to enlist in the Canadian forces where physical requirements were less strict, Ernest Hemingway, in the autumn of 1917 got a job on the *Kansas City Star* with the help of an assist from a family friend and from his uncle, Tyler Hemingway. In April 1918, a story came over the wire that the American Red Cross wanted volunteers to serve as ambulance drivers on the Italian front. Hem and his friend Brumback— who had already served as ambulance driver on the French front— cabled their applications. By May 12th they were in uniform and shortly afterwards sailed for France whence they entrained for Milan.

Ernest Hemingway, Bill Horne, a classmate of mine with whom he "palled" on the way over, and the other ambulance drivers were rated as honorary lieutenants of the Italian Army, though they continued to wear their American uniforms with a small cross on the collar; no bars.

Dissatisfied by the quietness behind the lines, Hem and Bill Horne volunteered for canteen service at the front. On July 8, 1918, after six days of service, Ernest was distributing chocolate bars in the forward trenches when a shell landed, killing several soldiers and wounding him seriously.

But let me permit Bill Horne to tell about it since he saw Hemingway immediately before and after the event. Bill wrote to me that:

The Austrians made one attempt to break through the Pasubio position into the Po Valley, but couldn't make a go of it—maybe early July, after that our front was very quiet. So when the ARC asked for volunteers to go down to the Piave and run soldiers' canteens for a couple of weeks a number of us volunteered. Among them Ernie. He went to Fossalta, I to the next town, San Pedro Novello. It was at Fossalta that Ernie got hit by that trench mortar shell; then was picked up by the Austrian searchlights and took several big machine gun slugs while carrying a wounded Italian soldier back from the advanced listening post to the front line. For that he got the Silver Valor Medal—next to the highest [first the Gold Medal] decoration a soldier could get.

They finally found him (quite by accident I understand) and took him to the American Red Cross Hospital in Milan—most of the way across Italy. He was an awfully sick boy, believe me. Full of scaggia (which means metal fragments), a 45 slug under his knee cap.

It was there in that American-run, American-staffed hospital that Ernie (he was 19 years old at the time) met Luz.[4] She was the nurse on that part of the floor. I would estimate that she was two to several years older than he, that is *only* a guess. She was an American girl; of South Baltic antecedents, I suppose . . . I rather think I remember she came from Milwaukee, but am not sure of that. Anyhow, she was American, *not* British as Catherine Barkley was. Nor as beautiful—not nearly as beautiful. Just a nice, cheery American woman. And Ernie at that time one of the best looking, big strong men you could want to see.

So they fell in love—very very much . . . and it lasted almost as long as the war did. Then I think Luz went off to another assignment and fell in love with somebody else. But that is only hearsay . . . You can draw your own conclusions from rereading "A Very Short Story."

The impact of trench mortar fragments and machine gun slugs, the bearing of a fatally wounded soldier to the rear while seriously injured himself, and the desertion by Luz, each in its way must have affected Hemingway. The explosion and bullets displaced a kneecap, and put fragments of steel in his leg. For a time afterwards he found it impossible to sleep in the dark, and was harrassed by nightmares. Also the shock brought on the depressions which haunted him on his return to the United States, and recurred in his late years. The rescue of the fatally wounded soldier, which earned him the silver cross, also gave his morale the greatest boost it was ever to receive. Thereafter he was confident of his courage "in the clutch." Luz's desertion shook his faith in women.

After putting down this passage and some of what follows, I read *Hemingway, A Reconsideration*, by Philip Young. In his brilliant study, Mr. Young finds that the wounding of Hemingway on the Italian front was a traumatic experience which affected his personality. It still seems obvious, according to Mr. Young, "that for Hemingway and the hero alike"—he was referring to Hemingway's fictive heroes—"the explosion at Fossalta was the crux of that life, and the climax to a series of like events which had their start up in Michigan and were to be repeated and imitated in various forms over and over again" (p. 64).

That, I believe, is the gist of Mr. Young's thesis. I do not question its essential validity. But I believe other aspects of experience beside the physical injury, and other life experiences beside the wounding at Fossalta, had as great or greater importance. Possibly Mr. Young would agree with me. Few things are as simple as they seem, which Mr. Young recognizes. Our difference, therefore, comes down to one of emphasis. The wounding at Fossalta may have been the climax of Hemingway's life, but I do not think it was the event most influential in shaping it. This occurred, I suspect, much earlier. By the time Hemingway and I met in the 1920's he was, I am now convinced, already too sick for friendship, and capable of its betrayal. He had de-

Hemingway in a more serious moment. *Collection of Gale Research Company.*

veloped defenses which blinded me—and I was not the only one to be deceived. And it may well have been that Hemingway himself was so deceived. Nothing in our relationship justified the distortion of the real friend that I was into the Robert Cohn of *The Sun Also Rises.* Without putting each of them into a novel, Hemingway came to distort all his kind friends. Finally, he trusted, it would seem, only Mr. A. E. Hotchner who, in turn, accepted everything that he was told and told everything.

NOTES

1 These articles were the forerunners of Mr. Hotchner's book, *Papa Hemingway*, to which later references are made.
2 According to Marcelline, Hemingway's sister, Hadley had a small trust fund. *At the Hemingway's* (Boston: Atlantic Monthly Press, 1961), p. 211. This confirms my remembrance of the situation.
3 A. E. Hotchner, *Papa Hemingway* (New York: Random House, 1966), p. 275.
4 Not her real name but the name Hem gave her in his story entitled "A Very Short Story."

Chapter 3   HAROLD LOEB

With Duff at Ascain

THE *auberge* was poised on the side of a hill. From our balcony we could see the line of the Pyrénées. Where the mountains fell away, a small triangle of sea was bounded by two green hills and the fragile blue of the sky. Below our windows, Japanese iris and a low stone wall enclosed a flagstone terrace with a tree in one corner. Man and Nature had combined to do their best.

For three days we talked and walked along the straggling lanes that led between curved knolls. I moved in a kind of trance that defied memory, incidents and sensations all running together. Duff was relaxed and happy.

On the fourth day I went down to the terrace while Duff was dressing for dinner, and forced myself to think about the future. Where, I asked myself, did we go from here? It was not that time was passing. Eleven days of idleness after six years of work did not matter at all. And I found the hours so sweet that I could not imagine anything more pleasant. But I had lost my sense of urgency, and this troubled me. Also, there were practical matters to decide. I hadn't told Hem and Bill that I was leaving Paris, and they were expecting me to go to Spain with them in about two weeks. Should I join them? Should we join them? Or should we just disappear?

Reprinted by permission of S. G. Phillips, Inc. from *The Way It Was*, by Harold Loeb, and by kind permission of Mr. Loeb. Copyright © 1959 by S. G. Phillips, Inc.

Ascain is near St. Jean-de-Luz, where Duff Twysden and Harold Loeb had spent the first few days of their two weeks in the south of France.

136

Duff came and sat beside me. A translucent stole lay across her
shoulders. Each evening she surprised me by achieving a new effect
with a minimum of means. I took her hand and said, "You are
beautiful, darling: more beautiful tonight than last night even." Her
fingers tightened ever so slightly and I could feel the glow of her eyes.
It was as if someone was speaking through me. I meant the words
though the usual me could not have said them.

"I'm worried," I said. "I'm far too contented."

"Darling," she replied. "It's good to be still. Things happen, too,
when you are still."

"But I don't do anything but look at you, and I don't entirely
approve of that. Ever since the bookshop I've been working hard.
Then came the magazine and finally the book. There never was time
enough to do everything that should be done."

"I know," she said. "You men must have ambition."

"It isn't exactly ambition," I objected. "It's just that there's so
much to be done. And I like to do things. You must know what I
mean."

She said, "I, too, used to dream of doing things. I was not at all
like the woman you watched from the corner of the Sélect. But I didn't
do a thing about my dreams. Things happened to me."

"They always will," I said sadly.

A waiter came up with a cocktail shaker, filled our glasses, and with-
drew.

"Are you ever jealous?" I asked.

Duff grimaced above the rim of her glass. "Have I cause to be?"

"Yes," I said, "there's always cause. I've known women who pulled
terrible scenes if one so much as mentioned another female; and there
are women who cannot bear a man's loving his work."

"I do not understand jealousy," Duff said quietly. "If someone is
gone, there's no point in being jealous. And if he is still yours, you
have no reason to be jealous."

"Perhaps; but jealousy is not rational."

We talked till twilight, then the waiters carried out a table with the
linen and silver in place, and set it down in the corner beneath the
solitary tree. After we had finished, silence fell between us. Then
softly, as if to herself, Duff said, "There's love or there's nothing.
When love is not, you drink or work or fornicate—it doesn't matter.
There is nothing, nothing at all."

I said, "Love comes and goes and there is little you can do about it.
But there are other things that we can do."

Then I asked myself whom I was protecting by sprinkling cold water:

was it myself or Duff? Since I did not choose to protect myself, it must be Duff. But that was pointless. Careless of the morrow, she believed in squeezing the last drop of rapture from the night. Perhaps she was right. But right or wrong, I did not want to waken from the trance.

I said, "Long before we knew each other I used to watch you, and what I saw was good. I suspect that we see most truly when we look through loving eyes."

She smiled, then asked, "But what if the transforming glass through which you see me should be lost?"

Could it be, I wondered, that she was concerned because, as she put it, I saw her as "someone she was not?" I saw her as good and beautiful. She did not think she was good or particularly beautiful.

I got up from my chair and stood before her. Then I took her hands in mine. "Darling," I said, quoting an Eastern poet, " 'All is darkness without you.' "

The moon rose like morning from the sea. Her hands were soft and tender. Yet I was troubled. For the time being all that mattered seemed to lie within our circle. But I knew that this condition was temporary. I looked for a way to tell Duff that love was the great miracle, but that life had to go on with love or without it. There were many other things. Hunger, for example, hunger which was no longer necessary.

"Let me tell you a story," I said, "that James Stephens told me. At the age of twenty he lost his job and could not find another. He wandered hungry through the streets. Sometimes he'd have nothing to eat but scraps of bread and garbage for an entire week. Most of the time he was weak and faint and could not get manual labor because of his build. A hundred times he tried to ask for a bit of bread, but his will power was never strong enough. Always he turned away, plea unexpressed. He slept in the parks and areaways through snow and sleet with no food inside him. Once he jumped off the bridge into the river, but the shock of the cold water was too terrible and he struggled out again.

"One evening he climbed over the rail of the park before the Shelbourne Hotel to sleep beneath the bushes. His mind was wandering a bit; it was one of his longest stretches without food. On passing the pond—he was quite alone as the gates were locked—he noticed that one of the big swans had a crust of bread in his beak, and snatched it away from him. This was the signal for a battle royal.

"The bird attacked with beak and wings and fury. Stephens' hands and face were bleeding and his breath entirely gone. Finally he ran out of harm's way with the spoils of battle. Then he ate half of it, though a loaf would not have been enough, and gave the rest back to the swan."

"Darling," Duff said, "I love to watch your eyes when you feel something strongly. They give out sparks." She smiled at me quizzically. Then she asked, "Do you think Stephens would have been a better poet if he hadn't known suffering?"

I said, "You cannot eliminate suffering, but you can hunger—at least in our countries."

"Darling," she asked, "did I ever tell you how we lived in Paris?"

I knew that she managed on a small allowance from one or both their families. But evidently it was more complicated than that. She said that her income, some ten or twenty quid a month, arrived erratically. Pat, too, got what came to him at unequal intervals. But when a check arrived, they moved to the Ritz. Everyone knew them there. She would get out her white gloves and evening gowns; he'd have his dinner jacket pressed. They'd have champagne and caviar and a wonderful time until their money gave out. Then they'd pack up their things and move back to the Quarter and poverty. Often they did not have enough to eat. But there was always someone to buy drinks ... and there was Jimmy behind the bar. He knew she would pay up when she could. It was fun, too, she said, a different kind of fun.

"You mean," I said, trying to put the best light on it, "that you believe in contrast? That by refusing to even out the good times and the bad you eliminate monotony?"

"Darling," she said, "you try to put everything into syllogisms. It can't be done. They don't come out the same." Then she added, "I've been thinking."

"So soon?" I asked apprehensively because I, too, had been thinking, and did not like where my thoughts were leading.

"Pat expects to find me in Paris when he gets back. We were out of funds, as I told you. He had to spend some time with his mother."

I made no comment. I had scrupulously avoided mentioning Pat.

She said, "Pat expected it would take him about two weeks."

"Yes," I said dully. Then I called for a bottle of champagne. "I did not know you liked champagne so much," I said.

Though I regretted my words, I did not tell Duff that champagne was the symbol of what I disliked about the way of life that I had rejected.

The waiter brought a bottle in a pail of ice, opened it, and filled our glasses. In the moonlight you could see the bubbles rising.

Duff said, "In Scotland when the Black Watch drink a toast, they throw their glasses against the wall so that no one will ever drink from them again ... To us! May we see each other always as we do tonight."

She hurled her glass into the darkness. I heard it shatter against the stone wall.

I drank and threw my glass with all my strength after hers. It hit a branch and deflected. We heard the thud as it dropped to the ground.

A dog barked in the distance. I wondered if he had been barking before. I shivered.

Duff broke the silence. "Darling," she said, "did I ever show you my sketches?"

I said I'd like to see them.

She went upstairs and came back with a large portfolio. Inside were drawings—clothed figures as you are taught to do them at school; a few nudes, unshaded; and a series of pastoral scenes.

Recalling from *Broom* days that artists were suspicious of undefined admiration, I told her that the clothed figures were excellent, that she had a flair for draping a piece of material about a body.

Duff was pleased. She liked best the ones I liked.

"Why don't you go on with it?" I asked. "It's good work. And you need something to fill the blank spaces."

"Blank spaces?" she asked incredulously.

"Dull times," I said. "Times when there is nothing outside to stimulate or amuse you, times when you have to draw on your own resources, the times you get down to work."

"Sweet," she said, "I don't have 'blank spaces.'"

I wondered about that. I knew she found something to laugh at in everything that happened, something of interest in every man's talk. Not so much in women's; she was not keen on women. Yet she had been charming to Ruth, who had followed her every movement with her eyes, and sweet and considerate to Mrs. Sanders.

"Yet you like people who work," I said.

"I like people," she answered.

"But if everybody enjoyed themselves and never worked, there wouldn't be any champagne or underclothing."

She said, "Different people need different things. The grasshopper had always managed, or some of us wouldn't be here."

"That may be," I said, "but I don't think human grasshoppers have the best time. It must be quite a strain to eat and jump and sing all day. You like Hemingway, don't you?"

"Yes," she said, "a good chap."

"He has exuberance, joy of life, what-have-you.... Yet he works like hell, seldom misses a day."

"I have nothing against work," Duff said, "for those who like it."

Wanting to show her something I had done, I hurried upstairs two steps at a time and dug down in my trunk until I came upon the issue of *Broom* that contained "The Mysticism of Money."

"You might glance over this article," I said when I got back to the table. "Don't try to read all of it. But parts of it may amuse you...."

Duff began to turn over the pages, looking at the illustrations: a stone camel from China, the elephant god as conceived by the Hindus, a carved ape from Siam. Finally she got to the article. I sat there in silence. When the waiter appeared I hurried him off with a peremptory *"Encore une bouteille, s'il vous plaît."* I was annoyed when he proceeded to clear the table.

Soon she handed it back with a whispered "It's very good, darling."

I was grateful though not certain that she meant it.

"It has a beautiful make-up."

That was not the praise I wanted. I told her I felt that the great artistic achievements in my country consisted largely of the forms and products turned out for the people. "Cars and dynamos. Jazz. The movies. Much of the work is anonymous, much of it is not associated with aesthetics at all."

Duff said, "But much of it is so vulgar."

"Yes," I said, "of and for the crowd. That's exactly what I was saying."

"But you're not like that," she said. "This magazine of yours, this cover by Juan Gris, this piece by Blaise Cendrars. They're not popular, my darling. Why do you sponsor one kind of thing and praise another?"

Broom, I explained, was a high-brow magazine that published individual expressions. But I had wanted our intellectuals to face the fact that many popular expressions were wonderful too in their way. "Let me show you some of Paul Strand's photographs...."

"No," she said, "I just want to feel the night. It is enough to be here with you."

She raised her glass. A smile was playing with her eyes, a smile so lovely it would have transfigured a homely face, and hers was not homely. I knew she wasn't interested.

That moment was the nearest we came to an argument. Duff seldom generalized. She never tried to convince anyone of anything. Yet she was quite firm about the things she believed in. She believed, for example, that behind appearances existed another more real world with which she was in contact. And because of this belief she did not question her inner voice, no matter what it told her.

Duff had told me that she was not sure I belonged to this esoteric circle. Sometimes she felt I did; at other times she doubted it. And the possession of an inner voice seemed to cause the possessor to distrust reason. She did not tell me this, but every time I used my mind to examine a concept, I felt her withdraw ever so slightly. It was as if she was not interested in that which she did not directly know.

I felt there was an incompatibility between the faith she professed and her actual conduct. If I was inconsistent, so was she. "How is it," I asked, "if your actions are governed by an inner voice, that you sometimes suppress this voice to obey the dictates of convention?"

"Do I?" she asked.

"Not always, but sometimes. You said that even if you liked Hemingway you wouldn't go off with him because of Hadley. But if you liked him, that would have been your inner voice speaking. The voice and the social conventions would have been in conflict. Yet you admit that you would have suppressed the voice in order to observe the convention."

"Darling"—although Duff used the word on everyone from chambermaid to lover, I was seldom able to resist its magic—"you have such faith in what the world calls logic. Maybe you are not one of us after all. Yet you are a dear."

I was slightly piqued. I did not think of myself as closed to all forms of mystical experience. I had always had a sense of the magic behind nature's screen. "Have you read *Green Mansions*?" I asked. "Even before I'd read it, the woods were mysterious. And your laugh, when I first heard it, reminded me of Rima singing."

The moon lay like satin on the flagstones. In the fold of the hills a grove of oak stood black and silent. A bird twitted. Duff said, "I never read *Green Mansions*. Didn't it take place in South America?"

"Physically," I said, "but it could have been anywhere."

"I have often thought about South America," Duff said. "Should we go there, darling? To a strange land, all new and different. To live as you want to live. Take a boat and go, just like that?"

"No," I said without hesitation, "not South America."

Her hand moved off. The night bird called again. The "no" I had spoken lingered on. I could feel the pulse in my temples. I was profoundly sad.

The next day we were just as we had been, just as affectionate, just as considerate, just as involved in the feel and look of each other. But before the morning was over Duff asked me would I go down to St.-Jean-de-Luz and reserve a place for her on the night train. She had promised Pat to meet him at the *gare*. And he was coming from London on Sunday afternoon. She would have to leave by Saturday night.

Till that moment I had not really faced the fact that our time together was soon to end. Now but three days were left to spend together. I was incredulous; it just could not be. Yet I went dutifully down to the station and bought the ticket.

Still, I was not unhappy; her nearness brought me too much joy. But now and then when I wasn't looking, the thought of losing her pierced like a knife thrust. I would pull my breath in. She had never seemed so beautiful.

I did not try to change her mind. I thought about it and the temptation was tremendous. But several considerations held me back.

For one thing, I did not believe that she would change her mind; there had been a finality about her gentle assent when I'd said "no" to South America. Then, too, I was not sure that I wanted her to change her mind; that is, my mind was not entirely certain. My heart was quite certain that I wanted her to stay. But I knew myself well enough to know that, should I ask her to stay and should she accede, I would be assailed by a legion of doubts. Her going away on her wedding night with the best man, a deed which at least amused her, eliminated a basic security. If she could "shove off" that way once, she could do it again. I knew that there was no security for mortal man, but I expected a few things from a loved one, some warning, some consideration. But when the voice spoke, Duff moved—as she had with the best man at the wedding, as she had with me.

And I feared the effect of her way of life. Would she live as I had to live? So she had intimated. But could she? I did not know. I doubted if Duff could change for long, but I wasn't sure.

Oddly enough, my refusal to take off for South America had not been induced by any of these considerations, not consciously. My "no" had seemed to slip out in response to stray trivia: to the fact that I knew no Spanish; that it did not rain in Chile where the copper mines were; that I had not liked the Cuban students at Mohegan. My "no" had seemed to come out as if by itself, but I knew it hadn't.

So we did not speak again of staying together. We made love furiously, as if we were trying to squeeze a life of love-making into three short days.

For the final afternoon we returned to Mrs. Sanders'. The *pension* was as it had been, several new guests but otherwise just the same. Ruth Ainsley and the Breton were still there; Ruth's eyes were, if anything, bigger. After dinner we took a cab down to the station.

We had one brandy and soda in the bar off the station platform. We

had three brandies and sodas. If we drank enough of them we would
not know when the train came in. I knew this; every particle of my
being was aware of this. Duff knew it too. Her eyes were moist and
glowing.

We drank and looked at each other. Our fingers were clasped. We
smiled at our secret. Each of us knew the other knew that the train
would come and the train would go and that nothing could touch us.
And should the train go, leaving Duff behind, there would be no taking
a later train; there would be no going back at all. Duff would stay with
me for good. For Pat would know if she wasn't on it, and the world
would know, and that would be that.

"*Garçon! Garçon! Encore deux cognacs!*"

Empty soda bottles littered the table. I felt a deep peace. The question I had been unable to answer was being answered for me.

The conductor came in, a stout, officious little man with a fluffy
mustache, eyebrows right under his visor, and a sheaf of tickets in his
right hand.

"Madame Twitchell," he called. *"Est-ce-que il y a une* Madame
Twitchell *ici?"*

He came over to our table. It wasn't hard to figure it out: Duff was
the only Englishwoman in the place, unmistakably English.

"Madame Twitchell," he said. *"Vous avez une reservation, n'est-ce
pas?"*

"*Oui,*" said Duff, "*je suis* Madame Twitchell."

"*Dépêchez-vous, alors, dépêchez-vous. Le train va partir.*"

Duff was trying to rise. I helped her up. Then there were bags to collect. The train was puffing and straining in front of the platform. The
conductor kept hurrying us toward the *wagon-lit.* The porter took her
bags.

"Good-by, my love," she said.

"Good-by," I said.

"Bless you," she said.

The car started to move. Gradually it got ahead of me. Then
another car came along. I walked as rapidly as I could; then I began to
run. The cars were going faster now. I could hardly keep up. Then the
platform ended; I had to stand there and look. The cars were passing
faster and faster. Now the last car was passing, a light on each side of
it. The lights got smaller and smaller and closer and closer together.
Then everything was gone and there was nothing left.

Chapter 4   KATHLEEN CANNELL

Scenes with a Hero

TOWARD the middling twenties in Paris, later to be known to some of us as "B.S." (Before *The Sun Also Rises*), I generally saw Ernest and Hadley Hemingway several times a week. We played tennis together, Hadley came "antiquing" with my sister and me—all the in-girls were collecting earrings—and with Harold Loeb[1] we had dinner together in some restaurant we all liked—a favorite was "Le Nègre de Toulouse" on the Boulevard Montparnasse.

I have always loved and admired Hadley; I instantly felt that Ernest was undependable and unpredictable. This was based on a physical proportion. From his big, handsome, almost hulking body weakness slanted out of wrists and ankles. The only other man in whom I had observed this had involved everyone close to him in real danger until he finished up insane in a military hospital. Some scenes in which Ernest Hemingway and I played parts proved me right—to my own satisfaction, at least.

The one which was crucially to affect the Hemingways' lives was pleasant enough. Pauline and Virginia Pfeiffer and a friend of theirs came to tea at my apartment to meet Hadley. They were all from more or less the same locality in the Middle West and were curious about each other. I remember it was a beautiful fall day—first fur coat

Reprinted from the *Connecticut Review* II, 1 (1968), pp. 5–12, by permission of the editor acting in behalf of the Board of Trustees for the Connecticut State Colleges.

145

weather—because Pauline had on a new chipmunk coat from a top
Paris designer. It was the only one any of us had seen and she looked
as cute as a little chipmunk in it. Pauline and Virginia Pfeiffer were
petite with bright black eyes and black bobbed hair cut straight across
the forehead like Japanese dolls. Their bones were as delicate as those
of small birds. As I have often remarked in the case of attractive sisters,
they were more than twice as cute as if there had only been one of them.
The one who was a little older (Pauline) benefited by the looks of the
younger, and Virginia shone in the witticisms of the one who was a
little brighter.

Pauline was then working as the assistant to Main Bocher, the editor
of French *Vogue*. She had a schoolgirlish crush on him and everything
about him was "ambrosial"—the superlative of the moment.

After tea Harold Loeb and Hemingway and, I think, Paul Fisher
came in, probably from boxing. The two hunters exclaimed about the
chipmunk coat. The Pfeiffers set the tone with light badinage, still
considered smart, and Ernest took his part with unusual geniality.
After the girls left he said: "I'd like to take Virginia out in Pauline's
coat."

The next time I saw the Pfeiffers they had been to call on the Hemingways. They remarked with delicate shudders that they found Ernest
so coarse they couldn't see how a lovely girl like Hadley could stand
him.

Then one terribly windy day I met Pauline in a wonderful new
Louiseboulanger suit. She was struggling along under a brand new
pair of skis. She was going skiing with Ernest and Hadley Hemingway—to Switzerland, I believe. I was surprised as I had not realized
they had been seeing that much of each other. It was particularly concerned for those bird bones.

It was some time after the return from the skiing holiday that I met
Hadley—I had wondered why she had not got in touch with me sooner.
Innocently I inquired how Pauline had got along. "Well, *you* know
what's happening," Hadley replied coldly. I didn't.

"She's taking my husband," Hadley said.

Because the Hemingways' adorable Bumby was still a baby, Hadley
had often to stay in the hotel with him while Ernest taught Pauline how
to ski. Hadley hadn't had a chance, she said. Ernest and Pauline made
each other sparkle—and they had their religion in common.

But I couldn't imagine two people less suited to each other. I hoped
it would be a phase. It might have been except for the fact that Pauline,
nearing thirty, was a virgin and a good Roman Catholic. She held out

inexorably for marriage. And opposition is proverbially considered to whet the appetite of hunters.

And Pauline was an heiress. She didn't need money from Ernest. So Ernest made all the profits of *The Sun Also Rises* over to Hadley and Bumby. Thus ironically, he didn't make a cent on his first financial success.

Harold Loeb liked and admired Hemingway; it sometimes seemed to the point of hero worship. Doubtless Hem represented some sort of ideal to him.

Hemingway always made a great thing out of being poor. One wintry day we had gone to his place with Miro to see his painting of "The Farm" which Hem had just bought. Hem claimed he couldn't live without it. Hem had on a sweat shirt and a raggedy pair of pants. He said in the half joking, half sneering way he sometimes adopted: "Some of you rich guys ought to buy the old man a pair of pants so he wouldn't have to freeze his a--- in this weather." (It actually was showing.) Loeb look stricken. He went home and brought back his own new flannel slacks.

Hemingway's first collection of short stories "in our time" sold two hundred copies. Harold was determined, if possible, to get it republished on better terms, and to place stories Hem had since written.

Leon Fleischman, an old friend of Loeb's, had been a partner of Horace Liveright and had come to Paris as a sort of unofficial agent of the firm, from which he had retired. He was an agreeable young Jewish intellectual. His beautiful wife, Helen (a classmate of Harold's first wife), had an attractive touch of nymphomania. She later married James Joyce's son.

Leon was more than willing to use his good offices on Hemingway's behalf. So one evening we took Hem to the Fleischman's lush furnished apartment, to which they had not yet had time to add a single characteristic element. Leon received us in a velvet smoking jacket. Harold later thought this might have prejudiced Hem against him. It certainly was the antipode of his poorboy pose.

Drinks were expensive and lavish and snacks delicious. Leon could not have been more conciliating. He said he would forward Hemingway's manuscripts to Horace himself, and implied that would be tantamount to acceptance.

Hemingway was unresponsive, Harold on tenterhooks. When conversation lagged Helen and I filled in with small talk.

In the street I made an anodyne remark about having spent a nice evening. (I easily reverted to my correct social upbringing.) Hemingway exploded into profanity: "Double god damned kikes!"—with a lot of picturesque explicit expletives.

Harold stood stunned while Hem strode away. "Well, Baby there's your future friend," I said. "Oh no," Harold replied. "If Hem thought of me as a Jew he wouldn't have spoken that way in front of me."

Ernest Hemingway and I had one thing in common: a passion for cats. I had taken in a wonderfully bad black kitten to oblige a friend who was leaving Paris. When I went away weekends, I had to leave my animals with my mother. The kitten had fun pushing large priceless Sèvres jars off the mantelpiece and gloating over the crash with a wide grin. Regretfully, I offered him to Hemingway. He accepted with joy and called him Kitty—not after me, but for identification till Bumby got around to naming him.

I saw Hem in a café soon thereafter. He was feeling terribly low, he said, "I have just one consolation in life." (I expected to hear Hadley or Bumby.) "My Kitty."

This led up to the next scene with the hero—the last one before the group departure of Hemingway and his sycophants for the bullfights at Pamplona.

Hemingway first heard about Pamplona from Gertrude Stein and Alice Toklas. But Robert McAlmon first took him there and paid all expenses. (This was, of course, unforgiveable, since Hemingway posed as the rediscoverer, exponent and scribe of bullfighting in our time.)

Robert McAlmon had come to Paris with a letter to me from William Carlos Williams. I was the first person he knew there. It was friendship at sight and lasted until after the beginning of the Nazi Occupation when I chanced to meet him and he told me he had arranged to get out. He said: "Thank God for German faggots." I never saw him again.

McAlmon, now well known to historians of the Twenties, married Bryer, daughter of Sir John Elliman [Ellerman], the British tycoon. It was a marriage of convenience, calculated to make Bryer independent of her parents. Thanks to a settlement Bob got from Sir John, he founded Contact Press which early published writings of Gertrude Stein, James Joyce and others. He also gave Joyce an allowance.

Bob and I had dinner together one evening and he, perhaps too casually, suggested that we should pass by the Hemingways and find out how Pamplona plans were progressing. I wanted to see my ex-kitty, so we went. If I had known at the time that Hem had a yen for Lady Duff Twysden (Brett in the "Sun"), I would not have affronted the atmosphere, especially as Bob enjoyed sticking verbal banderillos into Hem.

The Hemingways then lived in a cold-water apartment that gave on a lumber yard in the Montparnasse quarter. It had neither gas nor electric light.

After hearing who all was going, Bob remarked deadpan: "I'm thinking of taking Kitty with me to Pamplona next week." Bob, who understood me as well as any friend I ever had, knew I would not have gone for anything on earth. I have a horror of blood sports and those who practise them, which was naturally a prime reason Hemingway and I could never get along.

Hemingway turned a terrifying purple. He lunged toward me, seized a lighted lamp from the table at my elbow and hurled it through the window into the yard piled high with boards and kindling.

We took our leave, I trying to imitate my British mother and pretend nothing had happened, Bob looking as though he had swallowed at least two canaries.

This brings us to the last act (B.S.) as far as I was concerned. Things had been ostensibly patched up between the Pamplona combatants. Harold Loeb and Bill Smith were returning to America together. And they organized a farewell party for the night before they sailed.

Hadley may have come to dinner, but I know she was not with us when we walked to the café afterwards, Harold and Bill ahead, Hemingway and I together.

"Well, I've taken your advice at last, Kitty," Hem said. I admired Hemingway's style tremendously. He often said he went down on his knees to pencil and paper to achieve it (he wrote every day longhand in a cafe). "But if you'd only write about life instead of moods," I would tell him, "you'd have a sure fire best seller." Now he continued: "I'm writing a book with a plot and everything. Everybody's in it. And I'm going to tear these two bastards apart. But not you, Kitty. I've always said you were a wonderful girl! (sic.) I'm not going to put you in." To see whether I was buying it, he looked straight at me with what I called his "shining morning face"—rosy cheeked, with white teeth and the sudden marvelous smile of a good little eight year old boy. It made you feel like giving him an apple—or maybe your heart.

But, of course, he did put me in.

Hemingway couldn't wound me because I had never believed in him. But he certainly did annoy the hell out of me—I simply can't find a more ladylike phrase to express it.

All the characters in *The Sun Also Rises* were duplex. The hero was a mixture of Hemingway himself and Bill Smith. Cohn was Harold Loeb and everything Hem disliked in Jews—which was everything. In making me Frances Clyne, he teamed me up with a little Jewish secretary who had accompanied Harold Loeb and Alfred Kreymborg from America to found *Broom*, the expatriate magazine of arts and letters first published in Rome.

I am of English and Irish descent with a touch of Red Indian and mostly educated in France. Frances and I were poles apart in background, looks, manners, and temperament. But Hemingway gave Frances my conversation. From family wheezes, jokes and so on I had developed practically an individual language.

The evening of Hart Crane's arrival in Paris he came in to the Coupole where I was sitting at the bar. I said a few words to my neighbor. Hart exclaimed: "Why you're Kitty Cannell! I'd recognize you anywhere from descriptions."

So apparently did everyone in Montparnasse. If I had a dollar for each person who came up to me and demanded: "Did you really hold Harold Loeb up for such a sum, in such a place, on such a date and in such a way?"—it would have been unnecessary to hold anyone up for years.

NOTE

1 As a bow to the convenances, Harold Loeb and I let it be thought that we intended marriage. But I was not divorced, and, by the time I was, we had given up the project. In Paris we occupied separate apartments in the same building near the Eiffel Tower, where we quite comfortably led double lives.

Interview with Hemingway's "Bill Gorton"

WHEN Ernest Hemingway's novel, *The Sun Also Rises*, was published in 1926, there was a joke around Paris that the book was such a complete copy of life that the principal characters were in search of the author—with a gun apiece. The characters, of course, were:

> Harold Loeb, depicted in the novel as Robert Cohn
> Ford Madox Ford, depicted as Braddocks
> Lady Duff Twysden as Lady Brett Ashley
> Pat Guthrie as Mike Campbell, and
> Bill Smith as Bill Gorton.

All but two of these, in addition to Hemingway himself (Jake Barnes in the book) are dead now. Of the survivors, Harold Loeb has told his side of the story in his 1959 memoir, *The Way It Was*, and in his epilogue chapter in the *Connecticut Review* (I, 1967). That leaves only Bill Smith* from the "original cast" of a seminal novel that launched Hemingway into world fame, that became a kind of manifesto of the "lost generation" and which is still very much alive today in the bookstores and colleges of the world.

Smith is remembered not only as the "utilizer" of whiskey and the appreciator of "real country" in *The Sun*, but also as the Bill of two of

---

Reprinted from the *Connecticut Review* I, 2 (1968), pp. 5–12, and III, 1 (1969), pp. 5–23, by permission of the editor acting in behalf of the Board of Trustees for the Connecticut State Colleges.
*[William B. Smith died in March, 1972.— Ed.]

Hemingway's most memorable short stories, "The End of Something" and "The Three Day Blow." In *The Sun* Hemingway seemed to use Smith-Gorton as a kind of contrasting figure to the "heavy" role played by Loeb-Cohn. Smith-Gorton was made to participate in a certain amount of taunting and anti-Semitism directed at Loeb-Cohn, but in real life, as Loeb pointed out in the *Connecticut Review*, and as Smith confirms, he and Smith developed a close personal friendship that endures to this day.

In Loeb's essay, I was particularly interested in his search for Hemingway's motivations for bitterness, since his findings tended to tie in with theories of my own about Hemingway's "hero code" and its possible relationship to Bill Smith. As Loeb notes, Marcelline Hemingway

Bill Smith, Key West, 1928. *Collection of William B. Smith.*

Bill Smith, Petoskey, Michigan, 1920.
Collection of William B. Smith.

Sanford, Hemingway's older sister, pointed out in her memoirs that her
mother

always wanted twins, and that though I was a little over a year older than
Ernest ... she was determined to have us be as much like twins as possible.
When we were little, Ernest and I were dressed alike in various outfits, in Oak
Park, in gingham dresses and in little fluffy lace-tucked dresses with picture
hats.... We wore our hair exactly alike in bangs....

Loeb is the first one, to the best of my knowledge, to point to this
blurring of gender as a possible basis for the strident masculinity which
characterized Hemingway's life. As it remained for Malcolm Cowley
to develop the incantation theory behind "Big Two-Hearted River," for
Professor Philip Young to evolve the wound theory behind Heming-

way's writing tensions, and for Professor Carlos Baker to equate mountains and plains with the ebbing and flowing of Hemingway moods, so too must Loeb's theory that Hemingway overcompensated because of his role as a "reluctant little girl" be fitted into the forces that carved Hemingway's early development. It seems to me that Loeb's proposal of the twinship theory can be brought to bear on the evolvement of the Hemingway code itself.

This is where Bill Smith comes in. If the hero's code was a natural kind of compensation for Hemingway's enforced "girlhood," Smith, it would seem, was the right man at the right place at the right time to help in the code's development. About a year ago, I had a long conversation with Smith which may be of relevance now in view of Loeb's disclosures. I talked with Smith in his stylish Arlington, Va. ranch house just outside Washington. A foot of pure white snow had just fallen. Later, I jotted down some notes of my visit.

At 70, Smith (his full name is William Benjamin Smith) is very spare, a little stiff in the back and shoulders and he has about him a definite suggestion of fragility. Both his hair and mustache are whitish gray and there is a slate gray quality about his eyes. He has a retired English officer look. He seemed politely somber at first, and conservative, and it was hard for me to connect him with my image of a tall, blond, wide-shouldered, rather swashbuckling young man whom Hemingway had described to Harold Loeb as "one swell guy." Stalwart he no longer was, perhaps, nor a rebel; but after we had found a corner in his comfortable living room, I soon decided that he was still the same kind of person who had attracted Hemingway as a boy and man over 50 years before. Smith was reserved—but comfortably lacking in self-awareness—and while he was not given to easy talk, he was capable of sudden smiling, often sardonic emergences of banter. Most importantly, he was still possessor of that man's code of ethics that does not need to be written to be followed and which (I felt certain) had aided Hemingway in formulating his hero's code in the great literature that immediately followed the Michigan years. (Small example: I accidentally folded one of Smith's letters from Hemingway into my notebook. It was a particularly historic letter written from Italy in 1918 in which Hemingway told of his plans to marry Agnes Von Kurowsky, the Red Cross nurse after whom he patterned Catherine Barkley in *A Farewell To Arms* written ten years later. Smith hadn't missed it, but my embarrassment can be imagined when I found it among my things just before I left. "What difference does it make?" Smith said. "You would have mailed it to me.")

The code understands that there are some things a man does and does not do and if you have to have the code explained to you, it cannot be. One characteristic of the code is that it can be played with very low as well as very high stakes. If grace under pressure is a high point in the code, then ordinary decent manners, though spectrally lower, is still a requisite for full membership. It may well be, in fact, that a code violation, second class, caused the "falling out" of Smith and Hemingway.

St. John: Was there a falling out, Bill?

Bill: No. It wasn't so much a falling out as a falling apart—because of geography. We simply lived a long way apart and that always causes a drift of some kind.

St. John: I had always thought that you may have resented the use Hemingway made of his friends in creating his fictional characters.

Bill: No. I was never disturbed by any of this; it was never a complete copying; he was a true artist in piecing things together, rather than in trying for an absolute reality. In my own case of course, I guess everyone who cares knows that Bill Gorton in *The Sun* was modeled after me, but then the character was really composite, as so many of Hemingway's characters were if people would just take the time to examine them. Hem also used Don Ogden Stewart in creating this character. I explain it this way: I drank a lot in those days; I had a leg as hollow as Lady Brett Ashley's, but no one man could have drunk as much as Bill Gorton did in *The Sun Also Rises*. It had to be composite.

St. John: But what about other characters that were hurt, for example your friend, Harold Loeb who was portrayed as Robert Cohn?

Bill: That character wasn't all Harold either of course. I don't think people appreciate what an artist is trying to do when they look for literalness in Hemingway's characters. The real person was merely a starting point, but often there was a philosophical truthfulness about Hemingway's depictions that rose above the little factual discrepancies that people loved to look for.

St. John: Mr. Loeb wrote his own account of what happened on the Pamplona trip in *Sun*. What did you think of his book, *The Way It Was*?

Bill: I enjoyed it very much. But in fairness to everybody, you
             have to remember that this is the way it was to Harold.
             Everyone of us would write a different book. None would
             jibe exactly. That is only natural. The thing about Hem-
             ingway's account is that it caught a mood better than any-
             one else could. After all, it must be said to the detractors
             that Hemingway did not pretend to be reporting a kind of
             travelogue of our trip to Pamplona in 1925.

St. John: What about the "Bill" in my two favorite stories, "The End
             of Something" and "The Three Day Blow?" Was there
             anything upsetting in them?

Bill: Nothing important. They were good stories. The settings
             were accurate, if that means anything; some of the people
             were certainly recognizable; what happened didn't have the
             accuracy of a diary, naturally; that kind of thing wasn't
             intended. There was nothing objectionable to me in the
             stories.

St. John: I keep wondering what caused the falling-out stories.

Bill: I don't know. There was nothing either one of us said to
             the other. It was just drift, as I've said. I was in government
             in Washington; Wemedge was batting about all over the
             world. I kept up with him for awhile; Hem got me a job in
             Europe—long before he was famous I might add; that's
             why I was with him at the fiesta. The job fell through
             through no fault of Hem's, but the fact is he got it for me;
             there's a lot of that aspect of Hemingway that doesn't come
             out. Even in Harold's book, *The Way It Was*, which cov-
             ered the exact period, the point about my job is not men-
             tioned. I doubt Harold knew it. I met Harold because of
             Hem and have known him all my life because of Hem and
             we are still good friends. In Paris that year, 1925, I was flat
             broke and stayed in Hem's apartment with him and Hadley
             (Hem's first wife) for several weeks. I got there in March to
             go to work and then had to hang around until July, when
             the fiesta was to be held, and it was Hem who made this pos-
             sible even though Hem and Hash (Hadley) had very little
             money out of his writing and had this small baby, Bumby.
             But all this is disgressive. The fact is we were together in
             the early days and apart later. It is as simple as that.
             Maybe there is confusion with the falling out my older
             brother, Y. K. had with Hem. Y.K., as you know, played as

pivotal a part in the development of Hemingway as any single person, probably, although both he and I concede that with Hemingway's genius he would have made it whatever way his life had unrolled. But he did expose Hem to people like Sherwood Anderson and Hadley and started him in the direction of Ezra Pound and Gertrude Stein. This was in Chicago. Later, when Y. K. was handling Coca Cola for D'Arcy in New York, Hem and Y. K. became estranged because of a personal matter I will discuss in private but not in public; Hemingway was innocent in this case; it was a misunderstanding, but they didn't see much of each other after that. Drift again probably. In any case, none of this affected my own relationship with Wemedge.

St. John: Mr. Loeb thought if there had been a falling out it may have resulted from a Dos Passos book that alluded to Hemingway in an unfavorable way.

Bill: You mean *Chosen Country*?

St. John: Yes. I gather Hem was furious because he felt the material must have come from Dos's wife, your sister, Kate.

Bill: Of course it must have come from Kate. That's why it wasn't an effective book. It was second hand. Dos had never been to Horton Bay, and the book did not really come off; it didn't sell well; it could not have hurt anybody. It was a bad book. I doubt more than 20 people ever recognized the allusions to Hemingway. (He was Georgie in the book.) But it absolutely infuriated Hemingway.

St. John: Mr. Loeb would have been less than human not to have enjoyed that— seeing the shoe on the other foot I suppose.

At this point Bill's wife, Marion, who had been showing some of Bill's Michigan pictures and Hemingway's letters to my wife, Ruth, looked over at us.

Marion: Hem was as mad as a man could be. It was almost funny. He was so engraged about the Dos Passos book that he lashed out at Dos on his Christmas card to us that year.

St. John: Did he hold Bill responsible in some way for the Horton Bay background? I mean that it reached Dos through Kate after coming from Bill?

Marion: Oh no. There was no suggestion of that. Of course Horton Bay was before my time. I go back 33 years in Bill's life but not to Horton Bay.

Bill: Kate spent a lot of time in Horton Bay. She had all that
            background first hand. Our family had been coming to
            Horton Bay for many years. I guess Hem and I met there
            when we were boys under ten, and Kate was four years
            older than I (seven older than Hem). No. I don't think the
            old master held me responsible.

Marion: Kate hated Hemingway at the end because of Pauline
            (Hem's second wife). It was Kate who introduced Hem to
            Hadley at Y. K.'s apartment in Chicago and Pauline had
            taken Hem away from her, but Kate loved her anyway; they
            were both St. Louis girls, as was Hadley. Kate used to write
            us furious letters about the way Hemingway treated Pauline.
            Kate had met Dos at Hemingway's house in Key West, as
            you know, when she went there with Waldo Pierce, the
            artist, but she really hated Hem at the end and it is easy to
            see how she would want to hurt him. I guess Hemingway
            realized that and it was implicit in his Christmas card.

St. John: I gathered that Hem was unfaithful to Pauline toward the
            end of his marriage, but I hadn't realized there was any
            cruelty.

Marion: It wasn't cruelty in the usual sense, but that's what it
            amounted to.

Bill: Did you know that Hem was immune to mosquitos?

St. John: What?

Bill: He was immune to mosquitos, both Hem and his father. I
            don't know what it was, but mosquitos didn't bother him, at
            least not much. Pauline was exactly the opposite. She was
            very fair and very tender and if a mosquito so much as got
            near her she would swell up. Well Hem used to insist on her
            going out with him fishing and I remember seeing her back
            literally black with mosquitos. It was after the Paris days
            when I was visiting Hem in Key West.

Marion: That kind of thing. Unfeeling.

St. John: Then Hemingway did not criticize Bill in the Christmas
            card?

Marion: Oh, no, but he put hate into that card. I think it was a
            record for hate in a Christmas card. Hemingway was a
            genius about hate as much as he was about writing. He was
            the greatest hater I ever met and don't forget I'm from
            Washington. Here, I'll show you the card. This is one Hem-
            ingway tidbit that's not going into the Kennedy library.

Bill's giving all his other letters, of course, must be a hundred of them. The library can thank me for digging them out of the attic. They may be worth a lot to collectors [65 Hemingway letters to an Italian contessa were sold by Christie's of London on Nov. 29, 1967 for $258.46 per letter. Bill's letters are from Hemingway's brio period 30 years ago and hence more valuable.] But Bill's not much of a letter keeper and he certainly is not a letter seller. As a matter of fact we wouldn't have this material at all if Dos Passos hadn't gotten in touch with us when he had his accident— the one in which he lost his eye and Kate was killed—and asked us to organize things. Various writers and relatives had been storing their things in the Dos Passos' attic and I had the job of sifting through it. I found a lot of Hemingway's original manuscripts and sent them to him, and that's where I found Bill's letters from Hemingway, going all the way back to one sent from Milan, Italy in Dec. of 1918 in which he spoke of his great love for Ag and how it was the real thing and how they were going to get married. Of course this was the original of Catherine in *Farewell To Arms*, at least partly. He called Bill "Jazzer" in that letter. They were always using the strangest names for each other.

Marion had handed me the "Jazzer" and I read it.

St. John: Bill, I notice that Hemingway wanted you to be his best man when he married Agnes. Isn't it an oddity that you did show up at his first wedding but Agnes didn't?

Bill: Yes, I was best man when Hem married Hadley Richardson in Horton Bay three years later. The funny thing is that Hadley—we called her Hash even before Hemingway's day —was nine years older than Hemingway and I tried to talk Hemingway out of marrying her because I thought she was too old. I liked her very much and we became even greater friends after their marriage but I thought she was simply too old. I was three years older than Hem myself and Hadley was six years older than I. It didn't seem in the cards for it to last, and of course it didn't, but I doubt it failed because of the age factor. Now that I think of it I remember what Wemedge said when I brought up the age business. "At least she'll have lived," he said. But you mustn't take that too seriously. Hem was great for bombast. Too many of

St. John: Your advising Hemingway against marrying Hadley sounds
            a good deal like the "Bill" in "The End Of Something" and
            "The Three Day Blow" advising Wemedge against marry-
            ing Marjorie. Did you advise Hemingway against marrying
            Marjorie? Was there a Marjorie?

Bill: I knew Marjorie very well. She was a very nice girl I re-
            member, and pretty. I really don't remember advising Hem
            not to get involved with her, although I may have. Maybe
            he took my advice about Hadley's age and applied it in
            another way to Marjorie for artistic reasons.

St. John: About that name, Wemedge. I thought that was something
            made up for the story.

Bill: No, Wemedge was my personal name for Hemingway.

Here Bill got up and pulled a book from his library. It was *For Whom
The Bell Tolls.* He flipped it open and showed me the inscription:
"To Bill with affection from 'Wemedge'."

Bill: We were both great nicknamers. It seemed to be more the
            custom in those days. Like many others, we would change
            endings of words; it would be a fad for awhile. Eating
            would become eatage, reading readage, walking walkage,
            etc. and thus we spoke. It sounds juvenile now, but that's
            how these things got started. Hemingway's name became
            Hemage and then, somehow, Wemedge. I have another co-
            theory that my own name William became Willage and then
            Wemedge and that they somehow became reversed. There
            are those who think Hadley's name became Hash because
            she had a small inheritance and thus became Hem's meal-
            ticket but that is untrue. Hash was simply a corruption of
            Hadley. Most of these names vanished soon enough but
            Wemedge seemed to stick. Even that Christmas card Hem
            wrote us about Dos Passos was signed Wemedge.

Marion had finished going through a pile of material and now came out
with a neat-looking, biege Christmas card with a Hallmark stamp on
the back. Inside, on the left hand page, facing the printed Christmas
message, Hemingway had filled the space with about 15 lines of his
characteristic rounded hand sloping slightly downward to the right.

Marion: The material in the Kennedy library will be available almost

Hemingway and Bill Smith, Key West, 1928. *Collection of William B. Smith.*

immediately to scholars and that's as it should be but I think in the interests of taste, this card should be suppressed from publication for about 50 years. In any case, as I have said, we will not include it with the other material.

I cannot, of course, reproduce Hemingway's Christmas letter here, but I must say I did not find it particularly scurrilous. It was more sardonic than polemical. It does not breach any trust to confirm in the reader's mind that the card made sarcastic references to *Chosen Country*, which was referred to by another name, and characterized Dos Passos himself in an unkind way. (Since my conversation with the Smiths, incidentally, Dos Passos has, in turn, characterized Hemingway somewhat unkindly in his partial memoir, *The Best Times*). The language of Hemingway's Christmas card was not enhanced by references to Dos Passos' physical infirmity nor by allegations of paternal dubiety, but it was not all that bad as vivid intellectual lives go, and I concluded that the main offense to the Smiths' sensibilities had been its inclusion in a Christmas card. Bill did not say that; in fact he denied that the card had affected his relationship in any way, but while Marion was looking for the card he had recited it to me from memory, all 100 words of it and I was impressed that he had remembered it so well after 15 years. Marion's final comment, it seemed to me, was not without significance.

Marion: Hem sent us another Christmas card after that, from himself and Mary, but Bill never answered it. There was no further exchange of cards after that.

Thus did the code operate. It was a falling apart, Bill said, a drifting, and maybe it was. I couldn't help feeling, however, that Bill was offended by Hemingway's virulence and lack of restraint in a Christmas card. Hemingway was accordingly read out of his friendship in a way so ineffable that if Hemingway had sought readmission into the invisible society he would have been readily accepted and even the original expulsion would have been denied. One does not become messy about these things nor give them the importance of recognition.

St. John: I have a theory Bill that you helped formulate Hemingway's famous code.
Bill: I don't know about that. The code came later.
St. John: I mean you and Hem were close for more than 20 years, starting in childhood, spanning Hem's most formative years and surviving the fame of both *Sun* and *Farewell*. You had

much in common, your cultural background, your loosely knit families, your common devotion to English literature and the gentleman's code, your mutual teenage interest in symbolism, your common entrapment in Victorian values, your romanticising but non-acceptance of females, your love of sports and wilderness. It seems to me your friendship had much to feed on; it didn't wear out as other friendships and even marriages did. You never bored each other. All of this makes me think you must have rubbed off onto Hemingway to a considerable degree and helped him develop the values that underlay his writing.

Bill: It was nothing I was aware of.

St. John: Of course. That was part of it. What I mean was the unconscious development of values, ideas, the feeling for understatement, the not talking things to death, the not doing things too long, the concept of grace under pressure, the man's mystique, so to speak.

Bill: There may have been something. I don't know.

St. John: I was always puzzled, Bill, by the epigraph in *In Our Time*. I remember it goes:

A Girl in Chicago—Tell us about the French women, Hank. What are they like?

Bill Smith—How old are the French women, Hank?

What was that all about?

Smith: Hem and I were riding the El to Chicago (to buy fishing tackle at V.L. and A's—von Lengerke and Antoines) when some gal he knew got on the same coach and began to ask Hem such questions as "How was Paris? Were the girls very pretty, etc., etc." I finally said, "How old are the French women, Hem?" I wanted to talk about our forthcoming trip to Horton Bay.

St. John: I might have guessed the fishing angle, Bill. It seems to me there is another epigraph here—Let nothing, not girls, not family, not sacred honor interfere with the companionship of men. And it gets us back to my theory about your influence on Hemingway. He did quote you in *In Our Time* and *The Sun*. He was impressed, and I see now what he meant: Don't ask foolish questions, don't talk things to death, don't go on too bloody long, don't get side-tracked from the main chance. You've got to admit this is a kind of evidence that you helped Hem develop the code.

Smith: This is basically correct, but it was not as direct and fully conscious as you seem to feel. It grew like Topsy because we felt and appreciated things. We tended to buy the English gents' code of gallantry as revealed in fiction. The idea of being "under wraps" was part of it, particularly with me. I mean the kind of attitude Jake Barnes had about the newspaper business in *The Sun Also Rises*—one should never seem to be actually working or pressed—and yet the work must get done etc., etc.

St. John: About all those books you and Hem discussed in "The Three Day Blow." I notice they were all by Englishmen and had quite a bit of the gentleman's code in them. Do you actually recall these books?

Smith: Yes, very well; it was the kind of thing we read in those days, Chesterton, Walpole, Hewlett, Meredith. We exchanged books, as I recall. There were some other books that appealed to Hem and not all of them wound up on his published reading lists. I remember *The Psychology of Sex* by Havelock Ellis. (I hid that one under my mattress at the old Charles farmhouse but of course Aunty Charles found it, and I'm sure that didn't help Hem's reputation any.) Another one he liked was *The Case of Sergeant Grischa*, by Arnold Zweig, but I guess that came out a little later than the ones we're talking about. The only other one I can recall now after all these years is *Harmon the Butcher of Hanover*, which had to do with the sale of human flesh.

St. John: I notice that in Hemingway's memoir, *A Moveable Feast*, he talks of writing "The Three Day Blow" in a Paris cafe in the early 1920's and that since the weather was bad outside the cafe it was that way in the story.

Smith: That may be true, but the fact is the weather was pretty miserable most of that summer of 1919. It really was unusually cold and of course those blows off Lake Charlevoix and Lake Michigan were common enough. One day the leaves would be there with all that wonderful fall color and then they would be stripped clean and it would be winter.

St. John: My God, that sounds like the scene in Paris when he wrote that story. They were both fall scenes and in *A Moveable Feast* he wrote that "the cold wind would strip the leaves from the trees in the Place Contrescarpe." It probably was what brought the Michigan story to his mind.

Smith now spoke at some length of his earliest contacts with Hemingway and of their many summertimes together in the tiny lakeside resort of Horton Bay, Mich. I was able to follow his descriptions of the geographical settings and to relate what happened in those days to the action of Hemingway's stories because I had already interviewed the *real* Marjorie and gone over the *real* ground of the two Bill Smith stories. In the course of this earlier exploration I had been surprised to find that the settings for "The End of Something" and "The Three Day Blow" were approximately the same as those of Hemingway's earliest story, "Up in Michigan," which seemed to have involved Jim and Aunty Beth Dilworth, old family friends of the Hemingways, in a rather sordid tale of seduction.

Bill Smith and Hemingway met as little boys at Dilworth's Inn in Horton Bay during the first decade of the 20th century. Smith's mother had died when he was a baby and he spent the summers in Horton Bay on Lake Charlevoix with his "Aunty Charles" and "Unk" Joe Charles, of St. Joseph, Mo. The Hemingways, from Oak Park, Ill., had a summer home on Walloon Lake about three miles from Horton Bay. "We didn't like each other at first," Smith recalls, "but later we were brought together through fishing at the point by Charles Edgar, a good friend of both our families." The point was the setting for "The End of Something," and lies directly across the "lagoon" of Horton Bay from the mill wharf where the seduction took place in "Up in Michigan." From the heights of the town up the sandy road from the dockside you can look down on the point across the water and even now there are usually a couple of small fishing boats drifting off the small spit of sand. If, from this same position high up in the town you turn your eyes to the right away from the point until you come to slopelands beyond the marshy Horton Bay creek inlet, you can see the wood-edged meadows where the Charles farmhouse was once located. This was where most of the action of "The Three Day Blow" took place. In the old days there was a path leading from the Charles house to the mouth of Horton Creek and on down the wooded spine of the point to its jutting sandy tip across from Horton Bay. Part of the path remains today and you can still follow easily the route that Bill must have walked when he came out of the woods to meet Nick-Hem after the brush-off of Marge in "The End of Something." The three stories thus form a kind of triangle: the village ("Up in Michigan"), the point ("The End of Something"), and the Charles house ("The Three Day Blow"), and in their "locatability" illustrate how the physical settings of Hemingway's stories, whether they be on Lake Charlevoix or on Lake Maggiore in Italy, tend to be mirror-images of life—even though this "factuality" does not necessarily carry over to the scenarios that motivate them.

The action of the stories varied widely in time: the plot of "Up in Michigan" probably took place in the last century since one of the characters talks in a contemporary way about James G. Blaine, who was defeated for the presidency by Grover Cleveland in 1884. The action of the other two Horton Bay stories probably took place in 1919, the year Hemingway got back from the war in Italy, for there is a reference to a possible trip back to Italy, with Marge; and, of course, the Chicago Black Sox scandal occurred in 1919, thereby accounting for some of the cynicism about baseball in "The Three Day Blow."

For all the long spans of time to the present since the stories "took place," the area is virtually as unspoiled today as it was in Hemingway's time. The same ingredients of mood are there. The land is heavily wooded, the subdividers have been held in check and big fish still jump in the little bay between the village and the point. There is one change: the Rainbow trout of Hemingway's time have been decimated by lamprey eels that got into Lake Charlevoix through a narrow canal from Lake Michigan when the St. Lawrence waterway was opened up to the Great Lakes.

In Bill Smith's memory there is no clear line between life at Horton Bay and the substance of the stories, and one must always distinguish between authentic settings and what is taking place. Marge of "The End of Something" was real enough to Bill—she was Marjorie Bump whose mother owned Bump and McCabe's Hardware store—but the brush-off of the story is a good deal harder to get at, and there is a bit of Hemingway weaving in the drinking of the boys at the Charles house. Bill's "Unk," Joseph Charles, was an optometrist, and was away most of the time; he was not as firm an image in Bill's mind as the formidable Aunty Charles, but both Unk and Aunty were clearly anti-Hemingways, at least in the young manhood days, and could be classed in some ways with Hemingway's own highly Victorian doctor father and frustrated opera singer mother. Unk's father had been a fundamentalist preacher (the exact opposite of Bill's own professor father whose life-time avocation was dissecting literalness in religion), and Bill can remember how startled he was one time when the older Charles slammed his cane down deafeningly three times on the kitchen table to emphasize the various parts of the Trinity. But it was clearly Aunty Charles who ruled the roost at Horton Bay. She was not only anti-Hemingway. She was also anti-Bill's father, and it was Bill's theory that she somehow blamed Prof. Smith for the tubercular death of her sister, Bill's mother. Dr. Smith, who was teaching mathematics and philosophy at Tulane University in those days (1893–1915), came to Horton Bay only on rare occasions. When he did, he put up at Dilworth's Inn rather than at the Charles house.

Aunty Charles was generally in poor health, Bill remembers. She would go upstairs to bed early and Bill and Hemingway would stay up playing poker by kerosene lamp; it was unlikely they would ever have had the opportunity to do any tall drinking in the same house with Aunty. But it was likely enough there was much talk about literature and baseball in front of the fire. It's faintly possible that some liquor was stashed in the house. The truth of the matter is that the drinking described in "The Three Day Blow" probably was done down at the point. Bill and Hem spent a lot of time at the point. In those days it represented the values both liked best, privacy, a retreat from the farm work both were required to do, and a lovely place to fish, talk, drink and even to sing unrestrainedly if they jolly well felt like it. From the point they could look across at the prim little town of Horton Bay up on the hill and in the other direction the sweep of Lake Charlevoix (called Pine Lake by many in those days) and they could feel the ocean-like winds from the big sea of Lake Michigan. I suppose there is no other period that Bill remembers with more satisfaction than the times he spend on the point with Hem and the little forays they would take out into the lake or up the creek that emptied into Horton Bay. "We used to wade up the cold waters of that creek," Bill remembers, "in ordinary pants, since we couldn't afford the fancy waders the summer people wore; it became painfully, achy cold and we would usually refer to this condition as penal servitude." The drinking that was done at the point Bill remembered in terms of a transparent jug of some kind filled with hard cider from Dilworth's grist mill back up the slope of Horton Creek (the wheel of the mill still exists). The point of the drinking was to compete in taking very long slugs, that is, chug-a-lugs. The name of the manufacturing company was printed vertically on the jug—Bill remembered it was Hornsby something something manufacturing company. A good swig was to lower the bottle about two inches, say from "Hornsby" to "manufacturing."

As Bill talked about Horton Bay, it was easy to see how he might have fought in some perhaps unconscious way to preserve that way of life. Hemingway too might have seen in the situation (actual or extrapolated) the wrenchings and endings that plague the sweet things of life and keep them from becoming boring. Hemingway's Bill and Marjorie stories, therefore, are certainly not without relevance to the

Smith-Hemingway relationship, although determining what actually happened is a bit more difficult, it must be remembered, than merely checking the geography. The reader is cautioned to proceed at his own risk.

In "The End of Something" (clearly one of the best titles devised by man) Nick (Hemingway) and Marge have been trolling for trout in Horton Bay when an apparently spontaneous quarrel develops and Nick tells Marge that love isn't fun anymore. Marge rows off by herself, leaving Nick to walk home. Since almost immediately Bill comes out of the woods, it is clear that the quarrel between Marge and Nick did not just happen and that the two young men had rather cold-bloodedly planned the whole thing. There is some regret on Nick's part but not much. In the sequel, "Blow," the two young men have a wonderful time by themselves in Bill's father's cottage. While winds from Lake Charlevoix and Michigan howl sensually around the house, Nick and Bill sit before a glowing fire and get gloriously tight on the father's liquor. In the course of their drinking, they have lively discussions about English literature and baseball and, finally, "the Marge business." It becomes evident that Bill had counseled the breakoff because getting married "bitches" everything and, besides, Marge's family was not quite right for a doctor's son. Nick seems to agree but is depressed by the whole matter until Bill warns him not to slip back into the relationship again and this possibility surprises Nick and revives his mood somewhat. Finally, when the two boys go out in the storm to hunt, the wind seems to blow everything away from Nick's mind and he feels happy-go-lucky again.

St. John: Marjorie doesn't remember actually fishing with Heming-
            way as in the story. Do you think he may have fished with
            some other girl, perhaps one of his sisters?
Smith: I doubt it.
St. John: Do you think by any chance Hemingway substituted Marge
            for some guy who was going to get married and who would
            thereafter be unavailable as a fishing companion? I ask this
            because the disjointure of breaking up a good male re-
            lationship is strongly alluded to in "Cross-Country Snow"
            and in other places.
Smith: It's hard to know exactly what an artist has in mind, but I
            must doubt this theory.
St. John: I suppose the fishing Hem did at the point was actually
            with you?
Smith: We fished a lot out there. The Rainbows used to go up Hor-

ton Creek to spawn and feed and I remember all the time we spent trying to catch them up there. But we never caught a single one up the creek. The trouble is they were bottom feeders and when we tumbled to this we worked out a way to catch them once they got into the bay. We'd cut the head off a small perch, skin it back, put the hook through the tail and let it drift to the bottom. You could heave the hook out but it was better to drop them out about 50 feet or so, from a boat. We used to do that with my old Peterboro canoe. Then we'd bring the lines into shore, prop them up with log butts, set the reel and wait for a bite. We'd have several rods set that way and while we waited we'd play poker or "catch." When the reel started humming we'd drop everything and haul in the fish. Lost one or two rods that way I remember. Some of those trout were seven, eight pounds.

St. John: Bill, that description reminds me of a fishing story Hem wrote for the *Toronto Star Weekly* of April 10, 1920 in which he said: "We were fishing for Rainbow trout where a little river comes into a lake and cuts a channel along side the bank.... Every once in a while a big trout will jump clear of the water with a noise like somebody throwing a bathtub into the lake.... These monster trout won't touch a fly and we fish for them by casting out from the bank with minnows and letting them lie on the bottom of the channel...." This is the same scene isn't it, the mouth of Horton Creek? Another thing—I find in Hem's news stories he sometimes speaks of a fishing companion, Jacques or Jock Pentecost, who sounds suspiciously like plain John Pentecost, his high school friend from Oak Park, Ill. Would Hem Canadianize a name, that is angle it for his Anglo-French readers during those highly nationalistic days in Toronto?

Smith: Your hunch is 100 per cent right as to Jack Pentecost. And the action did of course take place at the point, but I do not recall the use of minnows. As I have said, I think it was skinned perch, that is why the click was set on the reel, as usual, and the "butt had been under a log and resting on another" as in the news story. That is not the way you cast with minnows in taking Rainbow. But no matter, Hem angled stories as does everyone. Particularly when they are fishing stories!

St. John: In that Toronto journalism, Hem mentions another news-

Bill Smith, Horton Bay, Michigan. *Collection of William B. Smith.*

man named Krebs, and I wonder if this is where he got the name of his principal character in "Soldier's Home?"

Smith: I don't know about the connection, but I knew Hem's friend, Krebs, had dinner with him once or twice at a place called Wurtzenzeps—something like that. [Wurz'n' Zepp's, Chicago, ed.]

St. John: I wonder if that Peterboro canoe you mentioned is the one referred to in Hem's poem, "Along with Youth": "and the canoe that went to pieces on the beach / The year of the big storm / When the hotel burned down at Seney, Michigan." You remember there is a burned hotel in Seney in "Big Two-Hearted River," and of course Seney really exists.

Smith: Same canoe, although row boats were used too, as in Hem's stories. I don't recall the big storm or when the hotel burned down.

St. John: You say you played "catch" while waiting for bites at the point. Was Hemingway much of a ball player? Aside from the baseball talk in "Blow," I've not heard too much about this interest of his. In one of his Toronto newspaper pieces he did speak of playing on a Petoskey baseball team, but I've never been able to confirm this.

Smith: We used to throw the ball around on the point, heave it at each other, talk about our "stuff." Baseball was a big subject and, of course, coming from Missouri I was a big Cardinal rooter. Wemedge was more interested in the Chicago teams, particularly the Cubs as I remember. We'd play on teams sometimes; I remember playing with Wemedge in Petoskey, so that checks okay. Usually he'd catch and I'd pitch. He wasn't so hot actually, but the picture he had of himself was pitching, not catching. He insisted on pitching in one game but I had to relieve him with three runs in and only one out in the first inning. He liked to follow baseball in those days but it was hard for him to become passionate about anything he couldn't do well himself. And I think he was disillusioned, like all the rest of us, by the Chicago Black Sox scandal of 1919, the first summer he was back from the war.

St. John: You don't happen to remember the Cards having a train wreck (as suggested in "Blow") and losing their talent just when it looked as if they might win for a change?

Smith: No. The Gas House Gang came later. In those days the

Cards thought of the First Division only during spring
training and for a few weeks after the season opened—then
they sank, sank, sank, usually to 7th or 8th. I don't really
recall whether Hem was a Cub or a White Sox fan, but he
did of course come from the Chicago baseball watershed.

St. John: During those sessions of yours on the point—someone told
me you two young men would recite the Lord's Prayer while
you were drinking or fishing. I gather both you and Hem
were well-tutored in the Bible.

Smith: We *sang* the Lord's Prayer in recitative very loudly when
very tight on hard cider. I wouldn't say that either of us
was well-tutored in the Bible, however. May I say one thing
here in defense of those poor jokers on the point? We
weren't absolute loafers you know. I had the Charles farm
to take care of, and Hem's father expected a very great deal
from him on the farm the Hemingways bought across from
their summer cottage on Walloon Lake. This Hemingway
farm was on the Horton Bay side of Walloon and so it was
convenient for us to "change work" from time to time. Of
course I wound up getting a B.S. in Agriculture; so the experience wasn't wasted, but to Hemingway chores of that
kind were pretty much torture and that probably accounted
for much of the friction with his father. In this connection I
might as well add that Hem always held it against his father
for taking out his tonsils without an anaesthetic.

St. John: Something bad happened between Hem and his dad when
he was 15—according to "Fathers and Sons." I wonder if
that was it.

Smith: I don't know just when it was, around there sometime.

St. John: To get back to the Marge story, Nick (or Hem) became
irritated because he felt that Marge was trying to top him in
fishing "in-ness." "You know everything," he said to
Marge. Dramatically, of course, this was said partly to start
a fight, but Hem *was* likely to be touchy in his own field of
expertness, wasn't he? I mean "in-ness" was important to
him, as in all that outdoor "in-ness" of his in "Big Two-
Hearted River?"

Smith: Hem set a good deal of store in his knowledge of hunting,
fishing, the outdoors. One time at the bay—at dusk—his
Red Cross friend, Ted Brumback, shot a night hawk with a
rifle. It was an impossible wing shot; it couldn't have hap-

pened in a million chances, but it did; the hawk dropped like a stone, and it broke the old master's heart. Sure, he had a bad eye and it was this that caused his rejection by the armed forces, but Brumback had a bad eye too [a glass eye, in fact, ed.] and in any case Hemingway could really shoot. He was the best shot I ever knew, and yet that night, when Brumback hit the night hawk it broke the old master's heart —and made him sulk a little.

St. John: Did you yourself ever fish the Big Two-Hearted River with Hem? Did Hem actually fish it or was that just an appropriate name for his story?

Smith: Hem and some friends went on a fishing trip to the Upper Peninsula of Michigan just before he left for the war in Europe in 1918. Brumback was on that trip and so was Hopkins, his editor from the Kansas City *Star*, the "Hophead" of the "Big Two-Hearted" story. I did not make that trip myself but I remember Hem mentioning the Big Two-Hearted when he got back.

St. John: Do you know whether Hem made another trip up the Two-Hearted (or perhaps the nearby Fox, as his brother Leicester suggests) after he came back from the war? I mean, to relieve the "workings" in his mind caused by his war injuries? That would have had to be 1919, I suppose, when Hem was still feeling his war nerves. But by the same token he still limped in those days when he got tired, and it is hard for me to imagine him carrying that Abercrombie and Fitch camping load that is itemized in the "Big Two-Hearted River."

Smith: No reaction to the first question. He could have carried quite a load though, limp or no limp. His legs were those of a very big man. He had the lower body of a 220-pounder, the upper of a 175-pounder. Still, I'll concede that load was probably exaggerated. Probably put in everything he'd forgotten to take on one trip or another.

St. John: Getting back to "End of Something," Marge thinks you may have noticed her waiting on tables at Dilworths and unconsciously relegated her to the servant class, thus making her unworthy, so to speak, of a doctor's son.

Smith: No, that simply isn't....

St. John: I mean at an unconscious level.

Smith: Of course it's possible. It was a long time ago. Thinking about it now, I consider it more likely that I said something like, "My God, Bump and McCabe's, a damn hardware store; it's like marrying into a hardware store." It could have been like that.

St. John: You mean you remember the company name, Bump and McCabe after all these years, about 50 isn't it? That is the store Marjorie's mother owned, but it wasn't mentioned in the story.

Smith: Yes. I remember the store very well. I used to buy my fishing tackle there.

St. John: Then you would have seen Marjorie's step-father, Charles Graham, "the fat one" referred to in early but not later versions of "The Three Day Blow?"

Smith: I suppose so. I don't particularly remember that now.

St. John: What was your premise? That a doctor's son was too good to marry a hardware man's daughter?

Smith: No. I don't honestly think it was that. It's just that I thought Wemedge had a lot more potential than that. I simply didn't associate him with the hardware business. There was certainly nothing personal about it—I mean nothing against Marjorie. And we are all certainly great simps at that age.

St. John: In "Blow," Bill says once a man's married he's absolutely bitched. Could this have been based, do you think, on your dad's marriage, or on your brother, Y. K.'s or Unk Charles'? Or was Hem talking about his own dad?

Smith: I think it was primarily that women, marriage, *et al* interfered with fishing, camping trips and other male pursuits. Hem believed in women enough to marry four times.

St. John: Do you remember the stories Hemingway was writing in those days? He read them to Marjorie and some others. Did he read them to you?

Smith: No. He did most of his writing that year after the 1919 fishing season had ended. He moved into Petoskey and I went back to Missouri. I had no personal knowledge of what he did that winter. But I saw some of his work the following summer of 1920 when he came back from his news job on the *Toronto Star Weekly*. I thought it was very good. The only trouble is he was sending it to the wrong magazines. The *Saturday Evening Post* would never have used that experimental writing of his (no matter how good it was)—and it was experimental even before he went to Paris. It belonged in *avante garde* publications and of course that's where it wound up—in Paris a bit later. In those days there was very little market in this country for experimental fiction and what little magazines there were were unknown to Hemingway at that particular point in his life, 1919–20. You know some of his early stuff Hemingway himself didn't like very much. I know for a fact he didn't care particularly for that first story of his, "Up in Michigan."

St. John: He liked it well enough to include it in his first 49 stories.

Smith: Well, it was his very first story, and it survived the great train robbery—I mean the loss of all his other Petoskey material at the railroad station in Paris; and it was about the bay. Probably some sentiment there.

St. John: Do you think there were sexual overtones in that title, "Up in Michigan," as some have suggested?

Smith: Of course. I remember kidding him about it and saying your next story should be called "Even Further up in Michigan."

St. John: Did Hem ever dream openly, in your conversations at the point, about becoming a writer and did he ever make impassioned speeches about the empty verbiage most writers used, the kind of talk for example that might have presaged his famous attack on Fourth of July words, like "sacred" and "honor" and "hallowed," in *Farewell to Arms*?

Smith: Yes, as to the dreaming, but I do not recall the speeches or what could be done about things. I remember one small thing: Over the years, Hem would say, "Now that could go in a book,"—as when something blew off the dock and sank before he could reach it. I would say: "Hemingway will save it, Hemingway will save it, too late for Hemingway." This referred to an old advertisement for Herpicide hair tonic. It seemed funny at the time but it's hard to remember why.

St. John: Marge Bump said something to me about Hem showing his stories to an established writer who stopped at Dilsworths. Marge remembered that the man said Hem had promise and it is my idea this may have been Hem's first professional encouragement as a writer. Does this ring a bell?

Smith: Hem showed his work to Edwin Balmer, I think his name was; Balmer later became editor of *Red Book* magazine.

St. John: Did you know Marjorie Bump well?

Smith: Not too well. I remember I saw her in swimming one time.
            I guess Wemedge logged his time with her after I left that
            year in the fall of 1919. In the story Hem was going to stay
            in Charlevoix to be near Marge, but, of course, that was just
            a cover for Petoskey where Marge really lived.

St. John: I met Ken Van Hoesen, the man you and your sister Kate
            sold the old Charles place to. He was a little boy back in
            1919 when Hem and Marge saw so much of each other, and
            yet his memory of Marjorie is still very fresh and glowing.
            He remembered her red hair and her bathing suit and how
            she seemed to him to be the prettiest girl in the world. She
            would have been 17 then and Hem 20. Of course Hem
            changed Ken's family name, Van Hoesen to Van Hoosen
            in "Up in Michigan."

Smith: Sure I remember old Stubs. He used to carry water to us
            out at the point.

St. John: Marge remembers carrying a picnic lunch to you and Hem
            out at the point one day; she supposes now that she made a
            big mistake in hanging around because you finally stalked
            back up the path toward the Charles house grumbling. She
            thinks this too may have made an impression on Heming-
            way.

Smith: I don't remember that. It could have happened. Probably
            nothing personal. Just a nuisance trying to fish with kids
            around. Something like that. If I was annoyed, it was more
            likely at Hemingway for not minding it. I don't know.

St. John: You thought of Marge as a kid?

Smith: More or less. She was—what was it—six years younger
            than I. That can be a big difference at that age.

St. John: Of course your being annoyed with Hem rather than with
            her is just what Marge means. She figures Hem equated
            your annoyance with her and since you could do no wrong
            that was that for young Mr. Hemingway.

Smith: Well, of course, this is all very speculative, and I don't
            know what it really means—now.

St. John: Of course. The only significance, I suppose, is in terms of
            the brush-off in the story, the motivation, etc. As to the
            luncheon Marge brought you, did people usually feed you
            out there?

Smith: Not that I recall. We either carried sandwiches or ate at my

Aunty Charles' or at Mrs. Dilworth's. That was a big tramp back to Hem's house.

St. John: In the "End" story, a knife is used to cut off the perch's head. Both you and Marge have told me Hem bit the heads off on occasion. I suppose I got the impression he was capable of eating raw fish out there on the point—or was that done just to shock?

Smith: We both bit fish heads off at times; mostly to shock I suppose, though on at least one occasion we were on the point without a knife. The Indian influence was strong out there in those days as I remember.

St. John: Getting back to basic influences on Hemingway, do you think you and Hem may have classed the Charles and the older Hemingways together sociologically?

Smith: I doubt it very much.

St. John: But they were both puritanical, weren't they? Didn't this account for the clash between your own father's liberality and the fundamentalist philosophy of the Charles?

Smith: To a certain extent. It was also a clash of personalities— Mrs. Charles was not a scholar and had no sympathy with my dad from any standpoint.

St. John: Did you see your own dad often enough to have been stimulated by him intellectually?

Smith: Yes.

At this point Smith went to some book shelves on the other side of the living room and brought back a rather slim volume with a blue dust jacket. It bore the title, *The Birth of the Gospel*, and its author was William Benjamin Smith, Bill's father.

Smith: My brother, Y. K. and I published this book after my father's death. Here, take it. But I warn you, it's not light reading.

I took the book and spent about 15 minutes leafing through it while Smith joined his wife, Marion and my wife, Ruth, in going over snapshots and letters that Marion had spread out on the coffee table. The book was subtitled "A Study of the Origin and Purport of the Primitive Allegory of the Jesus" and was finished in 1927 when Dr. Smith was 77, some seven years before his death.

St. John: After looking at this book, Bill, even this briefly, I feel more convinced than ever that the Smiths as a family have had a

Bill Smith, New York, 1935. *Collection of William B. Smith.*

greater overall impact on Hemingway's life and career than any other.

Smith: I would certainly call that a little excessive.

St. John: Well, let's start with your sister Kate Dos Passos—she introduced Hem to his first wife, Hadley and then rushed to the defense of his second wife, Pauline. And as an older and attractive girl she must have had some influence on Hem both at the bay and later in Chicago, though probably not very much by the Key West period. Then of course she was the source of Dos Passos' blast at Hemingway in his novel, *Chosen Country*.

Smith: Her greatest influence on me was her reading. And she was a handy source of books for both Hem and myself.

St. John: Then your brother, Y.K.—he certainly played a pivotal role in Chicago when he took Hemingway into his apartment in 1920, exposed him to a literary environment, and introduced him to Sherwood Anderson. Lord, it was that that led to Gertrude Stein and Ezra Pound and the whole Paris scene.

Smith: Yes, I'll say this for Y.K. He knew Hem was a genius even then.

St. John: That checks all right. Y.K. told me himself—I have his letter right here—that Anderson felt "the fires of genius in Hem and stoked it by overt lively interest." And genius wasn't the only quality that wise old Y.K. perceived, apparently. Here's the rest of that quote of his: "At this point Ernest began to take seriously his own talent as an alluring possibility. I think this was his first contact with a big-time artist and it gave him as it were a chance to measure himself. Gertrude Stein, etc. must have further escalated his self-esteem—put a firmer foundation under it. Ernest was never lacking in his feeling of being a worthwhile person...." By the way, Bill, did you yourself look upon Hem as a genius?

Smith: Of course not. Your buddy is never a genius.... This letter-writing business, I might add, is not the best way to unscramble this aged omelet, judging from my own previous contacts with Malcolm Cowley, Charles Fenton, Carlos Baker and others. It takes a face-to-face meeting, I think, to box the compass—to at least determine True North—the waters are tricky.

St. John: Did Y.K. discover any other geniuses during that one bel epoch of Chicago letters?

Smith: Y.K. got interested in one or two people, including a
            painter (Claud Buck) but none in the genius category.

St. John: Now about your father, I suppose he may have had the
            greatest influence of all on Hemingway.

Smith: I'm not even sure that they met, and if they did it was in the
            most casual way.

St. John: That doesn't bother me too much. Your father's great
            erudition, all the languages he knew, his translation of the
            Iliad from the original Greek into heroic verse, his antago-
            nism to the dogmas of Victorianism and now—above all—
            this book of his basic philosophy, *Birth of the Gospel.* All
            this makes me certain he must have had a strong indirect
            effect upon Hemingway. It may even be that only in an
            indirect way, that is, crystallized through the Smith chil-
            dren, could your father's influence have had its pure sublim-
            inal impact on young Hemingway.

Smith: Maybe, maybe, but let the record show that you said it—
            I didn't.

St. John: Well, in your father's book, the theme he chose was
            Goethe's phrase, "the deepest can be said in symbols only"
            —I remember Camus said that too—and he concluded the
            book by saying that man was prone to symbolize and then
            mistake the sign for the signified. According to Y.K., your
            father spent his life tyring to show that the refinements of
            Hebrew thought had been transformed into "the vulgar
            Christianity of today through the prolonged literalness of
            western interpretation." In his book, I notice, Dr. Smith
            even alluded to the same quotation from Ecclesiastes that
            Hem used to set the theme of *The Sun Also Rises* and to
            derive its name.

Smith: It's interesting, but I don't know how far you can go
            down that road.

St. John: Ok. Perhaps there is no direct connection, but in "Blow,"
            you, Bill, ask Nick (Hem) if he had read the *Forest Lovers*
            and Hem says yes, that was where they went to bed every
            night with a naked sword on edge between them; Hem
            didn't think this was practical because the lovers could roll
            over easily enough if the sword went flat. At which point,
            you said, "It's a symbol." Obviously that made a sufficient
            impression on Hem to remember and repeat as he had other
            things you'd said. And the symbol reference did come from

your father one way or another. Dr. Smith was after all a profound, one might say, a professional expert on symbolism. It seems to me that your father's preoccupation with the value of allegory as opposed to literal-minded fundamentalism must have spilled into your own philosophy and that you in turn exposed this kind of thinking to Hemingway.

Smith: Maybe, but this is a bit too involved for my memory patterns.

St. John: For anybody's I guess, after half a century. Still, it wasn't just the symbolism, although I don't know what could be more valuable to an embryo writer—particularly in the boondocks of Horton Bay, Michigan. Beyond that, surely it was a miracle that Hemingway was born to a Victorian-Calvinist family against which he would be compelled to rebel (this being the probable reason he was placed on earth) at the same time that he would be supplied with the kind of sceptical environment that the Smith family could provide.

Smith: Frankly, were I in your place I would not go off the deep end re the role of the Smiths in shaping the old master. He would have made it big no matter what.

St. John: I'm sure he would; the poetry was there, and the intelligence and the natural rebeliousness, but the direction his art took was certainly affected by the environment, and the Smiths were a handy gadget to have around—I mean they were unquestionably a large and sophisticated part of the environment in those important early years. . . . By the way, where did you pick up that phrase, the old master? Did you use it on Hem in the old Horton Bay days?

Smith: Hardly. He wasn't the old master then, not quite. In those days and for some time after we had a lot of special expressions for each other. Hem was "the massive woodsman" and would even sign himself that way sometimes—you saw it on one of the snapshots. Wemedge was the term both of us used most, of course, and the name he used in "Blow." Hem called me "Jazzer," "Boid" or even "Avis" and there was one period when I was the "Master Biologist" to Hem because I earned $200 a year from a student assistantship at the University of Missouri for chloroforming frogs, birds and such things.

St. John: Did you ever call Hem the "old master" or is that just some-
            thing you say now in retrospect?
Smith: No. We called Hem the "old master" in the early Key West
            days around the time he was becoming famous for *A Fare-
            well To Arms*. Dos Passos is the one who first used it, and
            of course he was a little older than Hem and had become
            famous earlier; so there was a certain irony in it. I first
            heard Dos call Hem that on a boat we both took to Key
            West out of New York on the way down to see Hem.
St. John: This was after the Michigan and Paris days of course?
Smith: Yes. After Paris and Pamplona. It was during this period
            that Dos met my sister Kate at Hem's Key West house.
St. John: Did Kate work in advertising as her prototype Lulie did in
            Dos' satire on Hem, *Chosen Country*?
Smith: Yes, for several years in Chicago.
St. John: I am puzzled by the Dos Passos image of young Heming-
            way in *Chosen Country*, which he must have gotten, nat-
            urally, from your sister, Kate. It is often said that fame
            spoiled Hem but I think Dos is the first to give the impres-
            sion that Hem was a congenital louse from the start. For
            example, would young Hemingway have baited a "furriner"
            as he is pictured doing in the book?
Smith: It is true that Hem and I both disliked some of the very well-
            heeled Jewish people who summered at Charlevoix, Michi-
            gan. Still, I think Hem got much more down on Dos than
            circumstances warranted.[1]
St. John: Dos Passos made Hem (or Georgie, as he called Ernie in
            the book) the villain of the shooting incident in *Chosen
            Country*. He has the sheriff catching Hem and the others
            and throwing them into jail for shooting out the lights in
            Boyne City, which Dos called Calumet City.
Smith: No one went to jail. What I remember about the shooting
            was the expression on the cop's face when he caught up to
            our car. He came tearing alongside us right after we'd
            engaged in some target shooting. He'd caught us practically
            red-handed, but then we stopped and he saw us, all bearded
            and tough-looking and carrying guns. "You guys don't
            happen to know anything about the shooting back there?"
            he said. We said we didn't and he smiled gratefully and
            drove off.
St. John: Did you young men actually shoot out some lights?

Smith:	Certainly not.
St. John:	Oh?
Smith:	The fact is they were insulators.
St. John:	You and Hem got together after the war obviously, but then he got married to Hadley in 1921 and went to Paris. Did you see him in Europe then?
Smith:	No. It was later, after he quit his newspaper job in 1923 and began devoting full time to creative writing. It was in 1925 that I went to see him in Paris; there was a job possibility that Hem had arranged, and when that fell through I went with him and Hadley and some others to the fiesta in Pamplona.
St. John:	And before the fiesta you went fishing with Hem in Burguete, as in *The Sun Also Rises*?
Smith:	Yes. I remember that country very well.
St. John:	Harold Loeb says in his memoir, *The Way It Was*, that the fishing was terrible, not wonderful as described in *The Sun*.
Smith:	That may be; it's hard to separate one fishing expedition from another after 40 years, but the fact is Hem had fished in Burguete the year before and it was perfectly reasonable for him to weave these experiences together in writing a piece of fiction.
St. John:	Bill, I know you have said Donald Ogden Stewart shared the "Bill" role with you in *The Sun*, but it seems to me the Burguete parts of that book are one hundred per cent you.
Smith:	We fished along the Irati all right. That certainly wasn't fiction. Don Stewart, of course, had been in Spain with Hem in 1924 as well as in 1925 when I was along.
St. John:	That expression of Bill's about "utilizing" the whiskey etcetera—it seemed typical somehow of the wonderfully natural banter in *The Sun*; and the odd thing is it stands up today. Was there any real basis for that talk or was Hemingway simply weaving again?
Smith:	You can get pretty silly when you're tight. Yes, I actually remember using that word, utilize, and I remember it catching on somehow, even with the Englishman. We all have our moments I guess.
St. John:	There was another expression that I liked—after Bill and Jake had seen a great grove of trees. "This is country," Bill said. That was all and that was enough. Does it come back to you?

Bill Smith, Horton Bay, Michigan, 1920. *Collection of William B. Smith.*

Smith: I probably referred to the area around Burguete and
            Roncesvalles, of Roland and Oliver fame, where we tramped
            and fished; very impressive country, and steeped in history.[2]

St. John: In rereading *The Sun*, I noticed some of Bill's expressions—
            "Let us rejoice in our blessings ... Let us utilize the fowls of
            the air ... Let us utilize the produce of the vine ... Will you
            utilize a little brother? Remember the woods were God's
            first temple ... Let us kneel, etc. etc." The biblical influence
            seemed pretty strong—where did all this come from—your
            fundamentalist Grandfather Charles? or your own sceptical
            but highly biblical father? It made a good blend for Hem-
            ingway it seems.

Smith: Your guess is as good as mine. As I have said—and I must
            insist on this—Hemingway was not a diarist; he was an
            artist.

St. John: You know that Burguete part in *The Sun* reminds me a good
            deal of "Blow." The short story came out in 1925, a year
            before *Sun*, so I suppose it was a kind of dry run for the
            novel.

Smith: Well, there was the drinking of course.

St. John: Yes, and the baseball and the fishing and the literary talk—
            this time about irony instead of symbolism—but it seems to
            me the most telling similarity of all was the way in which
            Bill brings up the subject of a special woman in practically
            the same way in both the story and the novel.

Smith: I haven't read the material as recently as you have, ob-
            viously.

St. John: Well, in "Blow," Bill says "You were very wise, Wemedge
            ... to bust up that Marge business." And in *Sun*, Bill asks,
            "What about this Brett business?"

Smith: Looking back, I suppose these matters were interferences of
            one kind or another. You'll remember how I explained
            Bill's remark that marriage bitches things—women and
            marriage interfere with male pursuits. Simple as that.

St. John: That gets us back to your part in evolving the Hemingway
            mystique, that is, the necessity of retaining the integrity of a
            man's world, not to be infringed by women, a world in
            which men were the only good companions—and yet, and
            yet, there being a place for women in man's life because one
            couldn't carry this man's world too far. I think Hem was

always clever about setting the limits on these things, that
faggot remark of his, etc.

Smith: You keep coming back to my involvement in the code. I
don't know how many times I have to say this. It was pretty
much all Hemingway and it certainly wasn't all me, in any
case. While we're on the subject of Smiths incidentally,
there is another Smith, Dorman-Smith, the British officer
friend of Hem's who was not without his influence on the
old master. He was Buckley of course in the original *in our
time*.

St. John: Yes, I agree, but he didn't grow up with Hem. Now about
Pamplona, after the fishing in Burguete, I've seen a couple
of pictures of you in the bull ring there.   In one shot, I
remember, you are being hotly pursued by a bull.

Smith: That was in a morning show and these were not really very
much. The "bulls" mostly consisted of cows, calves and old
bulls with padded horns.   By the end of the morning,
though, a lot of the padding had been worn off.   In one of
these little shows you'll recall Don Stewart was slightly injured.

After the fiesta in Pamplona, Hem and his wife stayed in Spain and
Bill went to Paris for a short time before returning to the States. While
in Paris, he received a letter from Hem dated July 27, 1925 and addressed to "Boid." No Hemingway letter may be reproduced verbatim,
but in the letter Hem gave some characteristically careful instructions
on how his mail should be handled while he was in Spain and mentioned he was expecting to hear from "Brumby" (his Red Cross friend,
Ted Brumback), "Liveright" (Horace Liveright, who was about to
bring out Hem's first American book, the short story collection, *In
Our Time*), "The Star" (*The Toronto Star* for which he had worked
until late in 1923), "Bank statements" etc. Hemingway said he'd been
having a swell time and that he'd been tight only once. He didn't mention *The Sun Also Rises* by name, since the title didn't come until much
later, but it was obvious he was working on that novel when he told
Bill that since leaving Pamplona he'd averaged 1,200 words a day and
that some of it might be bloody good. He'd gotten a lot of swell stuff
on the trip, he said, adding that the story was fairly funny and that he
had Ford Madox Ford in it as Braddocks. Ford went well as Braddocks, he said. The jacket for *in our time* had arrived from Liveright
and it looked swell. While in Spain he was interspersing writing with

going to the bullfights and was enjoying the matador Niño de la Palma very much. Palma, who was to serve as the model for the bullfighter, Romero, so dear to Lady Brett in *The Sun*, had knocked Madrid off its feet. Villalta had been good too; Hemingway was referring to the matador Nicanor Villalta after whom he had named his first child, John Hadley Nicanor Hemingway, otherwise known as Bumby. There was a swell beach where Hemingway was staying, he told Bill, and the water was as warm as you know what. He told Bill about a job possibility that he might look into and said he and Hadley expected to start back to Paris on August 2 and that it would be jake to forward mail before noon of the 31st. Hem concluded with a request that greetings be given his two Paris publishers, Bill Bird and Robert McAlmon, to Harold Loeb, to Paul Fisher and to Don Stewart. He signed the letter E. Miller, Miller his middle name. After a short postscript he signed off simply as Miller.

Earlier that July, the morning after the famous fiesta in Pamplona had ended, Hemingway had written a brief note directly to Loeb saying he had been terribly tight and nasty to him on the last night of the fiesta and that he wished he could wipe out all the meanness but that he supposed he couldn't. In any case he was terribly ashamed of the way he had acted and the stinking unjust, uncalled-for things he had said. Loeb had been mollified by the apology—until *The Sun Also Rises* came out the following year, in 1926.

St. John: I notice Hem told you he was using Ford Madox Ford in *The Sun*. Did he keep you informed on your own roles in his fiction?

Smith: No. No mention was ever made of that, and there was no need to as far as I was concerned.

St. John: What about *The Sun*, was it your favorite Hemingway work?

Smith: Not really. My favorites were *A Farewell to Arms* and *For Whom The Bell Tolls*.

St. John: Do you think Hem ever created a single character out of sheer fantasy?

Smith: I doubt if Hem ever used fantasy alone, or that any artist does for that matter, but he did use it to dress up and underscore people and places and events.

After his trip to Paris in 1925, Smith tried his own hand at writing short stories, but met with only modest success. He finally went to work for Harold Loeb as an agricultural writer in the National Survey of Potential Product Capacity. Then he went into federal service as a writer for various branches of the government and helped carry on the fight for the minimum wage and hour law. He is credited with writing some of Harry Truman's hardest hitting labor speeches.

While in his mid-thirties, he was married to Marion Freeman, who had worked for Loeb and whose brother, Joseph Freeman, had held great hopes for Hem as a proletarian writer in the late thirties during the time of the Spanish Civil War. There were no children.

St. John: You and Hem both liked words and made them work for you.
Smith: Yes. But Hemingway wrote the words for himself. I couldn't get anywhere until I started working for somebody else. A slight difference.

NOTES

1 Smith wound up marrying a Jew, and Hemingway's whole life, of course, belies the anti-Semitism sometimes charged against *The Sun Also Rises*. The anti-Semitism of the book was the anti-Semitism of the times and public reaction has tended to fluctuate. The offending phrases from the original book, for example, were expunged from a Bantam reprint of 1949 and then put back in again by Bantam in 1954.
2 I looked this up and Smith as usual was absolutely right. Roland and Oliver were paladins of Charlemagne, and Roland was particularly noted as a kind of Christian Theseus against the Saracens. Roland was killed at Roncesvalles in 778 after slaying 100,000 infidels.

Interview with
Donald Ogden Stewart

IN Ernest Hemingway's, *The Sun Also Rises*, the Bill Gorton who fished and drank and philosophized about literature and life with Jake Barnes, was undoubtedly Hemingway's boyhood friend, Bill Smith. But this was only part of that character. The other part, the flamboyant, wise-cracking Bill Gorton of Paris and Pamplona was unquestionably Donald Ogden Stewart, now 76 and living a pleasant expatriate life amid a houseful of art treasures in Hampstead, England, just inside of London.

No one doubts Stewart's association with the role of Bill Gorton, least of all Stewart himself (although he feels his role as well as his body has diminished over the years), but if there *were* any doubts they would be immediately dispelled upon meeting him, for the years that have stooped Stewart and frazzled his noggin have done nothing to slow his brain nor put a crimp into his compulsion for wise-cracks:

"I have to see the dentist today. You can come when I get back. You don't quite believe me? Okay, I'll show you a cavity."

"If this dreary story of my life is boring you all you have to do is yawn."

"Now that you've started coming around, St. John, I've had a burglar alarm installed. Would you like to have a burglar?"

They're not all boffolas, to be sure, and they may be irrelevant in

---

See Donald Ogden Stewart's "Recollections of Fitzgerald and Hemingway" in Matthew J. Bruccoli and C. E. Frazer Clark, Jr., eds., *Fitzgerald/Hemingway Annual 1971* (Washington: NCR/Microcard Editions, 1971), pp. 177–88.

today's naughty world, but the timing is good. Once I laughed out loud and Don became suddenly serious. "Thank you very much," he said.

"What?"

"The laugh. They don't make audiences like that anymore. In the old days I didn't have to worry. I remember my secretary in Hollywood—it was in her contract that she had to laugh at my jokes."

In *The Sun Also Rises*, Hemingway wrote, "Bill Gorton arrived, put up a couple of days at the flat [in Paris] and went off to Vienna. He was very cheerful and said the States were wonderful. New York was wonderful. . . . Bill was very happy. He had made a lot of money on his last book, and was going to make a lot more. We had a good time while he was in Paris, and then he went off to Vienna. . . . He was coming back in three weeks and we would leave for Spain to get in some fishing and go to the fiesta in Pamplona. He wrote that Vienna was wonderful. Then a card from Budapest: " 'Jake, Budapest is wonderful.' "

That sounded like Don all these many years later and besides, he *had* been in Budapest and Vienna prior to setting off for Pamplona with Hemingway, and his books *had* been best-sellers and he *was* destined to make a lot more money, more money than Hemingway could have dreamed of then when Hemingway was 27 and Stewart was 32. Beyond all that, the other model for Bill Gorton (Bill Smith) had not been to Budapest and Vienna before the bull fights in Pamplona, had written no books prior to that time and he was and is a relatively introspective, shy man of modest income.

Don, like Bill Smith, had been out of the public eye so long by the time that I saw him (1969) that most people thought him dead, and he was dead, perhaps, literarily speaking. If F. Scott Fitzgerald, Don's Hollywood friend, had been the high priest of the jazz age, and Hemingway its Ecclesiastian prophet, then Stewart was its widely acclaimed court jester. He'd made it big while Hemingway was a muttering nobody in Paris. He'd written a series of satirical best-sellers, and Hemingway himself had called Don one of the great white hopes of literature. Then Stewart had said goodbye to that kind of writing in 1930 and begun earning really important money in Hollywood. Thereafter, except for credits in movie titles and one Oscar for the scenario of *The Philadelphia Story* and, a bit later some notoriety (but not much) for association with leftish causes, Stewart dropped pretty much from the public eye. And when he left Hollywood during the Joe McCarthy era rather than "name names" (as some of his friends had) his burial as a public figure seemed complete. As a creative writer he's been dead for

40 years. Fitzgerald had "died" too before his actual death, but now, in death, Fitzgerald was very much alive, and Hemingway in death was very much alive; and Stewart, who was very much alive, was very much dead. So it might seem from afar perhaps, but on this clear, dry, rather pleasantly cool day in the middle of a London winter, Stewart seemed anything but dead to me.

We got into Hemingway then, and it was typical of thoughtful old Don that he should launch the subject without undue coaxing from me. What sprang first to Don's mind were his memories of the vivid Pamplona days that formed the background for *The Sun Also Rises*.

"There were two trips to Pamplona that I went on," Don said, "one in 1924, the other in 1925. The second was the one usually thought of as the model for *The Sun*. The first is the one I remember with the most pleasure. It was a masculine time. Things were great. Pamplona was ours. No one else had discovered it. I have nothing but the most satisfying memories of that trip. It was vintage Hemingway. It was a happy time. And then the lovers came along. On that second trip Duff Twysden and Harold Loeb were busily playing their roles as Brett Ashley and Robert Cohn, and Pat Guthrie was there as Mike Campbell. It wasn't just that a woman was along. Hem's wife, Hadley, and Sally, Bill Bird's wife, were with us on the first trip. It wasn't that. But by the second trip everything had changed somehow. Harold was having this affair with Duff; Duff was supposedly engaged to Pat and there seemed to be something between Hem and Duff. I don't mean physically, but something. Both Bill Smith and I noticed it. By the second trip, the establishment had caught up with the frontier. My God even the American ambassador was there in a big car. Things got cluttered and ordinary. I remember lining up with Pat Guthrie in front of a whore house and waiting an hour or so and then the whole thing being over in five minutes.

St. John: Don't you think, Don, in all fairness, that part of the disillusion of the second trip was simply that it was second.

Stewart: Some of that of course. But it was more than that. The lovers and their tensions dominated the second trip. It was good for the book of course, but not for the people.

On the first trip, in 1924, Pamplona was a staked-out place, with the Hemingway band the annointed blood brothers of the native revelers. Don remembered the wine slobbering down their faces as they tried to drink from the bladders in approved Spanish style. And he remembered the crowded, happy, swirling, dancing, friendly streets. There

Statue of Hemingway at Pamplona. *Collection of Leah Rice Koontz.*

was a sense of total fiesta; there was no other emotion. Even the pain that Don suffered when a bull broke three of his ribs that first year was remembered as a kind of honorable war wound sustained on behalf of Hemingway's tight little band.

Had Don ever run with the actual fighting bulls I wondered?

Stewart: Me? Let me get one thing straight. I'm a practicing coward. You had to be insane to run with those bulls. I mean they were right there behind those kids and all they had to protect themselves was the prescribed rolled-up newspaper. No. I wasn't stupid. The only reason I got into the ring at all was because Hemingway shamed me into it. The wives were there, don't you see, that was the thing. Sally and Hadley, people like that. What could I do? I was too cowardly not to go into the ring, although the wine helped some. It would have taken more guts to ignore Hem's example the way Dos Passos did. It didn't bother him at all. Dos was somewhere else most of the time and was probably in no need to prove the power of his cojones. Old Dos came around just once, as I recall; that was enough. You know this little alley they have around the inside of the bull ring. There are doors in it and it is low enough for a man to vault behind if the bull comes at you. Well, this one time, Dos saw the bull coming toward his side of the ring so he prudently got into the alley behind the barrier. The funny thing is the bull jumped the barrier outside of Dos's range of view and came up behind him just as he was feeling nice and secure. He got the hell out of there fast and I don't recall seeing him around the plaza anymore that fiesta. I gather from his own memoirs that he was proving his manhood during those fiesta days in a way rather more basic than getting into the bull ring.

St. John: I hear you busted those ribs in 1924 because of your misunderstanding of the veronica. How did that Stewart veronica go exactly?

Stewart: I thought you were supposed to stand there gracefully with the cape in front of your body and then move it tragically to one side, passing the bull away from you. Actually you were supposed to hold the cape to one side and stand there dauntlessly as he went past, your only movement being to lift the cape to let the bull pass under it. I compounded my error by waiting until the bull was an inch away; by that time his charge was unalterably established, and he bowled me ass over teakettle. Strangely enough—this made me angry instead of scared and so I got up and did the whole thing over again with the same results, except that this time my ribs were broken. That ended my bullfighting days forever, and no one could lure me back into the ring when *The Sun* crowd strutted their stuff the following year. Still and all, I became a kind of folk hero to the Spaniards and My God the story was carried in wildly distorted form in the Chicago and Toronto papers. They had me gored. Poor Hemingway had nothing to do with these reports; they must have come from Bird or McAlmon or Dos Passos. The next year it was Harold Loeb who took my place as a Spanish folk hero. The main difference between my performance and Harold's, both witnessed by Hem, is that Harold tended to make fun of the experience. I didn't have the nerve to, frankly. But Harold didn't care who knew how he felt and he didn't care for the cruelty to the horses, as neither did I. What infuriated Hem most was Harold's unpardonable crime of being bored with the bullfighting and of abandoning the brave company of men (at Burguete) to chase after Duff. Women were very important in Hem's code but it was a subdivision kind of thing that must not impinge on the solidarity of comradeship. Hem knew perfectly well why Harold had not met him for fishing at Burguete. These were all great sins of Harold's and help explain the book I suppose. I see Harold often nowadays when he comes to London on his way to South Africa and I have been trying to interest him in another assault on Pamplona, but he doesn't seem to be interested. It still bores him.

St. John: Those distorted accounts, as you call the Chicago newspaper stories, had you offering to blow smoke rings in the bull's eyes as you veronica-ed him past you.

Stewart: I hate to spoil that. It sounds like me, but I must plead not guilty.

St. John: The next year, 1925, when *The Sun* crowd arrived at Pamplona for the fiesta, I gather that Pat Guthrie joined you on the side-lines rather than participate in the morning fights with Harold Loeb, Bill Smith and Hemingway?

Stewart: That's right. Old Pat would have been too tight for that kind of thing. Incidentally, he was a heavy drinker all right, but not the all-around detestable louse who was pictured as Mike Campbell in *The Sun*. But it was true enough that he resented the presence of Harold Loeb as a rival for Duff, although it was equally true that Harold had helped plan the trip in the first place while Guthrie had dragged along later as a kind of bump on the log of Lady Duff Twysden.

St. John: From *The Sun*, I gathered that Pat was quite a man, liked by everybody except Harold despite his drunkeness, and yet there is a possibility raised by the Carlos Baker biography that Guthrie may have been some kind of latent homosexual, or reformed homosexual. This is suggested in an early, discarded treatment of Mike Campbell in *The Sun*, Baker says, and since so much of the book is probably roman à clef, consideration must be given, I would think, to the possibility that Guthrie was in fact a fairy—although not necessarily, since it is also provable that Hem inserted much fiction among his factualities. Actually, it is difficult for me to believe that Guthrie was homosexual for the simple reason that Harold Loeb, given the hostility he had for Pat, could scarcely have concealed a suspicion of this kind. All's fair in love etc. Furthermore, you told me Pat had lined up with you in front of one of those Pamplona whore houses and that seems an odd place to find a fairy.

Stewart: I missed that in Baker, and maybe it was true; it could have been another member of our gang who was with me at the whore house. These details get a bit fuzzy you know. I don't know. You can't always tell about homos. Pat seemed like a nice enough fellow for a drunk. Of course I don't know why he was doing all that drinking.

St. John: So he could have been queer but you have no evidence of same?

Stewart: Right.

St. John: I harp on the subject because I had always thought the fairies in *The Sun* were Duff's (Brett's) friends and were following her around. But if the man she was with was a fruit that would alter matters a bit; perhaps they were following Pat-Mike around. If this was so, then Hem did a lot more inventing than is generally imagined, and was not just reporting as so many people believe.

Stewart: I really don't know. I liked Duff. She was really quite a dish for a fairy to have, and yet it happens all the time. And she did pop off with Harold at St. Jean-de-Luz the minute old Pat's back was turned. But then if she were a nymph that wouldn't prove anything anyway. The fact is I really don't know.

St. John: Did Pat and Duff ever pay you back the money you lent for their hotel bill after the 1925 fiesta?

Stewart: Of course not. The only one who ever paid you back in those days was Hemingway. I helped finance his way out of Pamplona that year and he paid back every cent.

St. John: Getting back to bullfighting for a moment, I notice that the biographer Charles Fenton says Hem was much impressed with your early work as a satirist, particularly in the success of *Mr. and Mrs. Haddock Abroad*, and that he submitted a humorous account of bullfighting to you for publication in *Vanity Fair*, but that you rejected it. Is that true?

Stewart: No. I was in no position to reject anything at the time. I was no longer a staff member, and I wouldn't have rejected a piece of his anyway. I was submitting pieces to *Vanity Fair* myself at the time and might have suggested he do the same. No, that piece of his had to do with a ridiculous item that appeared in the *Chicago Tribune* in which it was claimed that Hem and I had been gored in an actual bull fight. That account for *Vanity Fair* was never published. Besides the *Vanity Fair* piece, Hem also wrote a letter of explanation to the *Toronto Star Weekly* since they had gotten the facts wrong too.

St. John: Oh yes, that is the so-called boastful letter that Carlos Baker talks about in his biography of Hemingway. Baker is safe in a way because an executive of the *Toronto Star*, W. L. McGeary, told me the letter was tossed out many years ago —they didn't know their reporter "Hemmy" was scheduled for fame. However, a copy of the story based on the letter reveals no boasting on Hemingway's part. Hem explained that he had failed to pass the bull and that when it hit him he seized its padded horns, not knowing what else to do, much as Harold Loeb did the following year. I remember Hemingway touched on these amateur fights in *Death in the Afternoon* and, far from boasting about his prowess, said the only thing dangerous about the whole affair was that many Spaniards had been in danger of laughing themselves to death at his clumsiness.

Stewart: I think people on the outside got the impression we were performing at a regular bull fight and that everyone in town turned out to see us; the fact is we were only two or three among a melee of 300 or so would-be bullfighters.

St. John: Maybe so, but you were news just the same and we can't forget that news was Hemingway's business; at least it had been the year before right there in Pamplona when he wrote up his first bull fight for the *Toronto Star Weekly* in 1923. By the way, let me clear up one thing—what were those bulls really like? I mean the ones you amateurs faced.

Stewart: They were bull enough for me, don't you see. I don't remember noticing the usual details. I was too busy looking at the other end. I thought of them as bulls and they charged like bulls, and of course one of them was mean enough to bust my ribs. I think Harold and others who demean these critters leave the impression they were little more than moo cows waiting to be milked. The fact is they were what the Spaniards call fighting cows or calves bred for this very purpose and, balls or no balls, they were mean as hell.

I asked Don if Hem's lack of a college education showed in the company of such educated people as himself, a Yale Skull and Bones man, Harold Loeb, a Princeton graduate, and John Dos Passos of Harvard.

"No, not at all," Don said. "He was far better read than the rest of us."

St. John: Tell me, what did you think of Duff Twysden?

Stewart: Duff was a fine person and she was enormously attractive to look at or to be with. She had a kind of style sense that allowed her to wear with dignity and chic almost anything— I mean a man's felt hat, or a matador's hat, maybe even a lamp shade—and bring dignity and charm to whatever she wore.

We talked then about A. E. Hotchner's book, *Papa Hemingway*, and it developed that Don had turned each page very warily, expecting to find himself cut up and bleeding. When Don noticed how paranoid Hem had become toward the end of his life, he began to wonder if perhaps some of these same symptoms had not been exhibited as far back as the early days in Pamplona. Hotchner had noted that Hemingway had been overly conscious of F.B.I. men lurking in the background as early as 1948, or 13 years before his death. And now Don wondered if some of Hem's lifelong little backward glances, as in his shadow boxing for example, might not have been the vanguards of the demons that plagued his end.

St. John: In Baker's biography, I notice he talks about Hemingway's
            "tirades" against you. Weren't you one of the chosen few
            who was never attacked by Hemingway?
Stewart: That's true. No tirades, either publicly or privately, aside
            from the Hollywood crack at me [on page 498, *Death in the
            Afternoon*; Stewart's identity was hidden behind the initials
            R.S. On the same page, Bill Smith is coded under the ini-
            tials W.G. which are the same as those of *The Sun's* Bill
            Gorton]. The only so-called blast I can recall occurred in a
            letter to Dos Passos, but this was also about my going
            Hollywood, and as I have told you, I agree with him com-
            pletely on that. I had written this early humor that Hem
            liked and then done the plays in New York, both wrote and
            acted in them, and did a musical for Joe Cook too. I guess
            Hem had visions of me writing the great American play.
            Writing was all he thought about in those days; he worked
            hard, I have to admit it. And here I was going off to Holly-
            wood and consorting with such gentry as Jock Whitney and
            making hundreds of thousands of dollars. It looked like a
            sell-out to Hem and I guess it was. I simply didn't know
            any better in those days. I had been trained to worship
            security and to consider society life in a rather noble light.
            This phase of my life ended eventually, but I didn't fit the
            the artist image. I was too successful, and it was perfectly
            natural for Hem to be disgusted with me.
St. John: But he never attacked you.
Stewart: That's true, but he was still a dangerous friend to have.

As an example of this dangerous element in Hem's character, Don cited an episode involving Dorothy Parker that occurred during a dinner in Paris in 1926, the year *The Sun* came out. Mrs. Parker was not present. Hem read a poem he had written about Mrs. Parker that rankled in Don's mind still, these many years later, even though he had long since forgotten Hem's motive or what the poem was about.

Stewart: There was just this mean streak in him. There's no doubt
            about it. It began to assert itself in 1925 when the critical
            acclaim started snow-balling. He hadn't acquired an audi-
            ence yet and had made no money, but those little Paris

books of his, and his short stories and his consistently great reporting had begun to create a critical ground swell. You were not to disagree with the Master in any way from then on. But in the early years, particularly during that first trip to Pamplona in 1924, he was a most charming wonderful man and I have nothing but the most pleasant memories of him from that period.

St. John: This character defect that you mention—the danger it posed for his friends—wasn't this a kind of force of nature to be accepted, the price you paid for genius?

Stewart: I suppose so. The trade works out very well for the public, which has the protection of distance, but with friends there is a difference. The mean streak was a booby trap kind of thing. There's no explaining it particularly, it was just part of his character along with the rest of him. It wasn't any dark secret known to a few. People talked about it. To look at it in a more charitable way, if Hem had been just plain mean you wouldn't have noticed it. But he wasn't mean; he was charismatic; and it was for this very reason that the mean streak startled you so when it came to the surface. The important thing to remember is that he didn't have to have a reason to be mean. It was more of a mood thing. The fact is it could be whimsical or simply inexplicable as in the case of that nasty scatological poem about Dorothy Parker. You wonder why he bothered to compose that damn poem, what he had against her, whether she had panned him in *The New Yorker* or whether he'd heard something she'd said about him. It was none of those things in my opinion. I think he wrote that damn poem and read it to his friends simply to be entertaining—to show how clever he was. I can at least say one thing. I told him off that time. No one else did. Not Archy [McLeish] or anybody else. I've always been known as the easy guy, everybody's Uncle Don, but I did tell him off that time, and of course you didn't do that to Ernest. This was in 1926, probably a little while before *The Sun* came out, late that year; he was already a bit of a master, as I have said. But the odd thing is he took my blast without a murmur, which is some kind of record I suppose. Nevertheless I don't think our friendship was ever quite the same. I don't mean we ceased to be friends; we were always technical friends; but it was a different kind of friendship after that. You know everybody talks about the Christmas checks I gave Ernest—as if this meant I had spotted his genius and was backing my hunch. It wasn't that way at all. Of course I admired Ernest's work and helped him get published, but the reason I gave him the money was simply that I liked him—and Hadley— very much—and I had the money and he didn't. After the Parker incident we saw each other occasionally under very pleasant circumstances. Both our wives were pregnant, my first, his second, when we sailed back to America together in 1931, and we had a jolly time with Jane Mason. Later still I saw him at the Writer's Conference in 1937 and we were glad to see each other. After that there wasn't much interchange, and, frankly, when I read the Hotchner book with all its blasts at former friends, I hardly expected to be spared the same fate. I suppose Bill Smith and I were two of the very few who were not dressed down by old Papa. The closest he ever came to letting me have it publicly was when he took that crack at me in *Death in the Afternoon* for going Hollywood, but even this jab as I have said, was hidden under some phony initials. Anyway I deserved it.

St. John: I find it odd that Hem's attack on Mrs. Parker made such a strong impression on you, Don, since it didn't seem to have any effect upon her. Alexander Woolcott described Mrs. Parker as being almost idolatrous toward Hemingway; in fact, he said her reverence was so pronounced that her reviews of his work sounded schoolgirlish and unprofessional. This was after the Hemingway blast at her which you describe and it seems to me she listed Hem as her favorite author as late as the mid-30's.

Stewart: I doubt Dorothy ever heard about Hemingway's poem. Her friends would have kept it from her.

St. John: Another thing that surprises me, Don, is that Hemingway's treatment of Harold Loeb in *The Sun* did not strike you as forcefully as his attack on Dorothy Parker, which enfuriated you so. It does seem trivial by comparison with what Hem did to Harold. An unpublished poem read to a tiny group of people is one thing, but Harold had his brains knocked out in a classic.

Stewart: It's hard to say, really, why some things hit you and others don't. For one thing, I was a kind of writing colleague of

Mrs. Parker. She was my friend. Harold was Hem's friend. It's hard to say. I was very fond of Dorothy, who was a Jew of course, as was Harold; but I have no doubt that I was really basically anti-Semitic in those days, as probably also was Hemingway. People had Jewish friends who, *mirabile dictu*, were nice people. I liked Harold all right, but undoubtedly I had a patronizing attitude to him and I don't find the anti-Semitism in *The Sun*, certainly as it may apply to me in the role of Bill Gorton, as essentially untrue.[1] The story was a true reflection of affairs, although it pains me to admit it now. Still, as Thomas Wolfe said in a letter to me about a thousand years ago, I am only saying what most everybody else would say if they spoke the truth. Not that any of this was the kind of deep-seated thing that helped give rise to Nazism, but it was there as a form of social snobbishness, something that people simply took for granted. In fairness to me, please you will have to mark down that I renounced all this claptrap a long time ago, that I later headed the anti-Nazi League in California and that I, like that other Bill Gorton anti-Semite, Bill Smith, married a Jew. But back in *The Sun* days I suppose I was anti-Semitic enough to have been cruel to Harold, perhaps not to his face, but even worse behind his back, since he remembers me with kindness. It's odd what you remember. I remember Harold was always coming out of barber shops and somehow went against my grain at the time. Furthermore he had the effontery to bed down a fine, noble Christian lady, namely Duff Twysden, and this was certainly a dastardly thing to do. Please make it clear which Don Stewart is talking. I don't claim any kinship today with that bibulous bastard of those dear dead days so long ago.

Aside from the Dorothy Parker incident, Don looked upon Hemingway's assault on Sherwood Anderson in *Torrents of Spring* as a prime example of Hemingway's mean streak. It was "a mean bitter book," he felt, which had been used to attack a man who had given Hem help when he most needed it. Don didn't believe in cruel parodies, only funny ones, and in any case not when they were directed at friends. Here it seemed was a clear line between the Stewart values and the Hemingway values: to Don, friendship was first and literature second; to Hem it was the other way around. Which may explain, perhaps, why one lives though dead and why one is dead though he lives; why one had a great audience and few real friends; and why the other has a host of friends and no real audience.

St. John: Don, do you think *The Sun Also Rises* will endure?

Stewart: At the time it came out it didn't make too much of an impression on me, certainly not as an artistic work of genius. I was surprised, really, at all the commotion it stirred up. It was so absolutely accurate that it seemed little more than a skillfully done travelogue. What a reporter, I said to myself. That's the way it really was—except of course for the matador getting beaten up by Loeb, which is to say, Cohn, and Hemingway getting together with Duff. He had to make some of it up, I thought, otherwise it wouldn't have been a novel.

St. John: What do you think of *The Sun* today?

Stewart: Disappointed I'm afraid. I read this copy you sent me a couple of days ago; it was my first rereading in 44 years. I had thought of my own part in rather inflated terms, but when I reread the book it seemed to me that the Bill Gorton part had shrunken considerably.

St. John: But don't you think the book rings true today?

Stewart: No, I don't. I can't say that I rank it as a classic, if that's what you're trying to get me to say. Of course you don't know how prejudiced you are in a matter such as this. However I simply do not think the book stands up.

St. John: And *Farewell to Arms?*

Stewart: That one was a big improvement; of course I admired Hem's short stories very much, perhaps better than anything else. I guess it was the stories that first attracted me to Hem as a writer.

St. John: That reminds me—it was you, wasn't it, who carried "Big Two-Hearted River" to Boni and Liveright and edited out Nick's inner monologue at Hemingway's request? That must have given you a twinge, I suppose, since the part you cut out had Hemingway calling you one of our literary hopefuls.

Stewart: Yes, I did the legwork for Hem since he was in Europe. But about his accolades for me, the context isn't quite right. I was much more successful than Hem at that time. I'd already had four books published and was doing a monthly column for *Harper's Bazaar*. Hem hadn't had his first book published in the states yet. Hem thought I was pretty funny,

Hemingway and Waldo Smith at Key West, 1928.
Collection of William B. Smith.

	but the point is I had gotten published in America and he hadn't.
St. John:	And *For Whom the Bell Tolls*—what about that?
Stewart:	Marvelous, but I did not think much of Hem's play, *The Fifth Column*. The only problem with *Bell* is that Hem came down damn heavy on the Russian adviser to the Spanish Communists. I think it unbalanced the fairness of the book. He was trying to be fair. It was obvious he was on our side, even though he was trying to seem the impartial novelist. However, his personal hatred for Marty came out so strongly in the book that it tipped the scales in a way that he did not perhaps intend.
St. John:	It seemed to me that the Left liked Hem's so-called bad book, *To Have and Have Not*.
Stewart:	Yes. He was really on our side in that one. But you know he was stuck half way through and didn't know how to finish it in a properly sociological way. He was absolutely at a dead end until Joris Ivens showed him how to go about tying it all together into something that would have social meaning.
St. John:	Oh yes, Ivens; he's the Dutchman who shot the film footage of *The Spanish Earth*, isn't he?
Stewart:	Yes, that's the one.
St. John:	And who made a film from the North Viet Nam point of view?
Stewart:	I don't know about that.
St. John:	I'd like to get back to *The Sun* for a moment. You mentioned the travelogue accuracy of *The Sun*, and then you cited the knockout of the matador by Loeb-Cohn and the getting together of Jake-Hem and Brett-Duff at the end of the book as provable variations from reality. There is one invention of Hem's that both of us have forgotten, another deviation if I may say so, from actuality. I mean Jake-Hem's sexual mutilation. It was a genius stroke, it seems to me, and brave too, to have the hero de-heroed in that manner. That was true guts and invention.
Stewart:	Yes, I've thought about that quite a bit while rereading the book. And for the first time I saw something strange developing that I hadn't gotten at all before. I mean, you know there is a small school of thought—to which I do not for a moment belong—that looked upon Hem as an unconscious

homosexual because of his stridently anti-homosexual stance and his heavy emphasis on good old buddy-buddy relationships. That was what Max Eastman seemed to be getting at with his false hair on the chest remark. Hem got almost too angry. However, if you follow the line of this school that Hem was a secret, possibly unconscious homo and that his whole life was a kind of counter compensation, you could argue that Jake's lack of the proper sexual equipment combined with his possession of a potent desire might symbolize the plight of the homosexual. The homo has the desire, but because it is unnatural he is not allowed to express his feelings in polite society. Jake had the desire for Lady Brett, but had no means of implementing it. There is a parallelism there. I don't know if this idea has been voiced before, but in any case I am not subscribing to it for Christ's sake; I am just indicating how the Jake situation could have tied in with the false hair theory. I don't believe it for a moment. Hem was all man as far as I was concerned, even though a bit priggish, and of course he did have these three sons which, I would say, is quite a lot for a pretender.

St. John: Let me ask you plainly if you are putting something politely out of deference to a dead friend?

Stewart: Oh my God. Now you've taken me seriously. I don't believe this theory. It's just a stupid idea, and one shouldn't speculate this way about real people. I shouldn't have mentioned it. In fact I will now state categorically that I do not believe a word of it.

St. John: Harold's theory about Jake's inadequacy is that this was Hem's way of saying that he couldn't have Duff because his wife, Hadley, was along, or perhaps simply because she existed. I myself go along with this and will add another factor; Jake's handicap meant that he couldn't have Duff in any important way because she was a drunk, a nymph and a friend's girl. Oh, there are a lot of possible barriers behind Jake's condition, I guess, including age. Lady Duff was eight years older than Hem (exactly the right age for Harold). Hem may have seemed a baby to her—and to himself in relation to her, although that theory tends to break down when you consider that Hadley was also eight years older than Hem.

Stewart: I'm inclined to go along with the idea that Hadley was the deterrent. She was a wonderful girl. I probably meant the Christcheck for her as much as for Hem. She was my favorite of Hemingway's wives. I knew the first three pretty well, but Hadley's the one I liked best. Maybe, after all, Hem did too.

NOTE

1 In a letter of April 16, 1971 Mr. Stewart wrote, "I certainly don't remember speaking unkindly to Hemingway about Harold Loeb" (Stewart to Editor).

"Montoya" Remembers
The Sun Also Rises

ANY admirer of Hemingway's art who has retraced the journey of Jake Barnes of *The Sun Also Rises* when he and Bill Gorton went fishing in the Irati River must certainly have experienced that sense of being a part of, not only the literary, but the real past. Coming over the Pyrenees to see the "gray metal-sheathed roof of the monastery at Roncesvalles,"[1] going into Burguete with its old inn and houses "along both sides of the road,"[2] following the same road that was there fifty years ago, winding up and down the mountains where the "grainfields went up the hillsides,"[3] coming at last to the ruined castle on the hill, one feels on this little-traveled road that nothing has changed. Critics have commented on the pictorial style of these scenes from *SAR*. Hemingway himself gave credit to Cézanne for some of his descriptive powers. But what startles one is not so much the Cézanne effect but that, riding along, phrase after phrase from the book comes to mind. Round a bend, and there it is! With his eye for a few selective details, Hemingway gives us a complete picture. One can hardly believe that forty-five years have passed over this land since the bus Jake and Bill were riding ground steadily up the hills.

The road leads into Pamplona, past the bull ring, with its bright red gates and sad-looking fountain, its bullfight done in mosaic, now fallen into desuetude. One thing here is new—the Hemingway statue erected in 1968 at the entrance to the ring, along the street now named Paseo de Hemingway. In the streets leading from the ring, workmen were erecting the barricades for the coming Fiesta of San Fermin, when young men would run down narrow Estafeta Street ahead of the bulls.

207

Juanito Quintana, 78, in San Sebastian. *Collection of Leah Rice Koontz.*

The sidewalks along these streets allow room for one person only. But going up a few steps into the Plaza del Castillo, one feels the cramped feeling give way. There on one side of the plaza is La Perla Hotel with its sidewalk café, where, according to the concierge, Hemingway often sat with friends during the Fiestas. Directly across the square is "Montoya's" hotel, which is now an apartment house, but with the Eslava café still there, the tables and chairs in their antiquity surely the ones of the 1920's. Here in those days sat all the characters from *SAR*, when they weren't walking across the square to the other café.

After the San Fermin and Jake Barnes's need for "cleansing," he went to San Sebastian to sit on the terrace of the Café Marinas and swim in the bay that the surrounding beaches encircle for miles, with the sawed-off pine trees along the promenade where Jake walked giving the whole scene an extraordinary aspect different from other beaches.

Here in San Sebastian I found Juanito Quintana, the Montoya of *SAR* and close friend of Hemingway. Fifteen minutes after I called him, he appeared at my hotel in a smart grey suit and blue shirt, erect and eager to talk of Ernesto. I confess that from Carlos Baker's account of his living in penury in a walk-up flat,[4] I expected to see a sort of decrepit old man. Not so. He is straight-shouldered and vivacious, with eyes that sparkle as he talks, and he talks of Hemingway continuously and lovingly. He told me he is seventy-eight. According to Baker, he would now be eighty. But whatever his age, give or take a couple of years, he belies it.

He first saw Hemingway in 1923 in Pamplona, where he ran the Quintana Hotel. The author, he said, was the first English-speaking tourist to attend the San Fermin. But Hemingway, not yet an *aficionado*, left Pamplona after one day and went back to Madrid. Raphael Hernandes, who wrote for the *Libertad Daily*, suggested that the next year he go to Quintana's Hotel. Hemingway wrote for reservations; thus the long friendship began, the author's infatuation with Pamplona growing into a life-long love affair. It was Quintana who initiated Hemingway into the art of bullfighting, which inspired not only the scenes in *SAR* but also led to the writing of *Death in the Afternoon*.

According to Quintana, the events of *The Sun Also Rises* are "told like it was." It was true that Hemingway and friends were "big drunks." An interesting anecdote concerned the night that "Brett" and "Mike," coming back to the hotel inebriated, ordered some consommé. The waiters by now were so fed up with their antics that they brought water in which lobsters had been boiled. These characters ate it, declaring it was exquisite! When I asked Quintana if he was really angry with Hemingway for the intrusion of these people into the world of *aficion* and if he had refused to speak like Montoya of the book, he said, "Not mad, but close to it. I loved Ernesto. But when he was too drunk he would disturb the other guests and I couldn't put up with that." Hemingway listened and wouldn't fight with "Montoya," declaring, "We're too good friends." As to the fight between "Romero" and "Cohn," there was one, but it was not so bad as the one depicted in the book.

When the Spanish Civil War began, Quintana was forced to leave his hotel in Pamplona, losing all he had. He remained in exile in France for eight years, returning to San Sebastian, where he lives in his fourth-floor flat on a street leading down the hill to the Bay of Biscay. Every July he goes back to the San Fermin at Pamplona, an honored guest.

Quintana had few kind words for A. E. Hotchner. He and Hemingway had stopped in San Sebastian in 1954 on their way down from France, and Quintana went on to Madrid with them. But he felt Hotchner was envious of him and treated him badly. Hemingway, however, couldn't tell Hotch (whom they nicknamed Pecas because of his freckles) to "go fry his asparagus." Quintana reaffirmed what others have said—Hemingway had a great timidity with some people, while with others he could be insupportable. But his great generosity was shown in the fact that when Quintana said he did not have the money to go on trips with him, he later found $500 in his coat pocket.

In 1959 he and Hemingway traveled to see all the bullfights featuring Ordoñez and Dominguin. If both were fighting the same day in different places, Hemingway would go to one and Quintana to the other; then Quintana would key Hemingway in on the one he had seen. From these trips came "The Dangerous Summer," published in part in *Life*.

Making a trip back to his flat, Quintana returned with the new book, *Hemingway and the San Fermins* by José Maria Iribarren, in which is one of his favorite photos of himself with Hem and Miss Mary and the inevitable wine bag. He also brought his framed autographed copy of the picture of Hemingway kicking the can in the snow of the Idaho mountains—"a picture no one had seen." I took this to mean the autographed one, since the picture has appeared in many publications. He was also proud to have had a part in a French TV production *Du Côté d'Hemingway*.

His gift to me was a 1967 copy of the newspaper *La Voz de España*, with a page and a half devoted to Hemingway, Quintana, the San

Fermins, and *The Sun Also Rises*, still titled in Spain simply *Fiesta*. In this paper he is quoted as saying, "Hemingway *era raro, muy raro; era raro.*" The old man with the young eyes who remembers so vividly has perhaps spoken the three words that say most to all of us who feel deep sensibility for his work: He was rare.

NOTES

1 Ernest Hemingway, *The Sun Also Rises* (New York: Scribners, 1926), p. 111.
2 Ibid., p. 112.
3 Ibid., p. 108.
4 Carlos Baker, *Ernest Hemingway: A Life Story* (New York: Scribners, 1969), p. 524.

Chapter **8**   SAM ADAMS

The Sun Also Sets

"SEÑOR Ordóñez, *mierda!*" the man said, pronouncing the name "Thenyor Ordonyeth." "I haven't been Señor Ordóñez or señor anything for 15 years." He laughed and then leaned across the dining table and shook hands.

"Call me Cayetano. Just Cayetano. The only Señores Ordóñez around now are my sons. You know. Like that great bullfighter. The great Señor *Antonio* Ordóñez." The man grinned, showing swollen gums and two yellow front teeth. Even three feet away, through the oily odors of food, I could smell his breath, sour and heavy from all the wine he had drunk at lunch.

"So you're an American?" he asked in a hoarse, phlegmy voice. I nodded and he picked up a bell-shaped glass jug with a large cone-shaped spigot sticking out one side, tilted back his head and. shot a long stream of red wine into his throat.

"Good," he gargled through the wine. "I like Americans. I've known a lot of Americans. Do you know Ernesto Hemingway, the writer? He's an American."

I said I didn't know Ernesto Hemingway personally, but that I'd read most of his books and liked them very much.

"He wrote about me in a book once," Cayetano said. "My bull-fighting name was Niño de la Palma but in this book Ernesto called me

Reprinted by permission from *Sports Illustrated*, June 29, 1970. Copyright © 1970 by Time, Inc.

Pedro Romero after Spain's greatest matador. Did you know that?"
I said that I had read the book several times and that it was my favorite
Hemingway novel. That seemed to please him.

"Too bad," he said after another long drink. "Too bad you didn't
know him. A good type, Ernesto." Cayetano pushed the wine over to
me.

I raised the jug, aimed the spigot down and then watched the red
liquid make a lazy arc to my mouth, stretched open wide like a baby
bird's—the sure sign of the amateur—but I did manage to cut off the
stream without staining my shirt, and only a few drops dribbled onto
my chin.

"You're learning," said Cayetano. "Ernesto was very good with the
jug and also the wineskin. But that was 30 years ago. We were both
young." He reached down and filled the jug from a giant straw-covered
demijohn on the floor.

I had seen a photograph of Cayetano Ordóñez taken 30 years before.
It showed a handsome young man in a bullfighter's ornate suit of lights,
standing very dignified with his dress cape hanging casually over one
shoulder, looking exactly the way everyone who has never seen a bullfight thinks a bullfighter ought to look. It was a photograph of Niño
de la Palma at 21, in his first season as a full-fledged matador, the Pedro
Romero of Hemingway's *The Sun Also Rises*.

"The best-looking boy I have ever seen," Hemingway said of Pedro
Romero. But by this time, in 1955, in this small pension in Madrid,
only the mouth—half pout and half sneer—and the dark eyes, slanting
down from the outside corners, were left. The young bullfighter of the
1920s was almost unrecognizable in the man who sat in front of me.
Cayetano Ordóñez was 51 but looked 70. He was bald except for
patches of ratty-looking hair over his ears that only accentuated the
baldness. His face was a map of dissipation, pockmarked and with
the cheeks and nose crisscrossed by hundreds of tiny purple lines. The
once-handsome brown eyes were watery and the whites mostly red. His
entire body seemed twisted, not wilted or disfigured, just a little out of
line from years of being battered by the bulls. He wore trousers and
a coat from different suits, shiny and frayed, and a badly darned tan
sweater over his thin chest. Yet he had a kind of tattered dignity—
that of a man who has lost but who somehow has managed to salvage
something good, some tiny piece of brilliance, from defeat.

After lunch the owner of the pension, Julia Hernández, a dynamic,
250-pound woman who had buried five husbands, took me aside.
Cayetano was a lifelong friend, she explained, and for the moment
was a little short of money. Would I mind if he took the other bed

in my room? Just for a few days? It was the only spare bed in the pension so I didn't have much choice.

"What about his family? Why don't they ..." I started to ask.

"Those types? They won't have him," Julia said disgustedly. "They pay him a little every month—the family. They pay him to stay away."

That afternoon I cut my classes at the University of Madrid and went to the American Library to see exactly what Hemingway had said about my new roommate.

In *Death in the Afternoon* Hemingway says that during his first season—the time of Pedro Romero in *The Sun Also Rises*—Cayetano "looked like the messiah who had come to save bullfighting if ever anyone did." But in that first year Cayetano was badly gored in the thigh and, "That was the end of him.... What had happened was that the horn wound, the first real goring, had taken all his valor. He never got it back."

Yet for almost another 20 years, until the early 1940s when he finally retired for the last time, Cayetano Ordóñez, Niño de la Palma, without his valor, afraid, fought the bulls. Only in Madrid, it was said, did he occasionally recapture some of his old brilliance, and then only because he forced himself—despite his fear—to perform well for the bullfight critics of the capital. It was simple economics. Good press in Madrid meant good contracts elsewhere.

When I returned to the pension I found Cayetano sitting on my bed in his shorts sipping *anis* out of a half-liter bottle. The sickly licorice smell filled the room.

"Hello, Samuel," he said and then smiled when he saw I was staring at his legs. They were remarkable, the calves and thighs almost the same size and covered with a cross-hatching of scars.

"Souvenirs of the profession," he laughed. "I got a few more good ones back here on my butt." Cayetano slapped his buttocks.

"Hey, student. What did you study today?" he asked after another long pull at the *anis* bottle.

"You," I answered and immediately was sorry I'd said anything.

"Me?" he said. "How do you study me? Are they teaching old Niño de la Palma at the university?"

I explained that I had gone to an English-language library and, just by chance, had come across the book in which Hemingway had written about Pedro Romero. Cayetano obviously was pleased. "What did it say about me ... about Pedro Romero?" he asked.

"He said that you—that Pedro Romero—had greatness. That your bullfighting gave real emotion and that you always worked very close to the bull."

"You see, Samuelito, what did I tell you? And it all occurs at the Feria de San Fermin in Pamplona and I make love to the English woman, right?"

I told him he was right and he seemed quite happy and drank some more *anis*. But then he got up and walked over to the window and for a long time stared down into the street.

"Ernesto wrote about me in another book," he said finally, still looking out the window, his back toward me. "It is a book all about bullfighting and he uses real names. Do you know it?"

I said I thought he must be talking about *Death in the Afternoon*, which translates easily but somehow poorly into Spanish.

"And what did Ernesto have to say about me in this other book?" Cayetano turned and gave me a smile. I realized I was embarrassed and showed it.

"Some of what was in the Pedro Romero book," I mumbled. "But it is mostly a general study of bullfighting, with drawings and a list of the Spanish bullfight terms explained in English. You know."

Cayetano winked at me and then sat back down on the bed and leaned over and slapped my knee. The sweet reek of *anis* was all over him.

"And does Ernesto tell what happened to me when I was badly gored during my first season as a matador? Does he tell you that I was no good after that? That the wound finished me? That I lost my nerve? Does he tell you all about that?"

They were not really questions but I had to say something. "He says you were all bullfighter but that after the goring you were not as brave as before." It was only half a lie.

"What would he know about being brave and having fear?" Cayetano spat. "From the wars? It's not the same. What does this American writer know of being afraid and alone out there with the bull and sometimes having to find your nerve again to please the animals in the expensive seats in the shade so they'll give you contracts for another season? What does Don Ernesto Hemingway have to say about that?"

Don Ernesto Hemingway had said that Niño de la Palma's occasional good performances after that first season were "the brave actions of a coward." I said nothing.

Cayetano emptied the *anis* bottle and seemed to relax. "Ah, what fear I had," he said. "What magnificent fear! Sometimes I shook so bad I could hardly control my legs."

He shook his head and then looked at the *anis* bottle and shook it. "Twenty years with the fear," he said. "Twenty years I fought so my family would have enough to eat, a clean place to live, and now I'm nothing to them. Nothing! And do you want to know why?" Cayetano laughed. "Because I have no shame. I'm a disgrace." A fine mixture of *anis* and spit sprinkled my cheek. "I'm just an old drunk and my family are all high society now and live where there are trees, while I stay in this whore of a pension in this whore of a town."

Cayetano studied the empty bottle again and then went out to the dining room and brought back a bottle of house wine. Board, even if you weren't paying it, meant free wine.

"What else did the good author have to say about me?" he asked after a long silence.

"Nothing," I started to say, but then I remembered something else and hoped it wouldn't be the wrong thing to remember. "He said you had too much imagination." Cayetano looked as if someone had knocked his breath out. He just sat motionless on the bed, gaping, but then the corners of his mouth began to twitch and his whole dissipated face cracked into a huge grin.

"He said that about me!" he roared. "That I had too much imagination?" Cayetano bounced up from the bed and yelled down the hallway, "Julia, listen to this! The American writer, Ernesto Hemingway, wrote in a book that I had ...," and he broke up laughing once again, "that I had too much imagination." I don't think Julia was even in the pension.

"Ah, what a good one that is," Cayetano laughed. "What a rare thing. Too much imagination! He knew, that Ernesto. He understood it. What an author, that one."

I wondered if he knew what else Hemingway had said about him in *Death in the Afternoon:*

"If you see Niño de la Palma chances are you will see cowardice in its least attractive form; its fat rumped, prematurely bald from using hair fixatives, prematurely senile form. He, of all the young bullfighters who came up in the 10 years after Belmonte's first retirement, raised the most false hopes and proved the greatest disappointment."

I roomed with Cayetano Ordóñez for three weeks. Three long, unpleasant and, for me, mostly sleepless weeks. In the early-morning hours he would stumble in, collapse fully dressed on the bed and begin snoring the loud, satisfied snores of a drunk who has drunk enough to sleep. Soon the whole room would be stinking with the rank sweetness of cheap cognac or, worse, *anis*. And later I'd hear the almost unhuman retching sound as he vomited into our white enamel chamber pot. Once he woke up vomiting and got half of it all over his sheets and pillowcase. And sometimes he'd just moan in his sleep, which was far worse than the snores or the violent discharges.

If I got two consecutive hours' sleep a night I was lucky. In the mornings I would stumble onto the streetcar for the university, which, fortunately, was at the end of the line, because I would have slept all the way to Lisbon if the streetcar had been going there.

I began to strongly dislike Cayetano which was too bad because outside of the ordeal of the long nights he was good company. He had a wry sense of humor and offered endless bullfight stories, which he told well, if somewhat with the cynicism of one who has failed. He knew just about everything about everybody who had had anything to do with bullfighting for the preceding 30 years. All the anecdotes. All the tragedy and failure and glory. All the dirt. "Bullfighting today is a mockery," he once said. "The bulls are half-size, with their horns shaved down, and the horses are padded to protect the tourists."

In addition, Cayetano Ordóñez was the only character from a Hemingway novel that I'd ever met, and I was 19 and in Spain. But none of this quite made up for having to live with him in that small room at night.

Finally I told Julia that either she put me in another room, which was out of the question, or I would have to find another place to live.

"Stay, Samuel," she said. "It's only for a few more days. Cayetano is just waiting for his money, and I can't put him out in the street. He has no place else to go." I agreed to stay for "a few more days."

"Who pays for his drinks every night?" I asked.

Julia just shrugged. "What sons!" she said, ignoring my question. "They care nothing for their poor sick father who risked his life a thousand times for them. High society. That's all they are now. Antonio and Pepe and the whole disgrace of a family. High society, in with the Dominguíns and all." Julia pushed up her nose with a thumb and then made a classic obscene gesture. "They have repudiated Cayetano when it is Cayetano who should disown them."

I asked if he were really great that first season.

Julia threw up her hands. "He was the best I've ever seen. The best! But after he got that first bad wound he was something to watch. Sometimes gray, really gray with fear. He could barely look at the bull. And when he had to kill he'd just stab it anywhere and hope. But that first season ... there's never been anybody like that. Just like the American writer said." Which was not exactly what the American writer had said.

The next evening Cayetano came into the pension wearing a new suit, cheap but definitely new, and carrying two bottles of expensive Carlos Primero cognac and a whole suckling pig stuffed under one arm, its head peeking out from under the brown butcher's paper.

"I'm leaving tomorrow, so tonight we have a party," he announced. It sounded like a command. The money, some money, obviously had come through.

The dinner was excellent. The little pig, head still in place, was unbelievably succulent, its pink skin cooked to a perfect amber, and crisp when you bit through into the sweet tender meat. There were eggs baked with spicy sausages, and a giant salad of tomatoes, onions and cucumbers soaked in fine Catalan olive oil. We drank a lot of red Marqués de Riscal that I contributed, partly because I felt guilty for being so relieved that Cayetano was leaving.

But in spite of the fine meal and good conversation, Julia was uncharacteristically quiet and looked worried. After coffee and most of one bottle of Carlos Primero, Cayetano, still quite sober, excused himself and said he was going out to take a short walk.

"Go after him, Samuel," Julia said as soon as Cayetano had left the dining room.

"What's the matter?" I asked. "He's just going out to get drunk."

"No, Samuel, this is different," Julia said, pressing her temples. "I know him. When he has money and puts on a new suit and buys the dinner and expensive wine and cognac, then it's going to be bad. I know him, Samuel. Go with him and try to keep him out of trouble."

"But he's already gone," I said.

"He'll be down the street at the Moya. He always goes there for one cognac before he goes on someplace else. They like him there. He goes there first and never is very drunk. Please, Samuel."

Julia looked so frantic that I got my coat and hurried down the two flights of stairs and out onto Corredera Baja.

Cayetano was standing at the marble bar in the cluttered little Café Miquel Moya, the kind of place that specializes in dealing out one or two fast drinks to men on their way someplace else—to work, home, an assignation, another drink.

"Well, what a coincidence," he said sarcastically. I started to order, but Cayetano motioned to the barman who pushed a saucer and a pony of brandy in front of me.

"Julia sent you after me, eh?" Cayetano was leering at me.

"No," I snapped. "What are you saying? I often come in here for a drink after dinner." It was a poor attempt at anger. And also a lie.

"Really?" Cayetano grinned. "Well, I've never seen you in here before." He turned to the barman. "Carlos, you ever seen this kid in here before?" Carlos shook his head.

Cayetano reached over and patted my shoulder. "That's O.K., Samuelito. Julia has no brains in her head, but if that fine woman sent you to be my bodyguard then that's what you'll do."

We drank our way out to Callao and down the Gran Vía, then through the side streets to the Puerta del Sol and across that giant square to Avenida San Jerónimo, stopping for only one or two drinks in each café.

Everywhere Cayetano made the grand entrance, effusively greeting owners and barmen as old, long-lost friends. And Cayetano was well known. Everywhere he was treated with suspicion until they saw he had money, and they saw that right away.

He would pay at once for the first round, pulling a crisp new salmon-pink 100-peseta note from a bulging wallet that showed more of the same, and then leave his change scattered carelessly on the bar. The result was always a warm greeting: "How's it going? It's been a long time." And then the offer of a drink on the house, which Cayetano would refuse curtly.

"The cheap bastards," he said as we walked across Plaza de Canalejas.

"They'll always buy you a drink when you've got money but never when you're broke and need one. And it costs them the same, the drink."

Suddenly he was very drunk.

In the next café Cayetano took one sip of his cognac and then carefully poured it on the floor like a chemist doing an experiment with a test tube.

"You call this cognac?" he yelled at the barman. It was the same cognac he'd been drinking all night.

We were asked to leave.

"What can one do?" the owner whispered to me, shaking his head and looking very sad.

On Calle Echegaray, a narrow street of cheap bars with whores and good food and bullfight ticket scalpers, Cayetano walked into a café where they did know me so I felt a little better about being with him. It was a café like thousands in Spain and quite a few on 14th Street in New York. It had a high ceiling with three very bright overhead lights that made the cigar and cigarette smoke seem thicker than it was. The walls were murals done in those mostly blue and some yellow ceramic tiles that you see too much of in Spain. Any wall space without a mural was filled with a bullfight poster. The bar was of the usual cheap orangish marble and behind it were countless bottles and two wine barrels. The rest of the café was cluttered with cheap wooden tables and chairs, and at one of the back tables the house guitar player, a friend of mine, sat with two other men. He was a left-handed guitar player who called himself El Zurdo—the southpaw—which was of considerable help in his business since he was not a very good guitar player. He smiled as we came in through the bead curtain at the door and then glanced at Cayetano and gave me a worried look.

The owner of the café had seen us too. He waddled over to the bar and started to say something but Cayetano slapped down a 100-peseta note and said, "What'll you have, *patrón*?"

It was clearly a challenge and the owner backed down, ordered a sherry, gulped it and excused himself.

"See," Cayetano said to me in a loud voice as the owner hurried away. "I know how to treat them."

Two men standing next to us at the bar turned and gave Cayetano a disgusted look. He had his back to them and didn't see it. The men were both well dressed, drinking Carlos Primero, and the barman had left the bottle, an honor accorded only the rich.

"Now this Antonio Ordóñez," said the first man, continuing their conversation, "I think he's...."

"You think he's what?" Cayetano had snapped around and was looking straight at them. "Just what about Antonio Ordóñez?"

The man was a little startled. "I said I thought he was, without doubt, one of the best today and probably would become one of the great ones."

"Ah, another Joselito, perhaps? Or a Belmonte?" Cayetano asked very pleasantly.

"It is possible," the man answered. "Very possible."

"No, señor, it is not possible," Cayetano said. "It is not possible because he is a fraud, this Antonio Ordóñez. All the bullfighters today are frauds. They don't fight bulls, they fight calves, and still they trim their horns."

"And just who, old man, the hell are you?" The second man was glaring at us.

Cayetano smiled. "I was Niño de la Palma," he said simply.

"Mother of God," said the first man. "The father?" He looked over at the barman. The barman shrugged and then nodded confirmation. "It's true. He's the father. Cayetano."

"So what?" said the second man. "He's just jealous." He turned back to Cayetano. "You're just jealous of your son. You were nothing. You were nothing as Niño de la Palma and you're nothing now."

Cayetano studied the two men for a while and then walked over to the end of the bar where a bullfight handbill was pasted on the wall. In brilliant colors, a slim, handsome *torero* was executing a perfect natural pass with his blood-red cape. The line formed by the man and the bull and the cape was perfect. Under the picture was advertised a "Grandiose Bullfight" and the poster went on to say that "with high permission and if the weather does not impede it, there will be rendered dead by sword thrust 6 handsome and brave bulls 6 ... by those great swordsmen: Julio Aparicio, Antonio Bienvenida, Antonio Ordóñez."

Cayetano stood for a long time looking at the perfect matador make the perfect pass. Then he spat on the poster.

"There, Antonio, my son," he said quietly. "You repudiate me and so I now repudiate you." Cayetano reached up and tore half the poster off the wall, tearing off the head and shoulders of the perfect matador and all of the bull. Then he sat down at a table and began to weep.

"Mother of God," said the first man and paid for their drinks and the two of them left, not looking at Cayetano as they passed the table.

I went over and sat down in front of him and said, "Let's go home." He just stared at me, the tears still running down his cheeks. El Zurdo and I managed to get him up and out the door.

Once outside, Cayetano seemed all right. We walked him up to Plaza de Canalejas, but as we were about to cross the square he suddenly stopped, pulled away from us and waved at something.

"My son Antonio," he said proudly. "There's Antonio. He's one of the best matadors in Spain now. Soon he'll be the best of all and not suffer many wounds and then retire with money and fame and honor. Hello, Antonio, I salute you. There he is."

"Where?" I asked stupidly.

"There," said Cayetano. "In that taxi." He pointed to a cab that had come out of Calle de Sevilla and was cutting across Canalejas, a black French-made Citroën like all the taxis in Madrid in 1955. He waved again as it passed in front of us and turned into San Jerónimo. "Hello, Antonio!"

The cab was empty.

Part **III**   FRIENDS AND EXPERTS

On the Characters in
The Sun Also Rises

March 31, 1951

Dear Pearson:

I have only a few letters from Hemingway and possibly later, when and if I get East, I'll hand them over to you, but they are of little interest. Soft soaping me, and as of his early years, before his big success, and he'd be apt to holler if he knew you had them. Beginning with the "Sun Also Rises" I found his work slick, affected, distorted characterization, himself always the hero. I haven't read the book since it first came out in about 1926, when I was surprised that he could be so efficiently slick, gelatine hard defeatism . . . , to match the mood of the youth of the time. I don't recall the fictional names of the various characters, but here goes.

Lady Duff Twisden was Lady Brett. She was in fact generally stinko with brandy, terrified of life economically, a mess generally, and at the time living with her cousin, Pat Guthrie (probably the Braddocks, you mention.) My time in Pamplona was a year or so before the scene of "The Sun" so some of the incidents I know of only from hearsay or from the book. Kitty or Kathleen Cannell was Cohn's gal friend, and of course Cohn was Loeb. Wescott was mentioned briefly early in the book. Who in hell Mike Campbell was I don't recall and shall cer-

Reprinted by kind permission of Ila Davis Wilson, Executor of the Estate of the late Robert McAlmon.

225

tainly not rr-read the book to find out. Probably a friend of Hemingway's name Smith, actually, forget his first name. Anyway I think Dos Passos married his sister. Harvey Stone and Woolsey I don't identify, but Count Mippipopolous, Zizi, were just characters around the quarter, not notable for action, work or personality, but I believe the count was Spanish and did talk of painting. Zizi, as I recall, played the piano occassionally in some night club, and possibly talked of painting too. Krum, I think was Krebsfield, and had been a friend of Hem's since their youth. Hemingway wrote a short story on him, but I forget

Robert McAlmon, a study by Berenice Abbott.
Collection of Berenice Abbott.

the title. Came out I think in Transition, or Little Review, not sure. Donald Ogden Stewart appears in the book, and I suppose was the Robert Prentiss you mention.

I did introduce Hemingway to Lady Duff and the title seemed to electrify him, and for weeks he was up with her in Montmarte, actually paying drink Bills for her and Pat Guthrie. He asked Mrs. Jo Bennett (now Brooks), myself, and perhaps others to take the weeping Hadley, his then wife, home while he stayed back with Brett. Looked like love or infatuation at least, and it was a surprise to many when he married Pauline, his second wife. Of course neither Jo Brooks or I DID take Hadley home, thinking if he was going to break with her that was his job, and we saw no reason of leaving our own drinks and companions.

When he had Bill Bird and I publish *three stories and ten poems* and *in our time* he was working away at other stories, and mourning the fact that Hadley had left a bundle of Ms. on a train, short stories, I guess, and his attitude was that they were, of course his best work. I judge he meant to use the material we published in a later and larger book, published by a house more commercial than our ventures.

That's the best I can do, except to say that I suspect most characters in his books are drawn from some actual person, although it would be impossible to believe of the nit-wit Italian countess in *Across the River*. She was him just proving himself the beloved hero throughout all. I couldn't get through the book but it was shoved at me in the Cosmopolitan installments by my sister-in-law and I skimmed one month's installment.

Hope this give you some info you want.

Yours as usual,

RMcA

Lady Brett Ashley and
Lady Duff Twysden

UNLIKE the historical drama or novel in which the living, or once living persons, are named by name, the *roman à clef* employs fictitious names for real persons; and part of the fun, of course, is to get the key to those who have been disguised.[1] More often than not, identities are fairly transparent, if not to the general reader, at least to some reviewers, and always to the author's intimate friends, some of whom might well turn up as among the fictive. And more often than not, their identities have been thinly concealed only to be heavily satirized or to have their intimate affairs intimately disclosed. Writers of such novels, one suspects, are hopeful of a *succès de scandale*. Ironically enough, those who have been the victim of the disclosed scandal frequently elicit our sympathy, or the scandal serves the purpose of raising from obscurity those whose reputations might never have spread beyond the circle of their acquaintances. In speaking of novels of this type, one must regard Hemingway's *The Sun Also Rises* as exceptional in at least one respect. The author has incorporated himself in the cast of characters, incorporated himself as the sexually incapacitated hero, Jake Barnes, and even consented to publicly identify the hero with himself. There are, indeed, people who exculpate Hemingway for his harsh treatment of Harold Loeb and Kathleen Cannell (the Robert Cohn and Frances Clyne of the novel, respectively) on the

---

Reprinted from the *Connecticut Review* II, 2 (1969), pp. 5–13, by permission of the editor acting in behalf of the Board of Trustees for the Connecticut State Colleges.

ground that he treated himself with far greater severity than these, his former friends.

The tendency of the foregoing remarks is not to encourage persons with a zeal for publication to defame themselves, or to encourage others to ask their literary friends to select them as fictional underdogs. In fact, if one were to respect current canons of criticism, particularly those of the New Critics, one should judge even a *roman à clef* with no heed to the key, with no concern for pairing up the living and the fictional, and with no obligation indeed for passing moral judgment on how justly the author has treated those identified. One should not go outside the text. One does.

For, perverse as it may seem to critical purists, the reader is not content solely to seek critical satisfactions; and even best-seller lists elicit widespread curiosity. We may concede at once that the private life of Ernest Hemingway has nothing to do with the value of this or that work he has written, but biographies of the writer continue to be written and read. It is asking too much of human nature to expect persons *not* to be interested in the author himself or the living characters who have been transmuted into a *roman à clef*. It is certainly to be expected that we will want to know how fair, or how malicious, the author has been to those persons. And if we pursue these interests in depth, we may find ourselves in areas remote from our original inquiry: the justice of the author's delineations. What we may discover is that characters fictionalized in a novel may become fictionalized still more in life. Hemingway, himself, it will be noted, underwent some such transmogrification. The myths created by an author about himself or other living persons are taken for reality and *that reality* is attested to by sober persons who not only confirm the author's fictive portrait, but improve upon it. In one way or another, the characters in *The Sun* acquired imaginative biographies—a myth here, a legend there.

Remember what consequences Hemingway brought on himself! Essays and critiques on the *real* Hemingway! Had he in fact like the hero of the novel, been incapacitated by a wound suffered in the war? Was he speaking of the shock to the entire man that he must have suffered at Fossalta when his body was host to some twenty dozen splinters of an exploded mortar shell? Or again, should we take the matter symbolically? Those who did, those especially with a Freudian orientation, concluded that Hemingway had problems, as the saying has it; and the analytic-minded sought to read Hemingway's assumed neurosis between the lines of his stark prose. Finally, when it became all too apparent—and very much more so since the appearance of Mr. A. E. Hotchner's book—that Hemingway the man, was, to put it

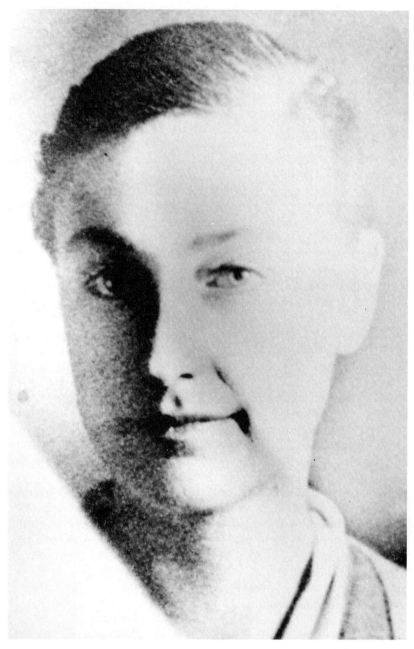

Duff Twysden, a passport photograph. *Collection of Carlos Baker.*

mildly, on this side of exuberance, a new myth replaced the old ones. The biographers settled on the theory that, of course, Hemingway was both virile and intact, and that his fictional counterpart, the wounded, impotent Jake Barnes represented imaginatively the blockade to a love affair with Lady Duff Twysden (the Lady Brett Ashley of the novel) which had to be foregone because of Hemingway's loyalty to his wife, Hadley. More on this legend to come!

So, several myths have been generated from *The Sun Also Rises*, some, as we have seen, concerning the author himself. But the truth about the living characters is far more astonishing—if it be the truth. It is said that there was, in the Hemingway circle of the Paris of the 1920's, a friend of Hemingway's who had been wounded genitally in the then recent war. He was presumably the sitter for that aspect of the portrait of Jake Barnes, and Hemingway did blurt out before the novel was published that, along with Harold Loeb, that friend too was destined for the slash. To Hemingway's ultimate credit, it must be said that he kept the friend's identity a secret; for when Hemingway gave Herbert Gorman a key to the characters, he set himself up as the model for Jake Barnes. However, concealment stopped there; for Hemingway did identify, among others, the rapacious Frances Clyne of the novel with Kathleen Cannell. A goodly number of expatriates in the Paris of the 1920's actually believed that Kitty Cannell was a gold-digger. But assumedly Hemingway was writing about someone else, a young woman on the periphery of his and Harold Loeb's circle. That was a young woman associated with *Broom* magazine who had been spurred on by a lady novelist to trap Harold Loeb into marriage. The lady novelist does not herself appear in *The Sun Also Rises*. Those with a zest for scandal might regret the exclusion, for the lady novelist was to achieve some repute as a writer—one of her works commanded an introduction by T. S. Eliot. It is as an intrigant that she remains mute and inglorious.

Hemingway apart, Lady Brett Ashley is the character that became the most legendary in life. She was drawn by Hemingway from Duff Twysden, and many of Hemingway's contemporaries assumed a one-to-one correspondence between the fictive Brett and the living Duff. Inevitably, in the memoirs of those who have recorded their Paris days of the 1920's, Duff is encountered fulfilling precisely the role Hemingway imagined for her in *The Sun Also Rises* where her natural habitat is given as either the bedroom or the bar. Historians of the era make it their business to report every glimpse they have of her at the Dingo or the Dôme or the Select. And we are left to assume that if her drinking is a fact, her promiscuity follows; for the latter is not as easily eyewitnessed as the former. Someone presumably knowledgeable like Robert McAlmon made it a point to interlard the autobiography of his literary life with his having arranged to lease an apartment for the "Lady Brett of *The Sun Also Rises*" who "had acquired an American boy friend, much younger than she...." Someone not knowledgeable at all like Jed Kiley told us that even before the novel was published, he had declared his night-club off-limits to her. "All that baby ever kept was the change when somebody gave her over two dollars." She was "hard-boiled," John dos Passos wrote when he recalled meeting her in Pamplona (she was not even there at the time). And in 1927, a year after the novel was published, Matthew Josephson recounted "how accurately Hemingway had drawn his friends and acquaintances." Josephson had gone to the Dôme, when he met "a tall slender woman" and "a tired-looking Englishman whom she called 'Mike'." They all chatted together and then went to Jimmy's bar. But even before then, Josephson sensed they were Hemingway's characters; "... the bantering manner with its undertone of depression; it was all there."

The two characters that Josephson had met were, of course, Lady Duff and Pat Guthrie, the Mike Campbell of *The Sun*. At Jimmy's, Harold Loeb was to appear out of the blue. Mike showed "little signs of irritation" as if Robert Cohn of the novel had appeared, and Josephson felt later that he had been through "a spooky sort of cocktail hour.... The characters were real enough and definitely not ghosts." So Josephson, like other writers of memoirs, bore witness to the accuracy of Hemingway's portraits; and years later, when he met Lady Duff in Connecticut on an occasion when she was drinking gin and coffee, he remarked that, "Nothing could stop her drinking." His few glimpses—perhaps they were no more than the two recounted here —confirmed his earlier description of Lady Brett Ashley: "alcoholic." He made no comment on the other adjective he employed for the fictive Brett, namely, "libertine"; its accuracy for the living Lady Duff is left for us to assume. But it must be said that Josephson, unlike some others, was not being intentionally malicious. As Santayana has said of creators of myth, he made "epicycles, as it were, on the reflex arc of perception." He remembered the novel, he saw parallels in real life. Like the others, he established a correspondency.

Such correspondency, according to the writers quoted here, allegedly struck them in a few months, or the immediate year, or instantly following the publication of *The Sun Also Rises*. But these were not impressions that faded with or were modified by the passing of time. The foregoing quotations are all from books published in the 1960's.

Nor were these writers the only corroborators of Hemingway's realism and the establishers of myths to come.

Historians of the '20's tell us that after the publication of *The Sun Also Rises*, Lady Brett herself became the ideal for Smith College girls whom she inspired to be depressed, and for whom she was the model for dissipation. Apparently, Lady Brett's influence was not limited to this side of the Atlantic. Robert McAlmon represented her to be the model of imitation for women of the Rive Gauche. One is tempted to imagine a bourgeois father and mother in the provinces wondering, "Where did we go wrong?," and one of them rejoining, "C'est la Brett," or a college president telling an irate Board of Trustees in Northhampton, "Gentlemen, it's that Brett Ashley."

It was inevitable that the influential Lady Brett Ashley and the living Lady Duff Twysden came to be identified. The identification lingered and was reaffirmed through Hemingway's suggestive words to Hotchner, "Her pallbearers had all been her lovers. Brett died in Taxco, Mexico. She was forty-three ... On leaving the church, where she had a proper service, one of the grieving pallbearers slipped on the church steps and the casket dropped and split open." Many years before Hemingway related this anecdote, another one had already been circulating. The rumor was that all of Duff's pallbearers were so drunk that the coffin they bore fell and rolled down a Taxco mountainside. The facts are that Duff, who died at the age of forty-six, in St. Vincent's Hospital in Santa Fe, New Mexico in June, 1938 was cremated (probably in Alberquerque). There was no coffin, there was no service, there were no pallbearers. Professor Philip Young mentioned to me that the sort of stories circulating about Duff were reminiscent of those that were current after the death of Andrew Jackson; and one recalls funeral myths associated with the charismatic of an earlier day: Marlowe, Shelley, and Ben Jonson for example.

But even the seemingly realistic accounts of Duff Twysden—those that highlighted Hemingway's accuracy—are open to serious question. Most commentators who observed her failed to take into account the times in which she lived and the milieu in which she moved. "She was young then," Lady Duff's friend, the eminent photographer, Berenice Abbott said, "and in those days everyone was gay, everyone drank."

We must bear in mind that those who saw her in the Dingo or the Dôme or the Select were not there themselves as sightseers. They too drank, and some of them, like Robert McAlmon, could drink her under the table. But there is good reason to believe that her drinking was essentially of that time and that place—not necessarily a permanent trait of her character. As for her promiscuity, let it be said that many of those who commented on her were themselves "free," and certainly, if they themselves were not, they had friends who were, and after all, it takes promiscuous men to make for promiscuous women. Once again, we must remember that there was a revolution going on—the sexual revolution did not begin in the 1960's—and we have every right to think of Lady Duff as merely a participant in that revolution. However, the stories of her license might well justify the retort of Mark Twain when told of his death, "Highly exaggerated." That is to say, we only know of two incidents, a very brief affair with Harold Loeb, a more extensive one with Pat Guthrie. Jimmy Charters, the barman who liked Lady Duff, believed that she was madly in love with Guthrie, who, he said, deserted her for an American girl. Loeb thought she wanted something more than an affair; she wanted to marry him. No other lovers have ever been named, although her friends concede that she had many affairs. But such friends may have been carried away by the evocative power of the fictive Lady Brett. Their assumptions may be gratuitous. If the accounts about her were true, one must recall that almost everyone who knew her agreed that Lady Duff was charming and captivating. That type of attractive woman, of course, would have more possibility of erotic experiences than the run-of-the-mill woman—and more possibility for gossip. Furthermore, one who knew her in the Paris days, and who herself was of English descent, pointed out that Duff was déclasse; and because she was, she suffered for a while that special instability from which American women are exempt, and from which English women suffer markedly.

All this is by way of saying that the fictive Brett Ashley, having become the female symbol of the Lost Generation, the living Lady Duff became the viable symbol of that generation. Through the creative offices of Hemingway, she became in the public mind not a participant in an uprooted group, but its exemplar. Accordingly, many who knew Duff made their estimate of her so as to jibe with her symbolic status. In the minds of the writers of memoirs, she became an abstraction. Heaven knows, as Brett Ashley she talked little enough in *The Sun.* Her dialogue was often flip, always laconic. Her most extensive utterances—and her most memorable—were, "Oh darling, I've been so miserable." and "Oh Jake, we could have had such a damned good time together." No one ever heard her speak that way in real life; Josephson, of course, caught an "undertone of depression" when he heard her bantering. One can not find a single sentence quoted from the living Duff. Equally astonishing is the absence of a recorded incident, other than a quarrel with an Apache in some bistro—precisely what we would expect to be recorded—that would indicate that there were events in Duff's life other than those prescribed by the novel, drinking and promiscuity.

So, Hemingway's portrait was taken for granted, and it was made credible because Hemingway in the novel had used some incidents drawn from real life. Apparently what Jake Barnes told Robert Cohn about Brett Ashley in Chapter V had some basis in reality. Duff was about thirty-four years old when *The Sun* was published in 1926, she was about to be divorced from Sir Roger Thomas Twysden, she apparently had been divorced previously, and she hoped to marry Pat Guthrie. A similar background was given by Jake Barnes to Robert Cohn. Subsequent events of the novel, especially those involving a love affair with Robert Cohn, were likewise based on reality, although Harold Loeb has issued his version of the events to indicate that Hemingway's accounts were somewhat wide of the truth. Moreover, the one-to-one correspondence between the characters of the novel and their reality is currently being questioned. Recently, Kathleen Cannell has also disclaimed—and with justification—the accuracy of her portrait in *The Sun*. And even Mr. A. E. Hotchner has pointed out that the incident of the bullfighter, Pedro Romero, tossing Lady Brett a trophy did not happen in actuality to Duff, but to Hadley Hemingway, the author's first wife. (Harold Loeb asserted that the bullfighter, Cayetano, who was the model for Romero, figured in the lives of himself and Duff and Hemingway for only a fleeting moment.) But in the main, Hotchner's quotations from Hemingway tend to support the established image of Duff. To the myth of the pallbearing former lovers, Hemingway added the fiction that, "Those days with Lady Duff ruined poor Loeb for the rest of his life," implying that Duff was very much like Brett Ashley, who made castration her hobby. But in the novel, Brett Ashley is finally able to exercise discipline out of respect for the bullfighter Romero.

If that gesture was a saving grace for the lady of the novel, Hemingway allowed no such exculpation for Duff. Loeb, himself, in a recent article, has denied that he was ruined; and I myself have seen the letters written to Loeb—kind letters—written by Duff after their brief affair in the South of France. Perhaps this is the time to make one fact clear between the real and the fictive Lady, and, indeed, between Hemingway the author and Hemingway the man. Some Hemingway biographers—and Harold Loeb himself—are to this day uncertain as to whether an affair between Hemingway and Duff had taken place. But it is quite certain that the Jake Barnes–Lady Brett Ashley affair occurred only in the pages of *The Sun Also Rises*. The living Hemingway, unlike the fictive Jake Barnes, was quite sexually competent. The living Duff Twysden, unlike the fictive Lady Brett Ashley, it remains to be added, was quite unwilling. Yes, she did tell Hemingway that she did not wish to break up a family—she told him this only to keep him at a distance, not out of regret. The excuse she gave was one of the oldest and the lamest, one of her friends told me. Hemingway was not her type, I was informed from still another source. That source was no other than the person to whom McAlmon referred as "An American boy friend, much younger than she...." That was her husband-to-be, not just a boy friend, with whom she planned to come to America, and with whom she lived happily for many years until her death in Santa Fe. He was a painter named Clinton King—by best accounts, her third husband.

In any event, the Kings came to America. Accounts of their life here are recounted from friends and acquaintances, some of whom had already thought of her in terms of the myth she had become through identification with Lady Brett Ashley. For example, Harold Loeb is quite certain that she met her husband-to-be by way of introduction from another painter, Sir Cedric Morris; but a close friend of Duff says that their meeting took place otherwise. King, that close friend said, was in a Paris bar, behind whose counter was a mirrored wall. In the mirrors he saw a beautiful face. It was Duff's and he fell in love with her. At once he introduced himself; they went off together; and eventually were married. So be it. Not really married, the friend added, "Duff would never do a thing like that." In the realm of fact was the King family's reaction. The Kings had a flourishing candy business in Texas, and the father was determined to stop the marriage. Lawyers were sent across the Atlantic to dissuade the young painter. Even five years later, to friends near Nyack, New York, he recalled with relish how he had defied the family. So, we can be quite certain they were married, and that they came to America with King losing his family's support. They were so poor thereafter, a friend of theirs said, that they had to live in a barn—the barn somewhat of an exaggeration, the dire poverty being just temporary.

Hereon, from all accounts, the Duff Twysden of legend—alcoholic and libertine, for whom false gaiety was a veneer for despair—is reported almost completely different. But even before her arrival here, Berenice Abbott repudiated Hemingway's fictive portrait. "He did not understand her at all. His portrait was superficial. Yes, he was fascinated by her old-world charm, her breeding and manners; but he saw her through the eyes of a boy from the midwest. He made her out to be a tramp—that was crazy. But he looked at women only sexually, not

Duff Twysden King, self-portrait with her husband Clinton, from a Christmas card, 1934. *Collection of Carlos Baker.*

as people. I grant that she was on a binge once in a while, but she was not alcoholic. As I said before, everyone was drinking then. She was attractive and charming and so she had many admirers, but she had talents. I saw some of her paintings. They were good paintings." Harold Loeb, too, remembers her paintings, and he too did not think she was an alcoholic. And that was the testimony of her New York friend, Mrs. John Rogers, and the testimony also of Dr. and Mrs. Edward Harkavy, near whom she lived for several months in New City, New York and who were in a position to know.

Duff and Clinton King had come to New City, New York to head an art school shortly to be opened. They worked in the spring of 1934 with the owner, a Mrs. Romaine. Quite unforeseen, there was a squabble over who should pay the postage to mail out brochures, and all at once the project folded. In New City were Duff and her husband, stranded without a cent. The Harkavys did what they could. They gave them shelter in a shack (not a barn) they owned; they gave them the use of their vegetable garden; and they sent their Korean houseboy with a drink of gin per day. The Korean servant, who had a passion for the stuff, saw to it that the limit was strictly observed. Dr. Harkavy, a practising psychoanalyst, is certain that Duff was not an alcoholic, not merely because she survived on that ration, but because, he said, she had none of that apparent greed nor the strained look so characteristic of alcoholics. Duff's friend, Mrs. John Rogers, also said that Duff was not an alcoholic; and when these friends were questioned about her fidelity to her husband, they were all certain that she was faithful and that theirs was a very good marriage. Apparently, during the many periods of occasional financial hardship, and an undetected tubercular illness, Duff was happy.

Mrs. Rogers vibrated smiles as she recalled Duff, "So captivating and witty. She was always witty, always delightful." Dr. Harkavy recalled "darting eyes and a mischievous look." His wife (known professionally as Millia Davenport) recalled one of Duff's harmless, though complicated pranks. "One day, at a gathering on the Carnochan Estate in New City, New York, a group had gathered to hear a lecture and to see some slides on the flora and fauna of Africa. The novelist, Bessie Breuer, was determined to impede the lecture and turn the gathering into a party. She began to undress the speaker, and then broke out into the score of an Italian opera. At this point, Duff unexpectedly dropped in; she sized up the situation immediately. Assuming the role of a desperate impressario, she addressed herself to those present and to an imaginary audience outside, imploring someone to volunteer to fill a role left vacant by a suddenly stricken member of the cast.

When by gestures, she made it appear that no volunteer was available, she braced herself suddenly and heroically joined Bessie Breuer in carrying on the opera. Duff was imaginative and was also musical; and in a later year, on inheriting a small sum, she spent most of it on the purchase of a piano." Dr. Harkavy recalled her always ready for sport. On one occasion, there were at a party three newly arrived German psychoanalysts, one of whom was Erich Fromm. Dr. Harkavy took an instant dislike to one of the trio, a Dr. C.—who bore himself with a holier-than-thou attitude, and who seemed to communicate the idea that he was the living Christ. Pointing him out to Duff, Dr. Harkavy asked if she would be so kind as to bring this divinity down to earth. She was to pretend to seduce him. But she did not have to. Dr. C. took one look at her and became mere man. It was not, Dr. Harkavy emphasized, that she was another Zelda Fitzgerald. "She liked fun," he said, "she wouldn't let a dare pass, but she wasn't reckless, she wouldn't endanger her life."

This then is a different Duff than the incurable alcoholic, the libertine, morbid character whom Hemingway depicted in *The Sun Also Rises*, and who was believed to have been represented with complete accuracy by those who knew her in Paris in the 1920's, and who recalled her in many parts of the world forty years later. The real person was about 5', 7", slender, long-legged, with luminous eyes that were always animated, a strong face—like that of a Norman soldier, Mrs. Rogers said. She was not voluptuous as Hemingway described Brett Ashley to have been. She did not have "curves like the hull of a racing yacht."

As we have seen, there were gross distortions made of the living Duff in the creation of the fictive Brett Ashley. But even those who disbelieved Hemingway's portrait—some of her friends and admirers in America—themselves created legends, or believed legends that they heard, or involved those who had once been close to Duff in myth and legend. One apocryphal item has it that Harold Loeb pursued Hemingway with a revolver, not as Hotchner passed on a similar item, just after the publication of *The Sun Also Rises*, but when Hemingway stole Duff away from Loeb. These fictions are part of a larger legend begun by Jimmy Charters in his *This Must be the Place*—with a preface by Ernest Hemingway. Charters said that after the publication of *The Sun Also Rises* the real characters depicted in the book went after the author with a gun apiece. One addition of this legend has it that Kitty Cannell, having acquired a boyfriend over six feet tall, ordered him to clout Hemingway on sight (Mrs. Cannell has said there is not a word of truth in this story). Still another, and a more romantic version, has

it that young Clinton King, then about twenty-two and some fifteen
years the junior of Duff, beat Hemingway to a pulp in a Paris bar.
Perhaps just as unfounded is the story that Duff was born a member
of the minor Scottish nobility. With that story goes the expected
sequel: the coming-out party, the superficial education, the marriage
into which she was forced by her parents to a drunken nobleman.
One variant has it that, in fact, she abandoned the groom at the wedding, and ran off with the best man—Duff herself told this to Harold Loeb. As one goes deeper into research for the facts of Duff's
life, one finds dubious testimony on both the friendly and hostile
sides. Even presumably objective records conflict. Her father's name
on the records of St. Vincent's Hospital, Santa Fe, New Mexico is given
as "Sterling." That does not correspond with the name of "Smurthwaite" given by *Burke's Peerage*. In fact, according to that source, her
original name is given as "Mary Smurthwaite."

To be sure, one must distinguish between ordinary errors and unusual myths. But the myths are plentiful, and there is no question that
they arose from the convincing magic of Hemingway's pen. We may, if
we wish, regard that evocative power as a gift, or a by-product of
genius. Or we may—the New Critics insist that we should—regard the
whole matter as really a sociological phenomenon. But if great works
of literature stimulate our imagination long after the book is closed, or
the play over, the superior *roman à clef* too has this persisting power.
It is, admittedly, another type of power. We are drawn, to be sure, not
within ourselves, but out there—to the world of the living. And as we
seek to establish if the fiction we have read corresponds to the way it
was, or the way the characters were, we may find ourselves encountering newly generated fictions remarkable enough to shift us once again
back to ourselves, so that the outcome may be a rekindling of our imagination. As for a particular living character, Duff Twysden, we find,
as we shuttle between the realities and the myths about her—often uncertain as to what were the realities and what were the myths—we become aware that she had some special quality, that quality that absorbs
us in spite of dry facts and statistics. Outside of the pages of *The Sun*
she possessed what Henry James called, "The real thing." He meant it
paradoxically, of course; it was that suggestive quality about a person
that could transcend his existential certitudes so as to stir the artist's
creative power. And it may be argued that the once-living Duff
Twysden—or as she might be called, Mary Duff Sterling Smurthwaite
Byrom Twysden King—possessed that compelling power even far more
than her fictional counterpart, the famous Lady Brett Ashley.

Chapter **11** JAMES CHARTERS

Pat and Duff, Some Memories

[*Editor's Note: The following memoir about Pat Guthrie and Duff Twysden (who later married an American artist, Clinton King) concerns those two persons on whom Hemingway drew for the characters Mike Campbell and Lady Brett Ashley in* The Sun Also Rises. *The passages which follow are parts of several letters to the editor and have been left in their original form.*]

I didn't become the bartender of the Dingo Bar until after Mr. Ernest Hemingway had written about his characters in *The Sun Also Rises* who frequented that particular establishment. I well remember observing certain characteristics about Duff and Pat which, from the time I took over the Dingo Bar, strongly impressed me and continued to do so for several years to follow. To begin with, I was struck and overwhelmed by their outstanding distinguished personalities which held me enthralled to the very end of my seeing them and serving them with food, drink, and cigarettes; chiefly drink, of course. From the Dingo Bar which I was persuaded to leave to go and open bars in the Montparnasse quarter, Duff and Pat followed me loyally like most of the rest of my clients and friends did. Duff and Pat arrived around early evening each day, about cocktail time, before dinner. Duff would always sit on a stool at the bar as erect as a broomstick. With a very

---

Reprinted from the *Connecticut Review* III, 2 (1970), pp. 24–27, by permission of the editor acting in behalf of the Board of Trustees for the Connecticut State Colleges.

241

James Charters, 1971. *Collection of James Charters.*

nice smile she would greet me, "Good evening Jimmy, how are you?"
Pat stood always at my bars, especially when he was with Duff. He'd
stand quite close to her, as though guarding her with his very life. Long
before I learned anything about their family problems, they gave me the
impression that they were a couple of newlyweds, and were spending

their honeymoon in Paris. They also seemed to me very much in love. Pat always appeared to simply idealize every move she made and every word Duff uttered. Pat, during these instances, often became elated, so much that he would look 'round with a happy smile to other clients in the bar for their approval. Then he would smile to me behind the bar when I was quick to return him a big grin as proof of my understanding and agreement. Duff could do no wrong in Pat's eyes during those years when they were together, neither by word nor deed. I can distinctly picture them, in my mind's eye, as though it was only a few days ago since I last served them with drinks in the several bars they came to. Yet it is almost 40 years past. I well remember Duff as she sat on the bar stool most times, with a pleasant happy smile, yet seemingly a sad, sorrowful smile very deep and far away as though she held several painful secrets. They seemed to be hurting her all the more owing to the fact that she was far too much of the real lady and gentlewoman to divulge them, and so easing her conscience.

She always wore on her head a cross between a Basque beret and a Scotch tam-o'-shanter. These were in different colors from time to time, placed on her head at a cocky-angle which I thought gave added attraction to her charming personality. Her dresses and suits were often of Scotch or Irish tweeds. I wouldn't be sure which, as I didn't know the difference between tweeds in those far off days. Sometimes she wore a tweed skirt and a colored pullover, to match her hat. The greens were my favorite, of course. Along with her tweed suits Duff almost always wore pretty brown shoes. She struck me as rather masculine physically, not unlike the English gentlewoman type of her day. I can just picture her riding to hounds with the pack. To me Duff typified the thoroughbred British aristocrat. At all times the perfect lady. To my mind she well and truly deserved the official title bestowed upon her. I never once saw her get angry with anything or utter a wrong word to or about anyone while drinking or otherwise. Pat was similar in some ways to Duff inasmuch as he came from a good family and was well educated. I was also given to understand that he'd been a young officer in a famous Scotch regiment in the 1914 War. Even though I knew him only in his civilian clothes, he gave the outward appearance of the British military officer out of uniform, from the way he walked and talked. I can just visualize him in his khaki tunic kilts, and the renowned Glen Glen gay hat. He must have been very kind and understanding to the men under his command, for he showed these tendencies, and more so, in his civilian life.

I noted these fine qualities he had right through the time I knew him. He was kind, understanding, well behaved at all times, unselfish, even

generous to a point when he had money. Unfortunately most of the
time he was hard up, and lived on credit where and whenever he could
get it. I could never say no or refuse Pat or Duff drink, food or cigarettes, in that order, though it was a strain on me as I had to bear most
of the credit out of my own pocket. However, I repeat, I could never
refuse them credit and they were continually hard up most of the time I
knew them. Anyway, they charmed me. I was awfully fond of both of
them, and they were of me too, I know. Some time after Pat died in
Paris, his mother came over to Paris to pay his outstanding bills. I
didn't know she was in town. However, I was sitting on the terrace of
a café one day having a coffee with a friend, just before going to my bar
to work, when suddenly a very distinguished, elderly lady came up to
our table and introduced herself as Patrick's mother, at the same time
inquiring if I was Jimmy the barman, who knew her son so well. I told
her I was, and ordered a drink for her. She had traced me from my
home address to the café. Anyway, she took me to one side and asked
how much did Patrick owe me. I gave her a reasonable bill without
taking any advantage of the situation. In fact, I felt like waiving the
debt as a token of good friendship and in respect to the memory of her
beloved son. I was about to begin on this line as I saw the chequebook
in her hand. However, she insisted on paying me and made out quite a
generous cheque. After we finished our drinks, we parted company
and, I must add, good friends.

A slight lead came to mind which I don't believe I've ever remembered to mention at any time before, not even to Mr. Morrill Cody
during the days he was ghost writing my Paris memoires. It might give
you food for thought and bring to mind a clue or two. What now
seems odd, curious, even strange to me, as I look back whenever Ernest
Hemingway was in Paris, which was very often in the early 20's and
well past the 30's while I was still a bartender in town, he would hardly
ever miss a day coming into which new bar I'd take over in Montparnasse for a drink and a chat with me. Yet as I think of it, I find it all
the more strange, for I have said earlier both Duff and Pat hardly ever
missed a day coming into whatever bar I was working at and still, curi-
ously as I remember it, neither Duff, Pat or Hemingway was ever in my
bar at the same time, so none of them clashed, or were obliged to walk
out on one another. Now I ask what might have been the reason for
Duff and Pat and Ernest Hemingway so conveniently missing one
another so often? Was their some animosity between them? If so, what
caused such animosity to people who, I believe, had been such great
friends at one time? Did the book, *The Sun Also Rises* cause the break-
up in their friendship? Was there some shame, fear, jealousy, or envy

grown up amongst those old-time friends after publication of *The Sun Also Rises?* Would this mean Duff and Pat had an adverse reaction to the book after reading it? Come to think of it, if my memory still serves me well, Duff and Pat for the most part often appeared extremely discreet within my hearing, though it was neither my nature nor habit to listen to client's conversations, in these early days, unless invited, of course. So owing to those discretions—and Hemingway was just as discreet and never mentioned Duff, Pat, or his book when talking to me—I find it regretfully difficult to record any of their true reactions to the book under the circumstances.

Did Mr. Clinton King, whom Duff later married, really knock Hemingway out? I certainly can't and won't believe it, though I vaguely remember a slight rumor going around Montparnasse to that effect. However, owing to the fact that Mr. King being much the younger man at the time, I wouldn't deny this completely. Still, my knowing what a tough man, physically, Hemingway was, I can only imagine Mr. Clinton King, bless his heart, having had to use a hammer, or a similar weapon for that purpose. Again, if it did happen, which I very much doubt, the fight could have been over-exaggerated and, I feel sure, didn't take place in Paris or I would have been one of the first to learn about it. On the other hand there might have been a row between Clinton and Hemingway through Duff's anger and pent-up reaction to Hemingway's description of her, and Pat for that matter, in *The Sun Also Rises.* You see, I felt then after the book had been published, that Pat might have wanted to get an apology, at least, from Hemingway, for whatever hurt he may have caused to Pat's and Duff's good name in pubic when, of course, it became widely known that they were Lady Brett Ashley and Mike Campbell, two of the main characters in the book. In my opinion, why Pat didn't wish to pick a row with Hemingway was because he was neither physically fit nor a violent fighting man. And so in case it might come to blows, Pat quite sensibly I believe, thought discretion in such circumstances would be the best part of valour. That's the reason I'm convinced today, that Pat didn't show outwardly his reaction to Hemingway personally. Yet I can still remember the strong undercurrent of feeling of both of them which today I could now interpret as their intelligent, silent, reaction. At the same time I'm far from indicating that Ernest Hemingway would have become violent with Pat had a row begun. Only should there have been a loss of temper on both sides then, anything might have happened.

However, coming back to Mr. Clinton King, if a fight had taken place between himself and Hemingway, I can easily believe that he was defending Duff's and Pat's cause. I agree wholeheartedly with others that Duff's love affair with Pat Guthrie was truly one of the famous romances of the Quarter. I would like even to go further and say, in my opinion and experience, the most famous love affair and romance of the Quarter. I believe I did hear or overhear from behind the bar on odd occasions, that Duff had been a Red Cross nurse during the war. I might easily agree, *now*, with Kitty Cannell when she says "though Duff Twysden was very much in love with Pat Guthrie, she would never have married him." I wouldn't have believed it for one moment until the day I learned they parted. It was a surprise and shock to me and to most of their many admirers, not only those in Montparnasse, but many others even further afield. Come to think of it now, perhaps they might have talked things over and agreed to separate, for marriage was out of the question as far as Duff was concerned. Though Duff had no intention of hurting Pat, neither did Pat wish to hurt Duff. And so Duff, I believe, took advantage of the situation when Pat found a new lady love—a most attractive young American lady. One of Duff's main reasons, I can now imagine, for not wanting to marry Pat might have come from his inability to keep her and give her the home that every wife is entitled to. I've used the above reason as one, of course; there could have been others for the final break-up. Anyway, it appeared all very sad when it happened. However, it must have been for the best, for Duff brought into my bar one day a very handsome young American and introduced him to me as Mr. Clinton King. He had a most soft, attractive voice plus personality and charm to match that of Pat's. Clinton and I became immediate friends, and what a sensible choice Duff made. A loving husband, a home of their own, and I'm sure they both lived very happily together until the Almighty chose to take Duff into his loving care. God bless her, and may her soul rest in peace.

Fitzgerald's *Sun Also Rises:*
Notes and Comment

Notes

READERS of Fitzgerald's letter who can neither remember the period in which it was written or qualify as serious students of the Twenties may need a little help with it—particularly toward the end where the names, not all of them famous, come thick and fast. At the start there should be no special trouble. "Bunny" is of course the Princeton name for Edmund Wilson (1895–   ) the critic, who wrote a novel later on. Maxwell Perkins (1884–1947) was Fitzgerald's editor at Scribners, and Hemingway's; he never wrote a novel. Neither did Katherine Tighe, who was a childhood friend of Fitzgerald's in St. Paul, Minnesota. O. Henry (William Sydney Porter, 1862–1910), mentioned a few lines later, was a writer of short stories, whose "surprise endings" Hemingway's stories did much to outmode.

As for trying to get Hemingway to "cut the first part of 50 Grand," it should be remembered that Fitzgerald succeeded. Its author regretted the cut a good deal later on, as he seems never to have regretted junking the first part of *The Sun Also Rises.* But he did drop three opening pages of typescript from the draft of "Fifty Grand" that his friend read. (A photograph of the original first page appears in the

Reprinted from Matthew J. Bruccoli and C. E. Frazer Clark, Jr., eds., *Fitzgerald/ Hemingway Annual 1970* (Washington: NCR/Microcard Editions, 1970), pp. 1–9, by kind permission of the editors and Messrs. Young and Mann.
The letter to which this article refers is reprinted below as Chapter 13, pp. 256–259.

trade edition of *The Hemingway Manuscripts: an Inventory*, 1969; all three pages are reproduced in the limited edition. Why Hemingway struck so much more than the very brief anecdote Fitzgerald—mistakenly?—thought stale is not clear.) Nor is the anecdote in the novel that Fitzgerald found "flat as hell without naming Ford" really all that flat, but since it appeared toward the end of the first chapter-and-a-half it disappeared when that did. Hemingway never forgot either anecdote, however, and this one was related at much greater length as "Ford Madox Ford and the Devil's Disciple" in one of the funniest parts of *A Moveable Feast*.

Now for some miscellaneous items. The mysterious reference to the "age of the French women" that comes just before the objection to the Ford business was not obscure to Hemingway, since it alludes to the epigraph he supplied for his pamphlet *in our time*, 1924, where he attributed an intentionally stupid line to his friend William B. Smith, Jr. (1895–   ), who had a bit of a reputation for wit:

> A Girl in Chicago: Tell us about the
> French women, Hank. What are they like?
> Bill Smith: How old are the French
> women, Hank?

Toward the end of the letter, "God! The bottom of p. 77 Jusque the top p. 78 are wonderful," refers to the scene in Chapter VI where Cohn's mistress, Frances Clyne, is giving him a very bad time and he is "taking it all"; "p. 87," where Fitzgerald says "The heart of my criticism beats," is the place in Chapter VII where Jake and Brett, alone in his flat, feel most acutely the hopelessness of their situation.

Annotation of the rest of the letter requires identification of seven women of fact or fiction and nine men, all writers of one sort or another. As for the writers, Fitzgerald's first objection was to the fact that Hemingway was calling in print three men by their own names (as in the first draft of the novel he had used the real names of virtually all the characters); if they are nobodies, the objection ran, then there is no point in mentioning them and if they are somebodies it is "cheap." All three were somebodies, especially Ford (1873–1939). (He is made foolish in the anecdote, but a typescript of his *No More Parades*, 1925, heavily revised in his hand, was—except for this letter—the only manuscript not by Hemingway to be found in Hemingway's literary remains.) "Allister Crowly," whom Ford described as a "diabolist," is Aleister Crowley (1875–1947), an English specialist in demonology and witchcraft. "H[arold]. Stearns" (1891–1943), long-time critic of American life, became Harvey Stone in the novel.

The other male authors were named to shame Hemingway into writing better. Michael Arlen was of course an extraordinarily popular English novelist (1895–1956) of Armenian birth and doubtful merit. Robert W. Chambers (1865–1933) was another best-selling writer of the period, whose influence on *The Romantic Egoist*, Fitzgerald's first (unpublished) novel, the younger writer acknowledged in a 1918 letter to Wilson. (We have Mr. Keen, *Tracer of Lost Persons*, 1906, from Chambers' pen.) "Dr. [Samuel Parkes] Cadman" (1864–1936) was the Norman Vincent Peale of his day. "Basil Swoon's" guidebook to Paris is only a slight invention, the sober citation being Basil Woon, *The Paris That's Not in the Guidebooks*, 1926. Stephen McKenna (1888–   ) is yet another once-popular novelist of English society. But in calling one of his own phrases a "Harding metaphor" Fitzgerald was, typically, hardest of all on himself; the prose style of President Warren Gamaliel Harding (1865–1923) was one national scandal among many.

Of the women whose names Fitzgerald invokes, three are characters from fiction, two were characters in fact, and one—whom he suspected of having "dramatized herself in terms of" fiction—was both. The last is Lady Twysden, Duff—the real-life Lady Ashley, Brett—of whom Fitzgerald was not an admirer. In June, 1926, he wrote Perkins that— "perhaps because I don't like the original"—he didn't like Brett in the novel; in *A Moveable Feast* he calls her "that girl with the phoney title who was so rude...." Rude or not, the title was genuine—acquired by marriage. And the lady who held it was such stuff as legends are made on. Bertram D. Sarason, editor of *The Connecticut Review*, and Edward Fisher, a novelist who knew her, have helped to straighten out her actual story.[1] She was born Mary Duff Stirling Smurthwaite in Yorkshire in 1892. According to her she was married for not quite two days in 1917 to an "older man" (apparently named Byrom), before eloping with his best man, Sir Roger Thomas Twysden, who is said always to have been either drunk or "away." (There was a son, however; born 1918, died 1946, no issue.) In 1926, shortly after the action of the novel, she and Sir Roger were divorced. She did not marry Pat Guthrie, the suitor called Mike Campbell in the Hemingway version, but a painter from Texas named Clinton King, who was promptly disinherited. A painter herself, she and her husband headed an art school in New City, New York, in 1934; the writer Jerome Bahr, for whom Hemingway once wrote a preface, remembers going out drinking with her in New York. The story Hemingway told the credulous A. E. Hotchner about her funeral in Taxco with her ex-lovers as pallbearers (who dropped the casket, which split in two) was pure apochrypha. Apparently tubercular, she died Mary Duff Stirling Smurthwaite

Byrom Twysden King in St. Vincent's Hospital, Santa Fe, New Mexico, on June 27, 1938, and was cremated.

In theorizing that Duff dramatized herself in terms of Arlen's dramatization, Fitzgerald has in mind Iris March, promiscuous heroine of Arlen's *The Green Hat*, 1924, a very best-selling novel about some "lost generation" British. Fitzgerald was a thoughtful student of such matters; in *A Moveable Feast* Hemingway wrote that once "He gave me a sort of oral Ph.D. thesis" on Arlen's work. And it is true that Iris and Duff/Brett had some things in common. Iris affects "bravely" a green felt hat; Brett's is a "man's felt hat," and when Duff came to see Edward Fisher in his Paris apartment ("very graceful," with a "musical laugh") the hat was green. More striking, Arlen's narrator remarks that Iris was "the first Englishwoman I ever saw with 'shingled' hair. This was in 1922." Hemingway's narrator says Brett's hair "was brushed back like a boy's. She started all that." The critic and literary historian Malcolm Cowley (1898–   ) also remembers Duff's "floppy-brimmed" felt hat as green, and he reports that she "was believed to be the heroine of... *The Girl in the Green Hat*." If so, then Duff did not dramatize herself in terms of Arlen's dramatization so much as play— or be—herself.

The other ladies of actuality Fitzgerald mentions are Diana Manners (later, and oddly, Lady Duff Cooper, 1892–   ), the English actress whom Colonel Cantwell in *Across the River and Into the Trees* recalls playing in Max Reinhardt's *The Miracle*, and "Station Z. W. X. square," which said goodnight at the end—if not Fitzgerald himself— might refer to Zelda. (A third lady of real life was deleted when Fitzgerald wrote "Arlen's dramatization ... of somebody's dramatization" and struck the words "maybe Nancy Cunard's." This was probably because she was not a writer or actress, but she was mistaken more than once for Brett's original. Of the Cunard Line Cunards, she "shocked society" by living among Negroes in Harlem, eventually marrying a black chauffeur. Publisher of some of Beckett's earliest work, her name crops up several times in *Waiting for Godot*. Not too long ago a correspondent to *The Times Literary Supplement* cited "authorities" to the effect that she was the model for the heroines not only of *The Sun Also Rises* and *The Green Hat* but of Huxley's *Point Counter Point* as well.)

As for the remaining ladies, all fictional. Beatrix Esmond is the lovely, fascinating but unstable coquette of Thackeray's *Henry Esmond* (1852), and "Jane Austin's Elizabeth" (Bennett) is the bright and spirited if prejudiced young lady of *Pride and Prejudice* (1813). Closest to Duff/Brett, however, is "the last girl in Well's *Tono-Bungay*" (1908):

Beatrice Normandy, a titled but "wasted and wasteful" lady who (recall Brett and Romero) refuses to marry George Ponderevo because she is "a woman smirched" and "spoilt." To wrap this thing up, if a little scantily, it should be reported that when Iris of *The Green Hat* is listing the three books she "most profoundly likes" she names "the last part of *Tono-Bungay*," involving Beatrice Normandy. (*Her* hat is "courageous.")

Comment

In his *Moveable Feast* Hemingway remarks that "Scott was very articulate and told a story well. He did not have to spell the words nor attempt to punctuate and you did not have the feeling of reading an illiterate that his letters gave you...." If anyone was not already in on this open-secret he is now, not that it matters. Hemingway's own spelling was idiosyncratic; this Fitzgerald letter was quite sufficiently literate; the effect of its taste and candor was permanent. Hemingway got the message. He tucked it away some forty-odd years ago, and it is a pleasure to untuck it, bestowing credit where credit is overdue.

It was not hard to swallow the story as we had it in the *Feast:* Fitzgerald did not see *The Sun Also Rises* until after Hemingway had sent it to his publisher; therefore he couldn't have had much influence on the book, Q. E. D. As Hemingway told it,

That fall of 1925 he was upset because I would not show him the manuscript of the first draft of *The Sun Also Rises*. I explained to him that it would mean nothing until I had gone over it and rewritten it and that I did not want to discuss it or show it to anyone first.... Scott did not see it until after the completed rewritten and cut manuscript had been sent to Scribners at the end of April.

(A note found in his papers reads, in part, "Mailed Sun Also Rises—April 25 -.")

A letter that Fitzgerald wrote John O'Hara in 1936 (Turnbull, pp. 537–38, where most of the mechanics are fixed up) once seemed to fit this account of things. Fitzgerald is talking about

the advice that Ernest and I used to throw back and forth at each other, none of which ever had any effect—the only effect I ever had on Ernest was to get him in a receptive mood and say let's cut out everything that goes before this. Then the pieces got mislaid and he could never find the part that I said to cut out. And so he published it without that and later we agreed that it was a very wise cut. This is not literally true and I don't want it established as part of the Hemingway legend....

This was Fitzgerald at his self-effacing best, and so far as is known the only person to dispute Hemingway publically on when his friend got to read the novel was Arthur Mizener. In a footnote to the 1965 revision of his Fitzgerald biography (p. 384) he quotes the sentence which says "Scott did not see it until after the ... manuscript had been sent to Scribners ..." and remarks "This statement cannot be absolutely true. ..." His reason: a letter from Hemingway to Fitzgerald, which he also quotes, to the effect that the novel had been cut to start with Cohn, that all the first part had been scrapped. In this it is clear that Fitzgerald knew what came at the start before Cohn; since in the book nothing does, he must have seen it when something did. It may appear unlikely that Hemingway and Mizener could both be right here, if unequally—and Fitzgerald too, if he is read "not literally." But that is pretty much the case.

The great bulk of the surviving manuscript of Ernest Hemingway is stored either in the vault of a New York bank or in the study of his widow's New York apartment. The *Inventory* of his literary remains was prepared in both places; single finds in each place clear up the confusion. The first was made early in the game at the bank. Inserted in the third of the seven French schoolboy notebooks in which most of the first draft of *Fiesta*, as the novel was then called, was pen-and-inked were ten pages of paper folded twice into quarters. On them was scrawled, with many deletions and insertions, some sort of unsigned letter to "Dear Ernest." Its author was easy enough to identify, but some of the phrases he cited from the book were not: "highly moral urges," "because I believe its a good story," "the Quarter being a state of mind." Surely they were not in the novel. But if they weren't what could Fitzgerald be quoting from? The letter in Mizener did not come to mind; it was not until later that James B. Meriwether wrote in to say that back in 1961 he had read a copy of what was not generally known to exist, the discarded opening pages of the book. ("Aren't they terrible, though!")

Of course the clue was in the letter itself: "Please see what you can do about it in proofs." Well then, the book had indeed been sent off by the time Fitzgerald read it; something happened after that. What that was became clear in the middle of a large stack of miscellaneous papers filed in a cabinet in Mary Hemingway's study. Here rested three galley sheets labelled *The Sun Also Rises*, which begin with the news that this is a novel about a lady named Lady Ashely. They print what was once the first chapter of the book and half the second, with the beginning of the story as we know it at the very end of the third galley. Fitzgerald was right beyond a doubt (not to mention Meriwether). The things he objected to are objectionable; given the brilliance of most of the rest of the book it is impossible to explain why it was feeble, irrelevant and misleading at the start.

First comes Brett, with her marital history, her present legal separation, and the fact of her son. Then we learn how she fell in with Mike Campbell one day at lunch in London, and went to Paris with him, where a hotel had only one free room and it with a double bed, which was the start of that. Mike's background follows, and Chapter I closes with a short account of their life together, mostly sleeping and drinking. Chapter II deals first with Jake—his undertaking this novel, his life in Paris, his newspaper job, his dislike of the Quarter and its inhabitants (which he has to go into, he explains, because Cohn had lived there for two years). Next we are told about Cohn himself, and his novel, and how Braddocks got Jake to read it so he wouldn't have to. This leads to the episode at the Closerie des Lilas which is told at more length about Ford Madox Ford (Madox = Braddocks) in *A Moveable Feast*, with one change. (Hemingway was alone in the nonfictional account; Jake in the novel is with "Alex Muhr"; in the first draft, before most people's names were changed, it was John Dos Passos.) Jake explains that he only tells us about Braddocks because he is a friend of Cohn's, and Cohn is the hero of the book. Then it is a little like coming into daylight to read the good old words, "Robert Cohn was once middleweight boxing champion of Princeton," which lead into the novel as we know it. (Of which Cohn is in no sense the hero, and Brett something less than the subject.)

The compilers of the *Inventory* had already told Mrs. Hemingway about the Fitzgerald letter, and with the second unearthing they showed her the uncorrected, unreturned galleys, reminding her of the way it was in the *Feast*. "Ernest lied?" she said quietly, with a bemused smile. "No, not exactly," was the response, then and now. What he did was tell the truth and nothing but the truth but not the whole truth.

Interest in this critique of Fitzgerald's has been such that the simple announcement of its existence made the pages of *Newsweek*, *The New York Times*, *The London Times*, and an uncounted number of other papers here and abroad. None of this did any harm, but a newsman from *The Washington Post*, jumping the gun without having been entered in the event, described the letter in detail on November 30, 1969 (pp. F1, F3). He further reported that Hemingway responded to Fitzgerald by getting drunk and composing an angry letter which compared his well-intended advice, unfavorably, to horse-manure. This letter, to go on with an unlikely tale, Fitzgerald unaccountably found "snooty,"

and when he wrote Hemingway to that effect the latter wrote back to
say he was sorry; he certainly hadn't intended to sound that way.

To misread this exchange so spectacularly requires special talents.
To begin with, the first Hemingway letter referred to was neither angry
nor drunken. And in the second place, none of the letters in question,
subsequent to Fitzgerald's critique, had anything whatever to do with
The Sun Also Rises. (They do have to do with an essay Fitzgerald
wrote for *The Bookman*, in which he praised Hemingway, who sent his
thanks, which the erratic Fitzgerald found "snooty," a reaction that
a friendly clarification presumably rectified.)

Then what *was* Hemingway's response to the letter about his novel?
Almost certainly it was never put on paper, save for the remarks quoted
by Mizener, since no reply in writing was called for. Fitzgerald pen-
cilled his objections, with quotations and page numbers, so Hemingway could look them up and reconsider. Except for the salutation and
the "good night," his was not in the ordinary sense a "letter" at all.
There was no envelope; the sheets do not look as though they had ever
been folded for posting; you don't normally mail things to someone
who is living practically next door. ("As I said yestiday," Fitzgerald
wrote.)

The two writers had come together this time on the French Riviera,
as Baker's *Hemingway* relates. The date was early June, 1926, some
five weeks after the book was mailed to New York. Hemingway had
gone that May to Madrid while his wife Hadley took their son John
to Cap d'Antibes, where the Scott Fitzgeralds—also the Archibald
MacLeishes and the Gerald Murphys—were in residence. There he
joined his family (so did Pauline Pfeiffer, his wife-to-be) and his friends.
He had written that he would have a carbon of the novel with him,
which Fitzgerald could read if the proofs hadn't come. On his arrival,
a small party of welcome was spoiled by Fitzgerald, who had started
to drink before he showed up, and eventually became rude and ob-
streperous. But not long after this Hemingway handed over the typescript and Fitzgerald submitted his opinions. The background to this
is supplied , again, in *A Moveable Feast:*

Scott was not drinking, and starting to work and he wanted us to come to
Juan-les-Pins in June. They would find an inexpensive villa for us and this
time he would not drink and it would be like the old days and we would swim
and be healthy and brown and have one aperitif before lunch and one before
dinner. . . .

It was a nice villa and Scott had a very fine house not far away and I was
very happy . . . and the single aperitif before lunch was very good and we had

several more.... It was very gay and obviously a splendid place to write. There was going to be everything that a man needed to write except to be alone.

It is fortunate for Hemingway and his book that he was not alone, but in rather good company that was not drinking too much on one particular night to remember.

NOTE

1 Sarason, "Lady Brett Ashley and Lady Duff Twysden," Connecticut Review, II (April 1969), 5–13.

Letter to Ernest Hemingway

Dear Ernest:

Nowdays when almost everyone is a genius, at least for awhile, the temptation for the bogus to profit is no greater than the temptation for the good man to relax (in one mysterious way or another)—not realizing the transitory quality of his glory because he forgets that it rests on the frail shoulders of professional enthusiasts. This should frighten all of us into a lust for anything honest that people have to say about our work. I've taken what proved to be excellent advice (On The B. + Damned) from Bunny Wilson who never wrote a novel (on Gatsby—change of many thousand wds) from Max Perkins who never (2) considered writing one, and on T. S. of Paradise from Katherine Tighe (you don't know her) who had probably never read a novel before.

[This is beginning to sound like my own current work which resolves itself into laborious + sententious preliminaries.]

Anyhow I think parts of Sun Also are careless + ineffectual. As I said yestiday (and, as I recollect, in trying to get you to cut the 1st part of 50 Grand) I find in you the same tendency to envelope or (and as it usually turns out) to embalm in mere wordiness an anecdote or joke

---

Reprinted from Matthew J. Bruccoli and C. E. Frazer Clark, Jr., eds., *Fitzgerald/Hemingway Annual 1970* (Washington: NCR/Microcard Editions, 1970), pp. 10–13 by permission of Harold Ober Associates. Copyright © 1970 by the S. J. Lanahan Trust.

thats casually appealed to you, that I find in myself in trying to preserve a piece of "fine writing." Your first chapter contains about 10 such things and it gives a feeling of condescending <u>casuallness</u>

P. 1.   "highly moral story"
            "Brett said" (O. Henry stuff)
            "much too expensive
            "something or other" (if you don't want to tell, why waste 3 wds. saying it. See P. 23—"<u>9 or 14</u>" and "or how many years it was since 19xx" when it would take two words to say That's what youd kid in anyone else as mere "style"—mere horseshit I can't find this latter but anyhow you've not only got to write well yourself but you've also got to <u>not-do</u> to do what anyone (3) can do and I think that there are about 24 sneers, superiorities and nose-thumbings-at-nothing that mar the whole narrative up to p. 29 where (after a false start on the intro-duction of Cohn) it really gets going. And to preserve these perverse and willfull non-essentials you've done a lot of writing that <u>honestly</u> reminded me of Michael Arlen

[You know the very fact that people have committed themselves to you will make them watch you like a cat. + if they don't like it creap away like one]

For example.

Pps. 1 + 2. Snobbish (not in itself but because the history of English Aristocrats in the war, set down so verbosely so uncritically, so ex-teriorly and yet so obviously inspired from within, is <u>shopworn</u>.) You had the same problem that I had with my Rich Boy, previously de-bauched by Chambers etc. Either bring more thot to it with the realization that that ground has already raised its wheat + weeds or cut it down to (4) seven sentences. It hasn't even your rhythm and the fact that may be "true" is utterly immaterial.

That biography from you, who allways believed in the superiority (the preferability) of the <u>imagined</u> to the <u>seen not to say to the merely recounted</u>.

P. 3.   "Beautifully engraved shares"
            (Beautifully engraved 1886 irony) All this is O.K. but so glib <u>when</u> its glib + <u>so</u> profuse.

P. 5.   Painters are no longer <u>real</u> in prose. They must be minimized. [This is not done by making them schlptors, backhouse wall-experts or miniature painters]

P. 8.   "highly moral urges" "because I believe its a good story"
If this paragraph isn't maladroit then I'm a rewrite man for
Dr. Cadman. (5)

P. 9.   Somehow its not good. I can't quite put my hand on it—it has
a ring of "This is a true story ect."

P. 10. "Quarter being a state of mine ect." This is in all guide books.
I haven't read Basil Swoon's but I have fifty francs to lose. [About this
time I can hear you say "Jesus this guy thinks Im lousy, + he can stick
it up his ass for all I give a Gd Dm for his 'critisism.'" But remember
this is a new departure for you, and that I think your stuff is (6) great.
You were the first American I wanted to meet in Europe—and the last.
(This latter clause is simply to balance the sentence. It doesn't seem
to make sense tho I have pawed at it for several minutes. Its like the
age of the French women.

P. 14. (+ therabout) as I said yesterday I think this anecdote is flat
as hell without naming Ford which would be cheap.

It's flat because you end with mention of Allister Crowly. If he's
nobody it's nothing. If he's somebody, it's cheap. This is a novel. Also
I'd cut out mention of H. Stearns earlier.

Why not cut the inessentials in Cohens biography? His first marriage is of no importance. When so many people can write well + the
competition is so heavy I can't imagine how you could have done these
first 20 pps. so casually. You can't _play_ with peoples attention—a good
man who has the power of arresting attention at will must be especially
careful.

From here. Or rather from p. 30 I began to like the novel but Ernest
(7) I can't tell you the sense of disappointment that beginning with its
elephantine facetiousness gave me. Please do what you can about it in
proof. Its 7500 words—you could reduce it to 5000. And my advice is
not to do it by mere pareing but to take out the worst of the _scenes_.

I've decided not to pick at anything else because I wasn't at all inspired to pick when reading it. I was much too excited. Besides This
is probably a heave dose. The novel's damn good. The central theme
is marred somewhere but hell! unless you're writing your life history
where you have an inevitable pendulum to swing you true (Harding
metaphor), who can bring it entirely off? And what critic can trace
whether the fault lies in a (8) possible insufficient thinking out, in the

biteing off of more than you eventually cared to chew in the impotent theme or in the elusiveness of the lady character herself. My theory always was that she dramatized herself in terms of Arlen's dramatatization of somebody's dramatizating of Stephen McKenna's dramatization of Diana Manner's dramatization of the last girl in Well's Tono Bungay—who's original probably liked more things about Beatrix Esmond than about Jane Austin's Elizabeth (to whom we owe the manners of so many of our wives.)

Appropos of your foreward about the Latin quarter—suppose you had begun your stories with phrases like: "Spain is a peculiar place— ect" or "Michigan is interesting to two classes—the fisherman + the drummer.

Pps 64 + 65 with a bit of work (9) should tell all that need be known about Brett's past.

(Small point) "Dysemtry" instead of "killed" is a clichês to avoid a clichê. It stands out. I suppose it can't be helped. I suppose all the 75,000,000 Europeans who died between 1914–1918 will always be among the 10,000,000 who were killed in the war.

God! The bottom of p. 77 Jusque the top p. 78 are wonderful, I go crazy when people aren't always at their best. This isn't picked out— I just happened on it.

The heart of my critisism beats somewhere apon p. 87. I think you can't change it, though. I felt the lack of some crazy torturing tentativeness or security—horror, all at once, that she'd feel—and he'd feel —maybe I'm crazy. He isn't like (10) an impotent man. He's like a man in a sort of moral chastity belt.

Oh, well. It's fine, from Chap V on, anyhow, in spite of that—which fact is merely a proof of its brillance.

Station Z. W. X square says good night. Good night all.

Two Essays on Ford Madox Ford

I

IN his illuminating afterword to the recent Signet paperback edition of Ford Madox Ford's great World War I tetralogy, *No More Parades*, Arthur Mizener reiterates his conviction that Ford and Ezra Pound between them propelled literature into the 20th century—by creating a "literary form that would enable writers to represent the appearance of their age in such a way as to reveal the inner quality that was for them its informing quality."

I first met these two in June, 1913, the year in which Ford was to write his best book, *The Good Soldier*. Ezra Pound dubbed my husband an Imagist poet and invited us to come over to London from Paris to assist in the launching of the Imagist movement. He took us straight to the Ford Madox Hueffers' for tea.

Impressed by the celebrities present, I was startled by Ford's first question: "Do you play lawn tennis?" When I said yes, he exclaimed: "Capital! A partner for Ezra!" As Ezra, then in his middle twenties, was considered the most influential man of letters in London, I was surprised there should be any difficulty finding girls to play with him.

Essay I is reprinted from *The Christian Science Monitor*, December 23, 1965, by permission of *The Christian Science Monitor* and Mrs. Cannell. Copyright © 1965 by the Christian Science Publishing Society: all rights reserved.

Essay II is reprinted from the *Providence Sunday Journal*, September 20, 1964, by permission of the *Providence Sunday Journal* and Mrs. Cannell.

Kathleen Cannell, publicity photograph taken in the 1940's.
Collection of Kathleen Cannell.

The next afternoon I understood H. D., the American poet, "a Greek
reborn into modern times," was to be Ford's partner. We three waited
on the emerald turf court adjacent to the Hueffers' South Kensington
house in the snowy whites then de rigueur.

Ezra ambled along in fawn pants and blue shirt. He motioned me
back court and lay down near the net. From this position he would

leap up and smash the ball over—marvelous when it came off. When it didn't, it was up to me. When I missed too, put off by blue streaks before my eyes, he would roar: "Partner! Don't just stand gawping like one of those Rossetti females. Play!"

As Ford had rightly judged, I was too young and too shy to protest. Ford chose from a bevy of lovely partners, but I was stuck with Ezra for the season.

After tennis the Hueffers held open house at gorgeous, substantial, sit-down English teas, specially dedicated to the famished young poets (for whom it might be their only meal that day).

Many already "arrived" people dropped in too. Douglas Goldring, who would later write *Trained for Genius* about our host; Frank Stewart Flint, a poet who spoke 10 languages; Wyndham Lewis; the opulent John Gould Fletcher from Arkansas; and once H. G. Wells, though I was informed that at the moment it was "not done" to read him.

Teatime conversation was priceless when one could hear it. Lady Gregory's tale of her vicissitudes with the Abbey Players, happily, was enunciated distinctly—how Yeats in rehearsal lay down with his ear to the stage to listen for cavernous voices; how Sarah Algood tore up her costume because she could not wear a velvet dress in a prison scene (she did not want foreigners to think the Irish were uncouth).

But Ford's breathy "interior" tones often diminished to a silky rustle. Ezra either whispered or roared, often quite unintelligibly. Two sturdy kitchen chairs were provided for them among the Victorian heirlooms, because of Ford's weight, and because Ezra invariably teetered on two legs, coming down on all four with a bang to make a point. Sometimes he fell off and then Mrs. Hueffer's very articulate parrot would cover him with ridicule.

I have never ceased to be amazed that the public images of these two men should be the diametric opposite of their private selves. Ford has passed as a mythomanic, a prevaricator, boastful, and overbearing; Ezra as a ruthless, egocentric arriviste—and worse.

Yet, though they hid their light under eccentric behavior, these two were probably the kindest men I have known.

II

During the London summer season of 1913 we had tea after tennis almost every day with the Ford Madox Hueffers in their big, comfortably worn old South Kensington house. We were on a literary honeymoon because Ezra Pound had discovered that Skipwith Cannell was an Imagiste poet and insisted that we come over from Paris to take contact with the movement.

Hueffer, whose father had been the distinguished German music critic of the London Times, was then editor of *The English Review*. Pound was his left, and sometimes right hand and (to quote Arthur Mizener) between them they were "helping literature" to leap into this century.

(A reminder: Hueffer changed his name after World War I to Ford Madox Ford because of the Germanic nature of the family name.)

From novels and poetry of his I had read and loved I imagined Ford as a romantic hero, and thus he always imagined himself. So I was totally unprepared for his appearance. His almost huge, pink roundness, his silky straight, canary-colored hair and moustache and very pale blue eyes gave him the air of an English country squire rather than the intensely sensitive and temperamental man of letters he was.

I later realized that Ford was only 40 years old, about my mother's age, but he seemed even more venerable to me and I treated him with respect, not dreaming in my naivete that his interest in any young female could be other than paternal, especially since he had lately taken a second wife.

This innocence piqued his amour propre, as he told me years later in Paris. (Our friendship, doubtless because founded on this Platonic basis, lasted until his death.)

The Hueffers held open house at teatime. We sat down at a large, beautifully appointed table. Upsetting protocol, I was placed at Ford's right hand "because she is the youngest." Authors on every rung of the literary ladder were apt to drop in, from Lady Gregory to Frank Stewart Flint, who spoke 10 languages, and his surprising Cockney wife who practically spoke none.

In a milieu bulging with balloon egos Ford's kindness and selflessness (like Ezra Pound's) in encouraging young talents were proverbial. Famished beginners were sustained by the lavish crumpets and sandwiches, nut bread and plum cake, possibly their only meal that day. And they learned about style from Ford, whose perception of their submerged word blocks was positively uncanny.

"Observe, listen, cut, polish, place," he would reiterate.

At that time I was a dancer with no thought of writing anything except letters. But the things he told me have kept coming back through the years to extricate me from entanglements in style. As he considered a jewel worthless without a proper setting, so writers who strove for continuous brilliance, Ford said, were likely to produce a desert of ennui—like too many sparkling grains of sand on a beach. He surrounded his climactic scenes in the novels with calm passages.

Conversation at teatime was marvelous when one could follow it. Mrs. Hueffer favored unexpectedly dry non sequiturs. Ford's silky breathy tones often diminished to a mere rustle, Ezra either whispered or roared. And he mounted a sturdy chair (specially provided for him among spindly heirlooms) as a Rosinante on which this contemporary Don Quixote charged the windmills of mawkishness, hypocrisy, and above all, bad writing. And sometimes like the knight, he fell off. Then the parrot would belabor him with oaths.

In spite of his kindness, Ford, could make one feel horribly immature and insignificant. Ezra consoled me by quoting what Stephen Crane had once written to a friend: "You must not mind old Hueffer ... He patronizes me, he patronizes Mr. Conrad, he patronizes Mr. James. When he goes to Heaven he will patronize God Almighty. But God will get used to it, for Hueffer is all right."

Ford's "tests" were, I believe, another reason he has left such an unpopular image. He tried on me a test joke he used to see whether Americans had a sense of humor. The only word that stood out from his confidential rustle was spinach. But I was watching Ford's eyes and when they flickered I laughed falsely, looking into them with what I hoped was an appreciative gleam in mine. I was in.

Ford also offended interlocutors by taunting them or making outrageous statements, hoping to break down their social guard and provoke reactions that would reveal their true feelings (to be duly recorded in his notebooks). And he has been called a bombastic liar. It is true that his stories were generally better than the facts. But often he was just seeing whether he could get away with something.

One example is Ernest Hemingway's report in *A Moveable Feast*. He relates how Ford at a café had claimed to cut Hilaire Belloc, when the passerby in question was Aleister Crowley—both of whom Ford knew well. I frequently heard him try his jokes on Hemingway, but have never been sure whether it really fooled Hem, or if he pretended it did so as to have an excuse for despising Ford, then his literary benefactor and editor of the *transatlantic review*.

The Sun Also Rises Revisited

WHEN a man tries to look back forty-five years to events that were at that time rather minor, he tends to mistrust his judgment. He must ask himself if he is really remembering facts and live impressions, or is he remembering names and faces and events which have somehow become enveloped in an unconscious embroidery of romance, hearsay, and innuendo. In these few notes I have tried to stay close to the facts and I have been fortunate in being able to confirm many of them with other persons who knew the people involved in some cases even better than I did.

The group that assembled in Montparnasse in the early 1920's was of course unaware that they would be the subject of hundreds and hundreds of pages of memoirs, conjecture, romance, and biography. And of course no one dreamed that one of Hemingway's stories would, in years to come, turn out to be a symbol of the whole "lost generation" in literary folklore. Who was Hemingway? A nice guy who called himself a writer, though almost no one had every seen anything he wrote in print. Hemingway was so little known that even Scribners, his publisher of *The Sun Also Rises*, in their first Grosset & Dunlop edition of this novel, misspelled his name on the front cover! They spelled it with two m's.

A few years ago I took the *Sun* with me to the San Fermin in

Reprinted from the *Connecticut Review* IV, 2 (1971), pp. 5–8, by permission of the editor acting in behalf of the Board of Trustees for the Connecticut State Colleges.

Pamplona and read it there while the fiesta was exploding all around me. I was interested in seeing if the events today had changed, perhaps been watered down, or whether Hemingway had really portrayed them as they were, "true" as he would have said. I was not really astonished to find that his description of every event, the religious procession, the *desencajonada*, the *encierro*, the dancing, the bull fight was deadly accurate, practically photographic, in the detail of its reporting. If you have ever been to the San Fermin and enjoyed it, you can live it all over again by sitting down for an evening with Hemingway's novel.

On the other hand the description of the characters in his novel and their conversations were a work of fiction and if they seemed inspired by real persons and real events, this was purely coincidental. At least that is the way Hemingway himself described it to me in a conversation we had on the subject in 1933. I was writing a novel, he said, not a biography. He was annoyed, he told me, at all the fuss that had been made about "the six characters in search of an author—with a gun." Even seven years after the publication of the book he was still threatening to punch Harold Loeb in the nose if he ever met him again because he was the one, he thought, who was complaining the loudest.

I am not so sure, however, that Hemingway was as unconscious of his use of real people and real events in the fiction of his story as he pretended. He enjoyed needling people, he enjoyed ranting a bit about persons he disliked. One might even say that he enjoyed disliking them. He repeated himself over and over again on Gertrude Stein, for instance, how she lied when she claimed to have helped him find a publisher and when she said she had encouraged him, even guided him, in his writing. He would pound the table and become very emotional over something that was long since past and not really very important in any case. Another example is the bitter words he spilled in *A Moveable Feast* about persons who had once been his friends. He nourished some deep resentment against some of the people he had known in Montparnasse. He wanted to "expose" them for what they were, a lot of trash. And yet for others he seemed to have a deep affection, as for instance Jimmy the Barman and even for myself whom he called, in 1953, "my oldest friend" which was manifestly not true. It was at this same meeting in Pamplona that he told me he was writing a book which would contain a series of sketches of Montparnasse figures (presumably *A Moveable Feast*) which would "show them up for what they really were."

In the *Sun* he probably enjoyed building a character that many would

identify with Harold Loeb because of a few obvious similarities knowing full well that the character of Robert Cohn in the book bore little
resemblance to the original. Harold as I remember him (and I have
not seen him since 1925 or 1926) was a far more intellectual, sensitive,
understanding person than the fictional character, though, like Cohn,
he was inclined to be tense, over-serious and humorless. Loeb was
generally considered rather aloof by most of the Montparnassians who
thought he took on unjustified airs of superiority. Little of this fits
the Hemingway portrayal.

In his description of Brett I find only a superficial resemblance to
Lady Duff Twysden. Duff was a queen bee in Montparnasse and the
Quarter was notoriously lacking in queen bees, for lady writers and
artists are not likely to be socially inclined. Duff, on the other hand,
shone with a wonderful lustre wherever she appeared. I can picture her
now sitting in the Dingo or the Select with a flock of men around her,
listening to her every word, loving her looks and her wit and her
artistic sensitivity. Some of them doubtless persuaded themselves
they were in love with her and it is just possible that Hemingway
was among them. Certainly he was one of her admirers and if in the
Sun he makes the "I" character (Jake Barnes) physically unfit, this
could have been both a joke on Duff and/or a way of emphasizing
his boasted virility which Duff may have spurned.

For Duff was devoted to Pat Guthrie and their love affair was a sort
of romance of the gods which everyone knew about and everyone
enjoyed. Pat too was most attractive as a person, a very kind and
gentle man, not too unlike the Mike portrayed by Hemingway. One
important difference existed between Pat and Duff, however. Whereas
Duff could drink everyone under the table and never really show it,
poor Pat was maudlin at the end of the second glass. If he persisted
in his drinking he might become belligerent too, though this was
seldom, I believe. In any case at the very early part of the evening Pat
might have to be led away, while Duff went on to other places, and
other drinks with other people. But she always went home to Pat. She
loved him and she expected to marry him some day when her divorce
came through.

This is not to say that Duff remained eternally faithful to him. For
instance she did have the brief encounter with Harold Loeb which
Hemingway has mentioned in the book, though it was greatly marred
(to say the least) by the unfortunate accident that her lover had a
shocking toothache during most of their time together. Duff has been
pictured as a nymphomaniac but I think this entirely unjust and untrue.

Morrill Cody, a recent photograph. *Collection of Morrill Cody.*

Nor was she an alcoholic even though she was certainly a devotee of the bottle. On the other hand she was a most competent pianist and a talented artist, traits which Hemingway omits in his portrait of her.

The only other queen bee in Montparnasse was Zelda Fitzgerald and it was normal that the two should not care for each other. This is in the nature of queen bees. And Scott absorbed this dislike from his wife, I suppose, for he later said so in a letter to Maxwell Perkins. My impression is, however, that Scott was quite attracted to Duff and that in the beginning the Fitzgeralds and Pat and Duff used to dine together rather frequently. At least I remember seeing them sitting together in the Dingo getting a "foundation" for an evening abroad.

But there is another possibility which offers intriguing opportunities for speculation, namely that Hemingway deliberately drew upon real persons in portraying Jake's group of playmates in order to produce a roman à clef which would help to sell his book to the public. This is hinted at in a letter from Fitzgerald to Hemingway when the latter jubilantly announced that the book had gone into a second edition. Fitzgerald tried to keep him from building too high hopes by saying that this probably did not mean a sale of more than a few thousand copies and assuring him that the chances of its finding a market in Hollywood was nil "unless book is big success of scandal." Well, it *was* a success of scandal, with everyone in Paris talking about it from the beginning and eventually the news spread to England and America by word of mouth and through the literary press. It was the best thing that could have happened to Hemingway from the point of view of launching him into the selling brackets comparable to those of Fitzgerald. But for a roman à clef, it had very big and obvious keys!

As for the real characters behind Hemingway's novel, they were not, with the possible exception of Harold Loeb, as unhappy with their portrayal as they pretended. I remember talking to Duff about it one evening in 1926 at the Trois et As Bar on the rue de Tournon. Of course he said nasty things, she told me, but after all he was writing a novel. Who cares? Not me. Pat, too, in another conversation, said much the same thing. He was far more concerned at that time with the breakup of his love affair and Duff with her discovery of a new and more stable attachment to a young American named Clinton King whom she insisted on calling George. She and King were soon married and lived happy ever after as in the fairy tales. "Ever after" was for some eleven years culminating in Duff's untimely death in America. Pat, after being pushed around for a couple of years, finally died by his own hand. Why he did this was never really known, I believe, though many thought that it was because he was still suffering from the loss of Duff. Pat was a gentleman by nature and instinct and he was intelligent, but he was utterly without ambition or talent.

As for other characters in the *Sun* the couple called Braddocks are easily identified as Ford Madox Ford and Stella Bowen because, both in real life and in the book, they took over a bal musette one night a week to which they invited all their friends. However that is where the resemblance stops. From the conversations of the Braddocks in the *Sun* they might have been almost anyone.

Harold Stearns, too, is easily identified as Harvey Stone in the book because both of them were always trying to borrow money and both were devotees of the race track. But Harold had a lot more to him than that. As Hemingway portrayed him he might have been anyone, but the similarity of name was used, of course, to point a finger at a particular man.

As to Hemingway's portrayal of Kitty Cannell as Frances Clyne, I find little resemblance. He draws her in a bad mood, in an unhappy emotional stage, and people are perhaps different under special circumstances, but I never saw any of this side of her nor did any of the friends whom I have consulted on the subject. Kitty was generally liked and admired by those who knew her, a person with more stability than most of the Montparnassians.

If however the fictional characters of Hemingway's book were not true pictures of real persons, the atmosphere of Montparnasse which he expressed and the portrayal of the English and Americans who lived there was indeed consistent with the life that all of us was living. We floated through those days in much the way Jake Barnes does, concerned with the things of the moment, running away from reality through alcohol or love affairs, working when the spirit moved or the creditors became too insistent. It was a good life for most of us, as long as we made an end to it before it undermined our ambitions and our spirit.

Duke Zizi

I'LL try to recollect what I can about Mitzy, other than what I have already mentioned in *This Must Be the Place*. I'm afraid that I may not be very successful in remembering more dope on him. You see, like the rest of my bar clients whom I speak of in my Paris memoirs, I rarely made notes other than mental ones. And as I haven't a copy of *This Must Be the Place* which might refresh my memory about Mitzy, I must trust completely and solely to my remembering way back half a century ago to the 20's. Anyway, I do trust that I am not mentioning deliberately anything I did say about Mitzy in the book. For that would be cheating and a cheap way out. So I will try to think up something I could have left out regarding his personality, character, etc. However, from what little I still remember of his personality, it was strong, pleasant, and effective, even to the point of being contagious. He was extremely popular with Americans and Englishmen, both outside as a guide and interpreter and also inside in the Dingo bar. He was very well liked there by all the clients and staff alike. Even Mr. and Mrs. Wilson, the owners of the bar, were quite fond of him and especially Mrs. Wilson, who was a very shrewd business woman. Yet Mitzy, if my memory serves me well, spent very little money at the bar.

In fact, I don't know whatever he did with his money, whenever or where or whom he received it from. He wasn't a drinker in the al-

coholic sense of the word, yet like Pat and Duff, he sat in the bar daily
for hours, engaging one or more clients in friendly, interesting, and
amusing conversation. He was very sociable with a nice sense of
humor. He charmed me in certain ways as he did most everyone else.
It was generally believed he was homosexual. Outwardly, his mannerisms gave one that impression too, though he was never vulgar or
suggestive in any homosexual way. On the contrary, always the tactful
little gentleman.

He wasn't very tall—about five feet three or four inches. Most times
he appeared smartly dressed and a little dandy dapper. I sensed he
must have come from a good family, even aristocracy; for, his breeding
seemed perfect. I often suspected, now I come to think of it, that
many days he had little or no money at all. Yet he would sit at the
bar entertaining others in conversation, though I'm certain he was often
very hungry but was too proud, unlike Pat and Duff, to ask for credit.
Occasionally, I wanted to pass a little money or especially some food
to him, but he was a very sensitive and proud man and I was afraid
of hurting his feelings. However, I think I did eventually get across
to him, particularly with the aid of the proprietess, Mrs. Wilson. After
all, he did bring clients to the bar from time to time, or told others
about the Dingo as he served as guide and interpreter round Montparnasse.

I believe he received a small check from home which, I think, went
to his hotel rent and perhaps a little food. I suppose he got by with
the rest as he guided tourists round town. I still can't understand
what he did with his money, for he was practically a teetotaler. I don't
remember him being a smoker either. He wasn't a gambler except for
playing small games of Poker Dice at the bar. And he didn't seem to
go in for the fast life as it was lived in Montparnasse and Paris generally in those days. He just seemed to enjoy the simple life, and when
he was not conducting people round the Quarter, he would make for
the Dingo bar where he spent many happy hours and days. We took it
for granted that he wasn't in the bar to spend money. We all accepted
him at all times as part of the family.

I swear, however, that by nature he wasn't a mean man. I believe
when finances permitted, he did order some light refreshments at the
bar. But never indulged in big meals with wine etc. He gave me the
impression he was on a permanent diet, taking care of his slim figure
which he did have in those days we all knew him and called him Mitzy.
I don't quite remember if I mentioned him in *This Must Be the Place*

as the Duke of Mitzicus of Greece. However, I believe it was generally
understood that he had some claim to that title. He looked every bit
a young Greek. And he certainly behaved like a Duke. I can well
understand Mitzy being the character Zizi in *The Sun Also Rises*.

One of his several hobbies and pastimes was that of portrait painter,
though I don't remember him being outstanding in any way in that
special art. Furthermore, I don't believe he really seriously tried to.
I think, like his interpreter specialty to the tourists, his portrait painting was simply one more means to help defray his overhead expenses.
Also, like his interpreting, it would seem a kind of free pass to meet
and to get to know people. He was on very friendly terms with Duff,
Pat, Hemingway, and many other well-known personalities and characters, both the heavy drinkers and otherwise. Mitzy didn't indulge in
very heavy drinking like many of the people he knew did, or keep up
with speed of night and day high living. Yet, I think he was to be
admired for the ease in which he mixed with everyone, and enjoyed
himself at the same time.

I remember vaguely making a joke, I believe in *This Must Be the
Place*, about Mitzy's bed manners when he was sleeping with a boyfriend. That is one reason why I want to look again through the book
to see if I mentioned the special boyfriend who might have been the
Spanish painter.[1]

I remember another discreet joke. Mrs. Wilson, the owner's wife of
the Dingo bar, and I used to signal between us. For instance, we
learned the common American term for homosexual was "fairy." Over
here they are known as "queers" or "puffs." Anyway, there was a well
known song on this subject often sung in the Dingo called *Fairytown*,
and, whenever Mrs. Wilson, who usually sat in a very prominent
position between the bar and the restaurant as cashier to give out
bills to the waiters, spotted what she believed to be a "fairy," she
would pass on a secret sign or facial expression to me, which I understood. Mrs. Wilson had a very shrewd eye at sizing up everyone
coming into her establishment, along with a keen sense of humor. In
fact, I thought she was quicker at it then me at times. When she
saw one of those coming in, she would make that secret facial expression at the same time miming the words to me from the song, "Oh
fairytown and fairytown." Mitzy was one of her chief targets for our
regular bit of innocent giggle, though we were all very fond of him.

He was near my own age group. You say he disappeared from
Montparnasse a long time ago. But Mitzy may still be alive.

NOTE

1 [The anecdote referred to is on page 121. Mitzy made it a point to shake hands with
his friend by way of bidding him goodnight. No mention of the friend's name is made.
Charters was trying to identify him with the Spanish painter who, McAlmon said, was
the model for Count Mippipopolous.—ED.]

Cavalier and Cowboy: Goodbye to all that, Mr. Ford Braddocks Ford!

AN active Anglo-American literary life had developed in Paris around Joyce and Sylvia Beach, Ford Madox Ford and Gertrude Stein, with a great deal of overlapping among the various groups. Little money was available and everybody was eager to find a publisher. Though Hemingway cultivated his Bohemian image, with a touch of the wild West (he was said to have survived on stray pigeons from Luxembourg gardens!), he was also very much involved in the literary game of the time. For instance, he accepted a post as sub-editor of the new magazine launched by Ford in Paris called *the transatlantic review*, and he even helped keep it alive for a while when he found a new backer, Krebs Friend, after John Quinn died and Ford's money ran out. He was responsible for preparing for publication a whole number of the review during Ford's absence. He also copied long sections of *The Making of Americans* to have them printed in the *transatlantic*, because Gertrude Stein would not let the manuscript out of her house. He may have learnt something by doing it, but admiration was certainly not his only motive. Though he never took his post as seriously as Ford would have liked him to, he thus occupied a key position in Paris as the coming young man of the new generation with the official blessing of an "old master." He read and annotated manuscripts which were submitted to the *transatlantic*, and Ford treated him as a sort of ambassador from the Middle West, a prophet of the new movement. Ford who, all his life, had played the part of the man who knew Conrad and Thomas Hardy, would have

275

liked some young master to act as his disciple, to create a legend around him. This was part of keeping a tradition alive.

In his dry matter-of-fact manner Hemingway defeated all these expectations. While Ford dutifully praised him, particularly when he told American magazine readers about literary life "on a Paris quay," and how talented he found their prodigal sons, Hemingway treated Ford's beloved review and its editor in a casual, almost offensive manner. As soon as Ford packed his bags to go to America in quest of money, Hemingway, his head already full of Spain, Pamplona and the bull fights, hastily put together the August number, an all-American issue, with the added spice of Surrealist poems by Baroness Freytag von Loringhofen, more in the tradition of little magazines than of a sedate international review. The serial publication of Ford's novel, *Some Do Not*, was interrupted. A letter from the editor was printed in a ridiculously garbled manner. Ford apologized to the readers and apparently took it all in good fun; though the British Consulate General cancelled its subscription. Soon after, in a special number devoted to Conrad, who had just died, Ford's dearest friend received only token praise from the sub-editor who, in addition, declared himself ready to immolate T. S. Eliot and grind him into fine powder in order to bring Conrad back among the living. More apologies from the editor. The style Hemingway would have liked was the free and easy tone of *The Little Review*, with a dash of French Surrealism, at least to the extent that it enabled the new generation to treat Anatole France merely as "a corpse." Ford, on the contrary, hoped that the *transatlantic* would become a modern version of the *English Review*, a prestigious monthly; his ambition was to present all forms of good literature, and, around it, all the complex loyalties of a *coterie*.

Everything in the two men's manners clashed violently. Ford-Braddocks, in *The Sun Also Rises*, appears as a convivial, easy-going man, who enjoys a meal with friends, or sitting at a café table talking endlessly. *Le Nègre de Toulouse* was his favorite restaurant and he had marked preferences for cafés with some literary flavor of the past. If only Joyce had accepted a joint patronage of the new generation to teach them how to write! In addition to solid pieces from confirmed talents the review could have devoted a section to experimental literature. Under the label "Work in progress" excerpts from Joyce's new book (to be called *Finnegans Wake*, but then merely known as "work in progress") could be published as well as young American literature, full of what Ford called Middle Westishness, and some watered down French Surrealism to give the review an international scope.

Ford considered literature as a sacred mission. He would rap-
turously talk about art as a family heritage. He had always hobnobbed
with geniuses, and, in his position of high priest of culture, wanted
to reform Anglo-Saxondom by injecting a dose of Flaubert into its
blood-vessels. In a broad sense, he culturally belonged to an English
social élite with a fondness for the old school tie, with loyalty to the
regiment, with a thorough knowledge of French (except for the accent
which must never be mastered), and with a taste for wine and winters
on the Riviera.

The stammering that went with the persona of the Old Tory was not
entirely affected. Ford was rather short of breath and the flow of
words was interrupted by wheezing sounds. It was also a way of looking for the right words, a Jamesian groping for the perfect form.

But what was the perfect form? That of novels written in collabora-
tion with Conrad two decades ago, and now the object of a cult?
("C'est toi qui dors dans l'ombre!" Ford solemnly wrote to introduce
an obituary article in the *transatlantic*!) Or that of the Jamesian
psychological novel, *The Good Soldier*, or that of the Tietjens family
chronicle, in its first stage now, with the serial publication of *Some Do
Not*?

His catholicity of taste, his sensitiveness to trends, to moods, and to
literary fashions made Ford into a perpetually *avant garde* writer who
never put his whole soul into the credo of the day. The contrast was
striking when Ford appealed to the editor of *The Criterion*, a fellow-
Tory with a clearly formulated policy, to help him launch the *transatlantic*: Eliot's letter was a real manifesto, whereas Ford's program for
the review was an act of faith. "*Fluctuat*" said the motto on the front-
page seal, but a direction, a new impulse was needed.

In spite of his professed dislike for the English "muddle through"
attitude, Ford himself was a great flounderer. He took up raising pigs
at one time, very much as he took up "imagism" at another. His
financial arrangements always proved shaky; he gave the impression of
belonging to the Establishment while his royalties merely kept him on
the relatively affluent side of Bohemia. His private life put Ford (at
one time Hueffer) outside the pale of conventional respectability; he
had unsuccessfully tried to get a divorce from his first wife by going
through the odd procedure of claiming German citizenship; he later
had a liaison with Violet Hunt, and was now living with an Australian
painter, Stella Bowen, by whom he had a daughter, Julie, Joyce's
god-daughter. But even this unconventional family life never made
him side with the sexually emancipated groups of the previous decade

or with the carefree members of the "lost generation." There was
about him and his *ménage* an air of respectability which Hemingway
acidly satirizes in the Braddocks couple.

The brief scenes at the beginning of *The Sun Also Rises* ironically
emphasize the "social graces" of Mrs. Braddocks, her lady of the house
style which, in her display of affability, clashes with Jake's cynical
parading of a prostitute as his fiancée. Her *faux pas*, lack of a sense
of humor and giddy use of the French language make her into a comic
figure, while Ford-Braddocks, perfectly unperturbed, and a great teller
of tall tales, saves the day: "Of course, darling. Mademoiselle Hobin,
I've known her for a very long time." This was a way of being a
perfect gentlemen, a concept Hemingway and Ford endlessly argue
about in *A Moveable Feast*. Hemingway made a big show of not understanding what the Englishman meant.

True to say, Ford never had a very clear understanding of Americans
either. He probably derived a composite picture of them from his
acquaintance with highly respectable Europeanized *hommes de lettres*
like Mr. James or Mr. Eliot, from no less a respectable banker and
patron of the arts as Mr. Quinn, and from a quaint genius from
Montana, Ezra Pound. He was now confronted with a new wave of
expatriates who loved whisky more than red wine, and wine more than
tea and conversation. He admired the bullish enthusiasm of that young
crowd, but, in his incapacity to place them on his literary chart, he
declared that they came from Chicago and had all been cowboys.

What surprised Ford was that these young men did not come to learn
about their craft by reading and talking, but, on the contrary, kept
clear of "influences." They all wrote grim stories about their childhood in America, in places like Nebraska or Iowa which, to Ford, were
incredibly far away. The very primitive settings described, the brutal
manners, the simple, down-to-earth behavior of the characters were
poles apart from the muffled forms of cruelty or from a despair soaked
in London fog that his English contributors favored. To him the
American Middle West was the Far West of the soul. He also felt
that this was new blood for English fiction and he wanted to channel
these sometimes clumsy literary efforts into a "movement." The relationship he established with young Americans was extremely ambiguous: father figure, friendly adviser, but also boring mentor and
stuffy Englishman.

His great "find" for the review was Ernest Hemingway, as he took
pride in having "discovered" Lawrence for the *English Review*. He

made him sub-editor, published him, sang his praises in other reviews
at a time when hardly anyone knew the talent of the *Toronto Star*
reporter. But Hemingway refused all forms of literary allegiance. He
wanted to be free to worship at the altar of Miss Stein occasionally
and even to create imbroglios between Ford and her (would any editor
in his right mind publish the whole of *The Making of Americans* as
a serial?). He had no need for Ford's advice or even for his paltry
five francs a page. This cowboy was a lone ranger.

Meanwhile Ford was engaged in making folklore. If tea parties did
not work, he would have a *bal musette*. The idea was always to have
a place where artists and their friends could get together informally,
both private and open, for entertainment and new contacts. It was
nothing but the old *salons* perpetually revived, as *cafés littéraires* at
one time or as *caves* at another. But in this case the Paris working
class atmosphere was artificial local color created for foreigners (with
the help of the *patron* and his family) by the foreign visitors themselves.
Americans, who patronized a wide range of cafés and bars in Paris,
made this weekly visit to the *bal musette* part of a tour of squaresville.
As a club of this kind quickly gets to be known, the parties were visited
by friends of friends, and the group with whom Brett makes her entrance in *The Sun Also Rises* belongs to the category of rich tourists in
quest of a good time. Jake himself brings along "Mademoiselle
Leblanc-Hobin" who is quite readily accepted by the group. (The
situation became even worse when Mrs. Krebs Friend, the not-so-
young wife of the new backer of the *transatlantic* proved more interested in having a gay time, while her husband tried to save on
royalties paid to contributors.) When Hemingway, who very soon was
not on speaking terms with Ford, once called with his wife, Hadley,
she was entertained at a separate table by the Fords, and her husband
bluntly said to her: "You pay for your own drinks, you hear!" To
Ford, the heir to Cavalier England, this was a scene from a Far West
saloon.

Mr. and Mrs. Braddocks have faded into oblivion, but many years
later Hemingway felt the need to give another portrait of "old Ford,"
and we read of the two men meeting again on a Paris street: the cowboy
from Chicago, the Cavalier from the Cinque Ports. This time, it was
during a *moveable* fiesta. But by now they are both ghosts. Farewell
to all that, Mr. Hemingway! Your mad friend Ford was already dead
when you blew your brains out.